THE PSYCHOPATH:

An Essay on
the Criminal Mind

WILLIAM McCORD
and JOAN McCORD

AN INSIGHT BOOK

VAN NOSTRAND REINHOLD COMPANY

New York Cincinnati Toronto London Melbourne

This book is a revised and abridged version of the authors' *Psychopathy and Delinquency*, Grune and Stratton, Inc., New York, 1956.

VAN NOSTRAND REINHOLD COMPANY REGIONAL OFFICES:
Cincinnati   New York   Chicago   Millbrae   Dallas

VAN NOSTRAND REINHOLD COMPANY INTERNATIONAL OFFICES:
London   Toronto   Melbourne

Published by VAN NOSTRAND REINHOLD COMPANY
450 West 33rd Street, New York, N.Y. 10001

Published simultaneously in Canada by
D. VAN NOSTRAND COMPANY (CANADA), LTD.

10 9 8 7 6 5

Foreword

Every society has its quota of trouble makers. Among
the least understood, and perhaps most destructive, are
the moral and emotional misfits known as "psychopathic
personalities." Their warped natures frequently thrust
them into the criminal segment of society. Even if they
escape the law, they bring misery and sorrow to their
fellow men far out of proportion to their numbers.

The psychopath often has bland and pleasing external
manners while on the inside he lacks those normal human
sentiments without which life in common is impossible.
The authors of this excellent volume describe him as an
"asocial, aggressive, highly impulsive person, who feels
little or no guilt and is unable to form lasting bonds of
affection with other human beings."

While the existence of such "moral insanity" has long
been recognized, it is only in recent years that psychological and social science has given it sustained attention.
Like other riddles of human personality, its solution turns
out to require the combined resources of genetics, child
study, psychoanalysis, electroencephalography, sociology,
and psychotherapy—to name only some of the specialties
involved. One merit of the present volume is its wide
survey of contributions from these and kindred sources.

Labels are perilous things. To call a destructive person
a "psychopath" does not, of course, prove that he be-
longs to a single well-defined nosological grouping. Indeed, the first question to ask is whether psychopathy is
nothing more than a semantic fiction. The authors face
this question and decide in the negative. The syndrome,
they say, is too well-marked and dependable for it to be
shrugged off as a figment. If, then, we are dealing with
a fairly unitary syndrome, does it have an identifiable
cause? Here to be sure our knowledge falls short of providing a final answer, but the authors give a guarded
affirmative reply, advancing a highly suggestive "neuro-
social" theory of its origin.

Next, the authors ask whether psychopathy can be treated successfully. Can normal sentiments of guilt and affection be planted and a modicum of self-control be instilled? It is now clear that severe punishment and half-hearted therapy do no good at all. But there is hope in vigorous total-push methods of treatment if they are inaugurated early enough—preferably no later than adolescence. Encouraging results have followed on the therapeutic efforts of Aichhorn, Bettelheim, Redl, and Papanek.

The most original contribution of this volume is its evaluation of the type of milieu therapy practiced at the Wiltwyck School, where psychopathic delinquents are studied in comparison with other types of young offenders. In order to carry through their evaluation the authors have devised several ingenious measuring instruments to tap relevant aspects of personality, including aggressive fantasy, guilt reactions, punitiveness of attitude, ego-ideals, and the boy's moral code. In a well-controlled experiment the McCords find that children diagnosed as psychopathic or as having behavior disorders actually respond to therapy more favorably than do neurotic and psychotic children. Whether the change is permanent cannot yet be told, but the demonstration has special significance. It shows that young psychopaths if brought out of their emotional isolation can come to hold more normal views of authority, of self-responsibility, and of social relationships. The discovery serves as a warning to those who have claimed without proof that psychopathy is incurable.

The authors ask whether psychopaths are legally insane or whether they may be held legally responsible for their acts. All discussions of this problem are necessarily inconclusive, but I find illumination in the McCords' treatment of the matter. Given time and determination we may yet find it possible to instill a normal structure of sentiments into lives that start out as loveless, insensitive, and destructive. The full achievement, however, will require further therapeutic discoveries as well as reform in criminal procedures, starting perhaps with the "treatment tribunals" advocated by Sheldon Glueck. Meanwhile we must accept Justice Cardoza's summing up of the situation: "Everyone recognizes that the present (legal) definition of insanity has little relation to the truths of mental life."

As a teacher I should like to add a further word. It has been my experience that the field of criminology holds the precise balance of intellectual and social challenge to which college students eagerly respond. A well-written volume on the subject, particularly if it includes illustrative cases, and if it deals with the personal causation of conduct, will have warm appeal. All these merits are found in this text, together with an especially fine lesson in evaluation. The McCords' report of their original experiment can teach the student much concerning the approach of modern social science to the difficult task of measuring change in human character.

I am persuaded that this volume is the most comprehensive and most dependable source of information available on psychopathy. And by virtue of their original research the authors have pushed forward the frontiers of knowledge in a perplexing field.

GORDON W. ALLPORT

Preface

Anyone who writes on the psychopathic personality faces a complicated, puzzling task. First, he must disentangle the various meanings of this ubiquitous term. The word "psychopath" has been absorbed into everyday language and has been used as a label for men as different as Whitaker Chambers and John Dillinger, Lawrence of Arabia and Hermann Goering, Rousseau and Rimbaud. Then, if the student finds—as this book contends —that there really is such a disorder as "psychopathy," he must evaluate a mass of evidence concerning the nature, causes, and treatment of the syndrome. This evidence is vast, sometimes conflicting, and continually growing. Between 1930 and 1940, 28 scientific articles appeared dealing with the problem. Between 1940 and 1955, this trickle of research became a torrent: 171 articles specifically dealing with psychopathy appeared, and hundreds of others produced facts relating to this strange disorder. Since 1955, authors in America, England, Germany, and Israel have produced numerous books devoted solely to explaining this strange disorder.

Why the flood of research? Many factors combined to produce it: the war brought thousands of psychopaths, with their disturbing behavior, into the army; political developments in Germany focused attention on the relation of psychopathy to Nazism; new techniques, like the electroencephalograph (E.E.G.), allowed science a closer look at the psychopath's neural state; research on child-rearing revealed some of the environmental roots of the disease; the rising crime rate drew public concern to the supercriminal psychopath. Most importantly, the ancient belief that psychopathy was an hereditary, innate lack of "moral sense" went into a precipitous decline. The supposition, created by new discoveries and theories in the behavioral sciences, that psychopathy might stem from the environment, opened new realms of investigation and new hopes that the psychopath might be "cured."

A few men played an important role in changing the concept. Sir David Henderson, the distinguished British psychiatrist, published his comprehensive *Psychopathic States* in 1939; American psychiatrist Hervey Cleckly followed in 1941 with *Mask of Sanity*, a book which did much to show the influence of the disorder and its socially-caused nature; psychoanalyst Robert Lindner produced, in 1944, a clinical portrait of treatment in *Rebel Without a Cause*; and, throughout the 1950's, the work of Anglo-American scientists such as Richard Jenkins and Maxwell Jones elucidated the nature of psychopathy and offered hope that the disease may be treatable.

We propose in this book to achieve several goals. We hope to clarify the nature of psychopathy—to define the disorder in a way that conforms to the experience of those who have been forced to deal with this type of man and yet avoids the sterile, dogmatic quibblings which have so often hindered the process of diagnosis. Another aim of this book is the synthesis and evaluation of our knowledge concerning the causation of the disease. An equally important purpose is the evaluation of those forms of treatment which can modify the psychopath, particularly those which can cure the psychopathic child before he becomes a social menace. In "milieu therapy," as practiced at the Wiltwyck School (and by such men as Aichhorn, Redl, and Bettelheim), society may have an effective treatment. At least, our evaluation of this school's effect on disordered children suggests that the method achieves important changes. Finally, we hope to indicate certain legal and social policies which may, in a more rational fashion than at present, reduce the cost of the psychopath to the community.

Like any discussion of the psychopathic personality, this book has controversial elements. Some may debate the concept of psychopathy itself and its independence from culture-bound judgments. Some may disagree with our causal explanation, which stresses environmental influences; others may question the optimistic conclusions drawn from the Wiltwyck research and other reports on treatment. Yet controversy often serves as the seedbed of scientific progress.

Dr. Sheldon Glueck and Dr. Gordon Allport of Harvard and Dr. Harry Levin of Cornell not only gave their advice and help, but also read the book in its various stages of completion. Dr. Glueck, with his wide experience as a criminological researcher, contributed substantially to the chapters on causation and legal policy. Dr. Levin's advice, particularly on the Wiltwyck research, its aims, statistics, and conclusions, greatly improved the project. Dr. Gordon Allport contributed unsparingly of his time and wisdom to every aspect of the book, from the definition of psychopathy to the recommendations concerning social policy. His discerning comments on the Wiltwyck experiment, his additions to the theory of causation, his correction of certain sentimental lapses, his suggestions of additional approaches, and his new insights—all were invaluable.

Ernest Papanek, the former director of the Wiltwyck School, made possible, encouraged, and helped to form the research on milieu therapy. Others on the staff of Wiltwyck, between 1953 and 1955, particularly Anna Chase, Francis Sims, and Malcolm Marx, gave important help throughout the research. We feel deep gratitude to everyone at Wiltwyck—the counselors, the psychologists, the Mennonites, the secretaries—for contributing their time and aid to the project.

WILLIAM McCORD
JOAN McCORD

Stanford, California

Acknowledgments

The authors wish to express their appreciation to the following publishers for permission to quote from these works:

"Durham v. United States," published in the *Federal Reporter*, 1954, by the West Publishing Co.

A Judge Takes the Stand, by Joseph N. Ulman, published 1933 by Alfred A. Knopf, Inc.

Psychopathic States, by Sir David Henderson, published 1939 by W. W. Norton & Co., Inc.

The Crime of Imprisonment, by George Bernard Shaw, published 1946 by Philosophical Library, Inc.

Encyclopedia of Criminology, edited by Vernon Branham and Samuel Kutash, published 1949 by Philosophical Library, Inc.

"Etiological Studies of Psychopathic Personality," by Anthony Symkal and Frederick Thorpe, published 1951 in Volume 7, *Journal of Clinical Psychology*.

"Psychopathology and Treatment of Delinquent Girls," by Florence Powdermaker *et al.*, published 1937 in Volume 7, *American Journal of Orthopsychiatry*.

Controls from Within, by Fritz Redl and David Wineman, published 1954 by The Free Press.

"Hermann Goering: Amiable Psychopath," by G. M. Gilbert, published 1948 in Volume 43, *Journal of Abnormal and Social Psychology*, by the American Psychological Association.

Wayward Youth, by August Aichhorn, published 1935 by the Viking Press, Inc.

Contents

Who Is the Psychopath?

This 'landowner' . . . was a strange type, yet one pretty frequently to be met with, a type abject and vicious and at the same time senseless.

DOSTOYEVSKY, describing Fyodor Karamazov

A sweaty crowd jammed the courtroom and gaped at a slender, passive young man sitting in the dock. He seemed detached from the melee, bored by the complicated legal process. If the papers had not splashed his picture across the front pages, few people would have known that this was the defendant, William Cook—"Billy the Kid"—brutal slayer of five human beings.

In his few years of life, Cook had been a terrible scourge to society. His youth had been spent in fights, homosexual orgies, and robberies. His adult life, short as it was, had culminated in the killing of a fellow robber, in the murder of an innocent man and wife, and—most shockingly—in the shooting of their two children.

This was the day the crowd awaited. Today Billy Cook would "get what was coming to him." What could he possibly deserve but death? The crowd had little patience with the legal process that led to this moment. They despised the hairsplitting psychiatrists who had maintained that Cook was "mentally ill, although not insane." Few of the spectators understood the esoteric arguments among the expert witnesses. Three defense psychiatrists had asserted that Cook was "psychopathic." The prosecution agreed but added, to the joy of the crowd, "So what?"

As the judge read the sentence, a dissatisfied rustle swept through the crowd. Not death, but "300 years in Alcatraz" was Billy Cook's fate. Few heard or cared to hear what the judge so solemnly added: "Billy Cook is a symbol of society's failure."

To save itself from other Billy Cooks, society must come to understand the psychopathic personality. Psychopathy, possibly more than other mental disorders, threatens the safety, the serenity, and the security of American life. From the ranks of the psychopaths come political demagogues, the most violent criminals, the riot leaders, sexual misfits, and drug addicts. Psychologist Robert Lindner has observed: "Hydra-headed and slippery to the touch though it is, psychopathy represents the most expensive and most destructive of all known forms of aberrant behavior" (151, p. 508). Not only does the psychopath cost society dearly, but he represents such a unique, fascinating example of the human species that the understanding of his disorder can contribute greatly to our general knowledge of human nature. For, as later chapters will show, he rests at one extreme of the continuum of human variety: he is the unsocialized man, the "lone wolf," the stranger to social intercourse.

Just what is psychopathy? For 150 years, science has known of the psychopath's existence; for at least 140 years, scientists have quarreled over the definition of his disorder.

A minority has maintained that the psychopathic personality, as a distinct clinical syndrome, does not exist. One of these dissenters, psychiatrist Olof Kinberg, commented a few years ago: "[The concept] should be abrogated as theoretically unsatisfactory, practically misleading and destructive to scientific thinking" (137). And Dr. Leo Kanner has commented, "A psychopath is somebody you don't like." Few of those who have dealt with criminals, worked in mental hospitals, or participated in social casework would agree with Kinberg or Kanner. Indeed, most investigators believe that the concept not only has meaning, but that it is indispensable. Even Kinberg surreptitiously recognized that certain individuals require a special classification. "In the good old times," he admitted, "one exported such cases to the U.S.A. where most of them went to the dogs or were sent back by their consulates" (137).

Although most social scientists admit the existence of the psychopath, they have extraordinary difficulty in defining his disease. As a psychiatrist with long experience recently exclaimed: "I know an elephant when I see one, but damned if I can define one!"

Much of the difficulty with definition has, however, been superficial and overly stressed. Hervey Cleckly, an American psychiatrist with vast experience with psychopaths, has observed, "At a meeting of the American Psychiatric Association, or a staff conference at a state hospital, if a physician expresses an opinion to one of his colleagues about a psychopath, it is clearly, and at once, understood that he is not speaking of a cyclothymic or schizoid personality or of ordinary homosexuality but of the grave character and behavior disorder so familiar to most psychiatrists as a distinct and easily recognizable entity" (39, p. 568). Below their surface argument, most social scientists postulate a common core of psychopathy with which many would agree: *The psychopath is an asocial, aggressive, highly impulsive person, who feels little or no guilt and is unable to form lasting bonds of affection with other human beings.*

The lives of two typical psychopaths, William Cook and Joseph Borlov, illustrate in more human terms the abstract definition. William Cook has probably been the most thoroughly studied psychopath of our times. Not only did Cook submit to a full psychological examination (by Anthony Smykal and Frederick Thorne), but he also wrote the complete story of his life (240).

Born in 1927, in a small Missouri town, Billy Cook never participated in the close family life of most Midwest farmers. His father, a pathological drinker, deserted Cook and the other children early in Billy's life. Although never brought to trial, Cook's father probably murdered his mother. When Billy was seven, he discovered her body. Later he described the event with a typical lack of emotion: ". . . one time my sister and me came home from playing at a yellow house and found her dead, laying on a cot. She had a large gash in the head."

A juvenile court judge split the orphaned family, sending Billy to a foster home. His new "mother," a brutal nymphomaniac, initiated Billy into the sordid side of sexual experience. When Billy finally ran away from the foster home, he was caught by the police and shipped to the Missouri Training School. He later wrote: "The training I got there was how to steal cars and pick locks."

Paroled, Cook lived with his elder sisters who shifted him from town to town. One brother-in-law taught him the burglar's skills and often took him on drinking sprees which ended in brothels. Another relative got a farming job for the boy, then cheated him out of his earnings. No one wanted him. His "family life" ended when a sister forced him into prison by declaring he had broken parole.

In prison, Cook developed into a confirmed homosexual and built up a record as a troublemaker. Upon release, he participated in several robberies and worked at odd jobs. Cook soon drifted westward—stealing when he could, working when he had to. An older man picked him up in a stolen car and offered to "pull some jobs." Cook turned him down, shot him, stole the car, and continued west.

When this car broke down, he hailed another, threatening the driver with his pistol. Cook later recalled: "I got in the car with these people. Moser was their name. I told them what had happened and I didn't want their money or anything. All I wanted was to get away."

The car raced across the Southwest with Cook holding a gun on the driver, his wife, and their two children. At a New Mexico gas station Moser attacked Cook, pinning his arms to his sides. Cook struggled free, forced the family back into the car, and made them resume the drive. Soon Cook, frightened by the attack, murdered all four. He stopped the car just long enough to stuff the bodies into an abandoned mine shaft.

Cook reached California, but the police had begun a six-state search and an alert local sheriff arrested him. In a last desperate attempt, Cook kidnapped the sheriff in a police car and dashed across the Mexican border. In a Tiajuana cafe, Mexican soldiers caught him. Securely tied, he was thrust on board a plane destined for the United States. The Mexican soldiers, jubilant over their victory, shot volley after volley into the air as the plane left the ground.

In a California jail, two psychologists gave Cook an intensive examination. Their tests, the Rorschach and the Thematic Apperception Test (T.A.T.), showed the killer to be basically immature, completely isolated from the human world, and impoverished in his emotional life. Because he couldn't profit from experience, he reacted to frustration with hostility and fury. Unable to identify with others, he seemed constantly preoccupied with "his feelings of rejection and underprivilege."

The psychologists asked Cook to make several drawings of the human figure. After "blind analysis," another expert concluded that Cook had an extremely low frustration tolerance and was explosive, preoccupied with sex, and psychopathic.

His examiners pointed to early rejection as the probable cause of his disorder: ". . . here was a child who suffered an intensive exposure to all of the pathogenic factors which are accepted by modern psychiatry as being etiological to conditioned character disorders."

Billy Cook exhibited a character unrestrained by guilt and barren of love—a personality so impulsive, so warped, that every frustration resulted in explosive, murderous aggression.

Another typical psychopath, Joseph Borlov,[1] covered his disorder with a more sophisticated veneer. I first met Borlov as his counselor and teacher in a segregated unit of San Quentin Prison. He was a handsome man, slender, wavy-haired, and always immaculately garbed in the prison dress. The English accent to his speech, his theatrical gestures, his well-timed sense of the dramatic tabbed him as an actor, which once he was. Nothing on the surface revealed his career as a forger, robber, liar, homosexual—and ultimately, murderer.

Because he felt no compunction about lying, it is difficult to disentangle Borlov's real life from his fabrications. The facts seem to be these: Born in 1900 as an illegitimate child in St. Petersburg, Borlov escaped the Bolshevik Revolution when his father took him to Paris. In France, his father deserted him. A vacationing American couple adopted him and brought him to the United States. During the twenties and early thirties Borlov lived by playing chorus parts in musicals and "walk-ons" in Broadway plays. Small robberies, forged checks, and fees as a homosexual prostitute supplemented his income. Bor-

lov later described these years with a grandiose disregard
for facts:

> In 1925, I first went to work for Florenz Ziegfield at the
> New Amsterdam in New York. The show was crummy;
> Marilin [sic] Miller, the star. I had a couple of bits in the
> show. Two years later, Ziegfield featured me in the Follies—
> I had arrived. For the first time in some years, I had a feeling
> of security—no more tank towns—I was eating regularly.
> After a few seasons with the Follies my old impatience and
> dissatisfaction appeared. I wanted to act; then I heard that
> Maude Adams and Otis Skinner were going to return from
> retirement and tour with a company in "Merchant of
> Venice." This was for me. I made tracks for Long Island to
> beard Otis Skinner in his own den. Fortunately for me, he
> had never heard of me—and was very nice. I fixed his sink.
> I think it was the sink that got me the part. Anyway, I was
> hired at the salary of sixty-five smackers a week. I was getting
> $1500 from Ziegfield. So much for money!

Everything, or almost everything, that Borlov described
about this period in his life was a lie, but intelligence
shines through the fabrication. Actually, he never played
with Marilyn Miller, Otis Skinner, Maude Adams. Instead, his biggest income came from petty robberies; his
greatest triumphs, from female impersonations.

After several arrests in New York, Borlov drifted west
to California. Late in 1940, in a drunken spree, he forged
$8,000 in bogus checks. Arrested in Santa Barbara, Bor-
lov was tried and sentenced to San Quentin for five
years. Released in 1952, Borlov "went wild" in San
Francisco. He robbed several grocery stores, successfully
charged $500 worth of perfume to a nonexistent account
at I. Magnin's, a luxury store in San Francisco, and, in
another burglary, shot a man to death.

During his imprisonment, several psychiatrists examined Borlov and agreed in diagnosing him as a psychopathic personality. His impulsive outbursts of aggression,
his narcissism, and his lovelessness singled him out as
pathologically different from other men. His lying indicated the possible existence of hallucinations. Yet all
who knew him agreed that Borlov, unlike the psychotic
individual, did not for one minute believe his own lies.
He lied, the psychiatrists agreed, because he enjoyed it.
If pressed, he would affably admit his prevarications.

His warped mind, although completely asocial, was capable of sparkling analysis. As philosophically as any academician, Borlov could rationalize the failings of his fellow criminals:

> A diseased mind will some day be cured by medicine— probably surgery—but never by conversation nor statistics. All crime is a product of environment, usually of civilization. No man is bad nor is any man evil—everyone is forced into a pattern by society. The very people who condemn his mistakes create his future crime. Since entering this particular prison, I have met many men—some are mentally ill—others just ignorant, while some are the victims of their own desires. Many sincerely know they have made a mistake and will not recreate one. Too many of them are of the belief that they must outsmart the authorities, the law, their captors. The pity of it: they don't have the mental equipment for the task they have set themselves.

Unfortunately for society, Borlov had the "mental equipment" for his task. He had the intelligence but no inner control. He had insight into his fellows but not into himself. He could talk of "guilt," of "misdeeds," of "mistakes," but the words were mere abstractions. Borlov could kill without guilt, lie without compunction, and steal without remorse. He said to me when I left the prison: "A lot has happened to me, a lot more will happen. But I enjoy living and I am always looking forward to each day. I like laughing and I've done a lot. I am essentially a clown at heart—but a happy one. I always take the bad with the good." Released after serving his full term, Borlov launched into a series of robberies and frauds. He successfully "conned" I. Magnin's out of many hundreds of dollars' worth of perfume and other goods. Later, while holding up a small grocery store, he shot and killed the owner.

Neither Borlov nor Cook would think of themselves as sick men—nor would society, its judges, its police, or its wardens. Yet beneath superficial differences, Borlov and Cook suffered from the same disorder. Whether brilliant or stupid, whether sophisticated or primitive, whether born to the purple or "on the wrong side of the tracks," psychopathic personalities have similar symptoms of maladjustment. Those who (to their sorrow)

have dealt with psychopaths would recognize the fundamental profile given in the following paragraphs.

I. THE PSYCHOPATH IS ASOCIAL

Society cannot ignore the psychopath, for his behavior
is dangerously disruptive. He may be robbing a store or
knifing another man; he may be peddling drugs or
forging a check. No rule, however important, stops him.
Since the bizarre, erratic behavior of the psychopath
antagonizes society, he is often found in the social waste
baskets: the prisons or the mental hospitals.

Because his behavior is so threatening, many people
lose sight of the disorder which causes it. Much of psychology's confusion over the psychopath can be traced
to a basic mistake: equating deviant behavior with the
psychopathic personality.

The actions of the psychopath are only outward symptoms of a sick mind. Many other deviants—the professional criminal, the gang criminal, the sexual aberrant—
exhibit dangerous behavior, but they do not share the
character structure of the true psychopathic personality.
Moreover, the definition of deviant behavior varies from
culture to culture. Borlov's homosexuality might have
been honored in ancient Greece, and Cook's murders
might have been overlooked if his victims had been
known German spies in the last war. Deviant behavior,
then, is an inadequate criterion of psychopathy. At most,
it may indicate the existence of a psychopathic character
structure.

In almost every culture, the psychopath can be found.
What he does will differ; what his society condemns will
vary—but the purposeless rebel, the unsocialized misfit,
the person who feels no guilt in breaking social mores
can be found everywhere. Consequently, any adequate
study of the psychopath must look beyond asociality.[2]

II. THE PSYCHOPATH IS DRIVEN
BY UNCONTROLLED DESIRES

There is no reason to believe that the psychopath has
been born with desires different from those of other men.

There is, however, evidence that the psychopath expresses his desires in ways different from other men.[3]

Hobbes said: "The wicked man is but the child grown strong." The psychopath is like an infant, absorbed in his own needs, vehemently demanding satiation. The average child, by the age of two, compromises with the restrictions of his environment. He learns to postpone his pleasure and to consider his mother's needs as well as his own. The psychopath never learns this lesson; he does not modify his desires, and he ignores the needs of others. In most respects, the psychopath is Narcissus, completely absorbed in himself, craving only his own pleasure.

Much of the psychopath's asociality can be traced to this quest for immediate pleasure. F. A. Freyhan observed: "The psychopath . . . is unsocial rather than anti-social" (72). He does not purposefully attack society, but society too often blocks his way to fulfillment.[4]

It seems probable, though not provable, that the psychopath has not learned to find pleasure in stability, for he seeks excitement in variety more than most human beings. The average man wants excitement, but he also wants security. The psychopath, however, often seems willing to sacrifice everything for excitement. His satisfactions have always been fleeting and highly changeable from childhood through maturity. Consequently, he seems to know no greater pleasure than constant change, and the search for excitement at any cost becomes an important motive.[5]

But if the psychopath maintains a desire for excitement which other men do not have, he does not seem to receive satisfaction from productive work. This characteristic has been described by Fromm, Horney, Riesman, and Maslow as an absence of the drive for autonomy and self-fulfillment which motivates the psychologically healthy person. This pleasure in productive action appears to be possible only when the individual feels loved and secure. Continually searching for a sense of identity, the psychopath often is too preoccupied by his insecurities to permit him to enjoy being creative.

III. THE PSYCHOPATH IS HIGHLY IMPULSIVE

Everyone wishes at some time during his life to ignore his responsibilities, restrictions, and duties. Once in a great while the normal person gives in to this whim, but the psychopath does so continually. His life seems an erratic series of unconnected acts, first leading one way, then another. Chornyak has quipped that with the psychopath, "The lid is off the id" (37).

Borlov, for example, often left his night club engagements to take whirling rides in fast automobiles. The clubs would fire him; he would get another bit part. Again and again he repeated this pattern. Billy Cook held a great many jobs, but never for more than two months: he couldn't stand the restrictions and boredom of regular work.

Unlike the normal person, or even the average criminal, the psychopath's adventures often seem purposeless. Even his crimes are rarely planned. He robs a store in a whim of the moment, not after careful consideration. He flits from woman to woman with volatile passion, never feeling prolonged attraction.

The psychopath has no stable goals. His life is dominated by fleeting desires which leave no space for farsighted planning. After many years of experience with criminal psychopaths, Robert Lindner observed: "Determined progress toward a goal—unless it is a selfish one capable of immediate realization by a sharply accented spurt of activity—the dynamic binding together of actual strands, is lacking" (153, p. 13).

Lauretta Bender, a child psychiatrist who examined 800 psychopathic children, concluded that the most prominent trait of the psychopathic syndrome was "diffusely unpatterned impulsive behavior" (17) (18, p. 373).

IV. THE PSYCHOPATH IS AGGRESSIVE

The psychopath's asociality often expresses itself in brutal aggression. He is not the passive neurotic who hurts no one but himself, nor the anxious psychotic who withdraws from human contact. The psychopath's uninhibited search for pleasure often clashes with the restrictions of his society; the conflict frequently results in aggressive action.[6]

A notorious Baltimore murder illustrates the psychopath's quick-triggered aggression. Two men held up a milk wagon. Both carried loaded guns. The driver resisted. One criminal did not pull his gun. The other robber, a psychopath, used his gun to shoot and kill the driver. The panic which any animal experiences when faced with serious frustration more often causes the psychopath to react with aggression.

Why is the psychopath so inordinately aggressive? His childhood may account for the phenomenon. The psychopath is usually severely rejected, physically beaten, and emotionally deprived by his parents. (See Chapter 4.) As a child the psychopath has received pain from almost every part of his environment. Studies repeatedly indicate that painful treatment results in what has been called "aggressive action." [7]

The normal man has learned to control aggression. He reacts to frustration with sublimation, with constructive action, with withdrawal—less often with aggression. The psychopath, on the other hand, characteristically reacts to frustration with fury.

Psychopathic aggression may be the result of early reward for such behavior. Often, the psychopath gained attention through aggression when other methods failed. Admittedly, the attention was usually retaliatory, but many a child prefers punitive attention to total neglect.

Does aggression make the psychopath any happier? Objectively, it seldom solves his problems and often increases them. But, subjectively, does hurting others somehow give the psychopath an inner satisfaction? Lindner believes that it does. He feels that the psychopath's aggression is an attempt to overcome anxious fearfulness: "Typical psychopathic manifestations are tensional discharges aimed at restoring a disturbed organismic balance" (152). Lindner's "homeostasis" theory must postulate a rather high degree of tension within the psychopath.

Yet most observers would maintain that the psychopath has relatively little anxiety, worry, or inner conflict. Bender, for example, found her psychopathic children to be without anxiety. "There are conflicts, and frustration is reacted to immediately by temper tantrums" (18).

Some scientists believe that the psychopath is confused by his own behavior. Kirson Weinberg has observed: ". . . the psychopath frequently seeks others to limit his random aggressions. . . . Actually he too is puzzled by his waywardness and unwittingly may want to put limits to his random, appetite-fulfilling and destructive behavior" 266, p. 269). Our experience partially confirms Weinberg's observation. The psychopath may temporarily seek control over his indiscriminate aggression, but this desire, like so many others, soon passes. Any control, however mild, again irritates him, and he rejects it.

V. THE PSYCHOPATH FEELS LITTLE GUILT

When the normal man violates the moral strictures of his culture, a gnawing uneasiness grips him: his conscience hurts. But the psychopath—and this is a crucial trait—has few internalized feelings of guilt. In the usual sense, the psychopath has no conscience. He can commit any act with hardly a twinge of remorse.

William Cook illustrates the psychopath's guiltlessness through his dispassionate description of three murders: "The two little kids started crying, wanting water. I gave them some and she [their mother] drove a while—and I turned around and started shooting in the back seat and then turned back and shot her. She fell over against me and onto the floor" (240, p. 311).

In the world of psychopathy, William Cook is no exception. After quenching the children's thirst, he shot them. It is this heartlessness of the psychopath which most strikingly sets him apart from the normal human being. The psychopath has the same desires as others; he dresses and talks in the same way. Yet a most important human element is missing: the sense of guilt.

Not only does this deficiency of guilt set the psychopath apart from the normal man, it also distinguishes him from other cultural deviants. Non-psychopathic criminals, for example, internalize an "underworld code of morality." For them, there can be "honor among thieves." If he breaches this code, the "normal" criminal feels remorse. The psychopath, however, has few values—either those of society or those of a gang. Dreikurs ascribes this to a lack of (Adlerian) common sense: ". . . our thinking in common, our participation in general ideas, in values and morals accepted by the whole group to which we belong." [8] The Freudian labels the trait as an underdeveloped "superego." Both interpretations point to the psychopath's lack of inner controls. This guiltlessness is one of the central features of psychopathy.

Some psychopaths exhibit a deceptive shell of remorse, but the shell is empty. They talk of morality, but inside they feel none, and their words do not hinder their actions. Borlov, for example, philosophized about his "tears" and the "lessons of the Bible":

> Life can at times be a problem—and a laugh. For me, there have been a great many laughs and the tears only made the laughter sweeter—a very little tragedy offsets and highlights the good. But all men, whatever their fate, could take a good lesson from the Bible—the fundamental truths of religion must guide us all.

Yet Borlov could steal and kill with conscienceless abandon. Sometimes his unconcern showed through the hyperbole:

> There have been times when they [society] have been frantic—but I, amid the riot I have created, remain calm and usually collected. I have always landed right side up—from the Village to the Hotel Pierre.

Hervey Cleckly, the neuropsychiatrist, has noted this cleft between the psychopath's understanding of morality and his amoral actions. Cleckly believes that the psychopath suffers from "semantic dementia," a severe form of dissociation between rational faculties and emotional inner control.

At first glance, there seem to be areas in which the psychopath is detained by conscience. Weinberg asserts: ". . . he does internalize in mild or marked degree such elementary restraints as incest, murder of his parents, cannibalism, and dress" (266, p. 268). Yet in several of these areas of "elementary restraint," the psychopath has no desires pressing him into deviance. The desire to be a cannibal, for example, is by no means innate; it is a learned cultural custom which psychopaths in our society do not acquire.[9]

Nevertheless, psychopaths—or at least some psychopaths—do adhere to some of the customs of our culture. They brush their teeth, they drive on the right side of the road, and they wear clothes. Why, then, do they not develop a mature conscience, feelings of guilt, or consistent life goals?

Gordon Allport has made a distinction between two types of learning, "opportunistic" and "propriate," which may explain this feature of psychopathy.[10] All human beings learn "opportunistically." That is, they absorb through continual conditioning a subsystem of habits and "tribal conformities" which help them to adjust to their world. Psychopaths, too, go through this brute learning process. As a result of punishment and repetition, they apparently develop the rudiments of social behavior. It is in another area, "propriate learning," that psychopaths seem deficient.

Most human beings pass beyond the "opportunistic" stage. They develop a "proprium," [11] a style of life, an inward unity, which is uniquely theirs. Here the psychopath falters. For various reasons—particularly, as a later chapter shows, because of his warped childhood—the psychopath apparently does not learn "propriately." He fails to develop a consistent self-image, or long-range goals, or, most importantly, a mature conscience. He does not pass beyond the animally conditioned stage of learning.

The vast majority of social scientists have found that the psychopath, whatever crime he may commit, feels little guilt. This consensus of opinion cuts across theoretical orientations. Sociologist Weinberg concluded: ". . . the psychopath can experience shame but slight guilt" (266, p. 266). Psychologist Robert White says that the psychopath "does not accept blame for his conduct nor feel shame about it" (269, p. 403). British psychiatrist Sir David Henderson, after long experience in the treatment of psychopaths, concluded: "They rarely if ever show any particle of remorse . . ." (111, p. 67). From the viewpoint of psychoanalysis, N. Thornton summarized this striking psychopathic trait: "The chief distinguishing feature in psychopathic personality is nothing but a conspicuously defective or else completely underdeveloped superego" (258).

Like the beast in Tennyson's "In Memoriam," the psychopath "takes his license in the field of time, unfettered by the sense of crime."

VI. THE PSYCHOPATH HAS A WARPED CAPACITY FOR LOVE

The psychopath has often been characterized as a "lone wolf." He seems cold and compassionless. He treats people as he does objects: as means for his own pleasure. Though he may form fleeting attachments, these lack emotional depth and tenderness, and frequently end abruptly in aggressive explosions.

Joseph Borlov was such a lone wolf. He had worked with partners, but only for particular crimes. He had several homosexual "affairs," but none lasted. He had taken a wife, but soon deserted her. In prison, Borlov gained the reputation of cold unapproachability.

This warped capacity for love is so obvious that most social scientists regard it as the core of the psychopathic syndrome. A. H. Malsow connects lovelessness with the psychopath's aggression: "I have found it helpful in understanding psychopaths to assume that they have no love identifications with other human beings and can therefore hurt them or even kill them casually, without hate, and without pleasure, precisely as they kill animals who have come to be pests" (163, p. 173).

Maslow, along with some other writers, makes the assumption that the psychopath is incapable of love. Certainly the psychopath's shallow and volatile relations show a severely blunted capacity for affection, but there are indications that the capacity, however under-developed, still exists.

Recent therapeutic experiments show that the psychopath does seem to identify with his therapist. A few therapists have reported the establishment of rapport with the psychopath.

Some observers maintain that the psychopath does not need love. "In the psychopathic personality," Maslow wrote, "the needs for being loved and loving have disappeared and, so far as we know today, this is a permanent loss . . ." (163, p. 131). Maslow bolsters his conclusion by citing animal research showing that certain basic instincts can be permanently extinguished through severe frustration. According to this theory, severe rejection has extinguished the psychopath's need for love.

There is, on the other hand, evidence showing that the normal child's need for love is not diminished by rejection. Instead, his striving for love actually seems to increase when the need is unsatisfied.[12]

Either because he is incapable of forming them, or because his experience has not shown him how to form them, the psychopath wards off close attachments. Perhaps, as some psychoanalysts maintain, the psychopath fends off close relations because he fears being hurt. In any case, his lovelessness sets him apart as a uniquely isolated individual.

VII. THE PSYCHOPATHIC SYNDROME

Putting all the foregoing traits together, we see a picture of a dangerously maladjusted personality:

The psychopath is asocial. His conduct often brings him into conflict with society. The psychopath is driven by primitive desires and an exaggerated craving for excitement. In his self-centered search for pleasure, he ignores restrictions of his culture. The psychopath is highly impulsive. He is a man for whom the moment is a segment of time detached from all others. His actions are unplanned and guided by his whims. The psychopath is aggressive. He has learned few socialized ways of coping with frustration. The psychopath feels little, if any, guilt. He can commit the most appalling acts, yet view them without remorse. The psychopath has a warped capacity for love. His emotional relationships, when they exist, are meager, fleeting, and designed to satisfy his own desires. These last two traits, guiltlessness and lovelessness, conspicuously mark the psychopath as different from other men.

In this chapter we have discussed each of these traits separately. Although necessary for a clear analysis, such separation tends to create an artificial, unconnected picture of the psychopathic personality.[13] Another case study of a typical psychopath may serve to draw these disparate strands into a unified portrait of the psychopathic character structure.

In 1953 I spent many hours with "Howard Dever," discussing his life and future. Throughout our interviews he talked freely, controlling the situation with a glib stream of sophisticated conversation. His business suit, his conservative tie, and his clipped mustache proclaimed him as a successful young man "heading for the top." The setting of our talks—the Boston Psychopathic Hospital where Dever underwent observation before his trial for fraud, robbery, and impersonation—belied this promise.

Dever, 35 years old, was born in a rural Vermont village. He hated the town and dismissed his childhood years with: "I got into trouble a lot, but they never put me in jail—not for a night." He disparagingly described his parents as "dull, stupid farmers." He pictured his father as a taciturn, forbidding person preoccupied with a country bank. His mother—"colorless, weak, lethargic" —didn't have the "gumption" to oppose his father's episodic rages. He added: "My parents really weren't so bad, though we were never close. They sent me money."

Although abnormally aggressive throughout childhood, Dever's official criminal record began during his high school years. His first job, when he was 14, ended abruptly as the town grocer caught Dever stealing $50 from the cash register. Despite his father's intervention, Dever's reputation as a "sneaky kid" grew until most townsmen ostracized him: "I became the scapegoat for everything that happened. Inspector Crooker would pick me up even if I wasn't doing a thing, just sitting on the curb."

At 16, Dever ran away to New York, where he led a life of larceny and dope peddling. His Manhattan career ended in 1941 when the Army drafted him. After three weeks in a Missouri boot camp, Dever went A.W.O.L. Military Police retrieved him in Vermont and sent him to a large Army prison at Vincennes. He hated the Indiana heat, his "crooked" companions, and the rough handling by Army police. "But I was lucky," he jovially admitted, "I was assigned a real Chicago lawyer for my court-martial. Boy, was he a slicker. He sent to Missouri for my company records, proved my name was still on the roll during my A.W.O.L., and got me released."

Immediately after his acquittal, Dever walked from the courtroom and again deserted. Retrieved, he repeated the pattern. His record shows 14 absences without leave.

The Army shipped Dever overseas. In England, after more desertions, he was sent to the Oxford psychiatric hospital. From there, too, Dever escaped. Each episode involved alcoholic orgies in London, fist fights, and bizarre aggressive behavior. The baffled doctors tried insulin shock, electric shock, and Sodium Amytal analysis. These brought temporary improvement.

Dever was released and, through a military bureaucrat's mistake, given a plush assignment as a clerk in "Torch" headquarters. During the day, he intermittently fulfilled his duties as a filing clerk. At night, he retired to his own London flat (in direct violation of Army regulations). During his evening wanderings through Piccadilly, Dever met an English girl whom he later married.

In one of the last Nazi bombing raids, an explosion smashed one of Dever's legs. Given a medical discharge, Dever headed back to America—leaving his wife on the day she delivered their first child. Several months later, his wife traced him to New York. She flew across the Atlantic and after an emotional reunion forgave him. Dever swore eternal faithfulness.

A week later he left for Florida without notifying his wife: "I met a guy in a bar, and he said he wanted to pull some jobs in Florida; would I go along? I said 'O.K.,' but I forgot to tell my wife. She didn't know where I was, but she took me back when I came home. It wasn't that I didn't like her—we got along O.K. I just had other things to do."

Dever's asocial behavior continued with almost monotonous regularity. He entered the automobile black market for a while, then moved to the selling of fraudulent bonds. He committed many burglaries and topped his career in Boston with the impersonation of an F.B.I. officer and the forging of a $5,000 check.

At the time of our talks, Dever faced trial in Boston on a 15-count indictment. New Jersey, Florida, and New York awaited his extradition. Summarizing his life, Dever said: "Hell, I didn't need the money. I just would get an idea and I'd go out and do it. Maybe I hurt somebody doing it, but I've had fun."

A comparison of Howard Dever with William Cook or Joseph Borlov shows the basic similarity in their character structures. Their malformed personalities expressed themselves in superficially different ways: Borlov, in pathological lying;[14] Cook, in brutal aggression;[15] Dever, in sophisticated "confidence" crimes.[16] Beneath these symptoms, however, they possess the same basic traits: an inability to control aggressive impulsiveness, persistent anti-sociality, a craving for primitive satisfaction, and a striking lack of guilt with a seriously defective capacity for loving others.

"Borderline" cases who combine certain psychopathic traits with other mental aberrations can, of course, be found. As we will have occasion to point out several times in the course of this book, the psychopath lies at one extreme of the so-called "behavior" or "character" disorders. It would serve no useful purpose to insist upon an *absolute* dichotomy between the psychopath and other behavior disorders. As Richard Jenkins has pointed out in discussing the problem of diagnosis:

> . . . if one divides the human race into persons of short stature and persons not of short stature, the number in each category will depend entirely on the cut-off point and different qualified observers will find widely different numbers of

short persons, for there is no natural cut-off point. All ·observers will agree that a few extremely short persons are short (122).

Similarly, the psychopathic disorder melds, at the borderline, into other forms of criminal or mentally disordered behavior. Consequently, the much abused term "psychopathic" should be reserved only for those extreme cases upon which most qualified persons would agree. Unless an individual exhibits the two critical psychopathic traits —guiltlessness and lovelessness—he should not be categorized as psychopathic. Indeed, as the next chapter indicates, confusion and controversy have plagued the concept of psychopathy.

NOTES

1. "Joseph Borlov" is a pseudonym. Since Borlov's future has not been settled as irrevocably as Cook's, it would be unfair to reveal his true name. The facts of his case are, however, presented without alteration. Quotations from him are taken from his letters.

2. In 1930, G. E. Partridge (191) advocated the term "sociopath" in place of "psychopath." His definition of the "sociopath" emphasized social maladjustment to the exclusion of other criteria. By lumping many varied types of criminals, sexual deviants, drunkards, and even unsavory politicians into one mass, such thinking buries the very real differences among them.

Sir David Henderson, an influential British writer, unfortunately described psychopaths (111) as those "who throughout their lives, or from comparatively early age, have exhibited disorders of conduct of an anti-social or asocial nature." Henderson qualified this definition and compiled an excellent study of the psychopath's character. Yet his words, used out of context, further muddled an already confused field.

3. S. B. Maughs, after intensive study of five psychopaths, concluded that their sexual desires were less pressing than the average man's (165).

4. Phyllis Greenacre (101) traced the psychopath's primitive drive for pleasure to distortion in his "sense of reality" and his perception of cause and effect. She maintained that the psychopath does not comprehend what course will ultimately satisfy him, so he takes immediate, and often disastrous action to satisfy his desires.

5. The psychopath, says Greenacre (101), views the world as

"magical." The insecurity of his childhood and the volatile inconsistency of his parents gives the psychopath a distorted view of reality. Because of the parents' changing whims, "What works for the child at one time, completely fails at another." Thus, the psychopath's life has been one of constant surprises.

6. Sir David Henderson (111) believes that "inadequate" and "creative" psychopaths exist, as well as the typical aggressive psychopath. The "inadequate" type, according to Henderson, is narcissistic, immoral, emotionally blunted; but he is passively, rather than aggressively, abnormal. The "creative" type is eccentric, impulsive, often egocentric. It seems more likely that such people belong to other diagnostic categories (acting-out neurotic, neurotic, or "cultural deviant"). Henderson's evidence will be more fully analyzed in a later chapter.

7. See Gordon Allport's (9, Chap. 22) criticism of the concept of an instinctive aggressive drive.

A study by Holzberg and Hahn (118) indicates that the psychopath's aggressive need is no more intense than that of the average delinquent.

8. Quoted in Milton Gurvitz (104, p. 96).

9. The psychopath may not have the incestual desire which many psychoanalysts believe to be universal. Freyhan (72) believes that the psychopath feels unconcern rather than hatred for his parents. Stafford-Clark, Bond, and Doust (237) indicate a conflicting opinion, i.e., that the psychopath does hate his parents.

10. For a complete discussion of this complex problem of social learning, see Allport (7).

11. Gordon Allport (8) depicts the "proprium" as consisting of a variety of functions and properties: a bodily sense, self-identity, "ego-enhancement" (self-seeking), "ego-extension" (the feeling that certain objects and loved ones belong to the person), rationality, a self-image, "propriate" (ego-involved) striving, and the "knowing faculty" (that part of the self which judges and observes the other functions). In at least three of these areas—consistent self-image, propriate motivation, and the "knowing faculty"—the psychopath seems pathologically deficient.

12. Recent research by the Harvard Laboratory of Human Development indicates that rejection leads to more "dependent" behavior and a greater striving for love. See Sears, Maccoby, and Levin (217).

13. In 1952, the American Psychiatric Association replaced the term "psychopathic" with "sociopathic." We have continued to use the label "psychopathic personality" because its use in the last 75 years has made it more familiar. Further, a

variety of disorders which we would not consider under the rubric of "psychopathic" are classified as sociopathic. In terms of the official psychiatric nomenclature, we follow Richard Jenkins (123) and Hervey Cleckly (38, 39, 40) in limiting the concept of "psychopathy" to the disorder characterized as "sociopathic personality disturbance, antisocial reaction."

14. Pathological lying, while often associated with the disorder, is not a central trait of the psychopath. Persistent lying can come from causes other than psychopathy.

15. Cook's aggression was more brutal than that of most psychopaths.

16. Some psychopaths appear charming. This superficial social poise is by no means a necessary correlate of the disorder. Even those psychopaths who do have a pleasant exterior cannot long hide their inner aggressiveness or guiltlessness, nor can they form deeper relations than can other psychopaths.

2

From Moral Insanity to Psychopathy

[The concept] is an attempt to return to belief in demon possession. . . .

J. ORDRONAUX, 1873

Psychopathy has now emerged as the most important of the great transitional groups of mental disorders.

British Journal of Delinquency, 1951

"Enraged at a woman who had used offensive language to him, he precipitated her into a well" (135). With these words, a French doctor of the early 1800's introduced an unusual case which had long puzzled him. His patient, the son of a "weak and indulgent mother," came from a powerful noble family. As a child, he had been given everything he wanted; as an adult he had inherited a fertile estate. Although highly privileged, the patient could never satisfy his desires. Obstacles aroused terrible fury: when a dog got in his way, he kicked it to death; when his horse jerked at the reins, he whipped it unmercifully. The patient's mania had worsened until, in a fit of exasperation, he had "precipitated" a peasant woman into a well.

Pinel, the psychiatrist, took charge of the patient when he arrived at the famous Bicetre. Since none of the usual psychiatric classifications seemed to describe the symptoms, Pinel concluded that this patient suffered from "manie sans délire."

With Pinel's description and diagnosis, the concept of psychopathy began. Pinel's patient (who probably was not a true psychopath) initiated a flurry of psychiatric speculation. Psychiatrists throughout Europe had often encountered such individuals, but Pinel was the first to build a conceptual scheme of the disease. Pinel's *"manie sans délire"* was more inclusive than the modern concept of psychopathy, for it mixed together a welter of very different disorders—paranoia, the "epileptoid personality," neurotic hysteria—as well as some cases of true psychopathy (135).

Confused as it was, Pinel's article shed new light on previously unexplained phenomena. Other psychiatrists, interested in Pinel's observations, reported their experiences with such personalities. In England, Dr. J. C. Pritchard coined the phrase "moral insanity" to describe those in whom "the moral and active principles of the mind are strongly perverted or depraved; the power of self-government is lost or greatly impaired and the individual is found to be incapable, not of talking or reasoning upon any subject proposed to him, but of conducting himself with decency and propriety in the business of life." [1] Although Pritchard's 1835 definition came closer to the modern picture of psychopathy, he too included such disorders as manic-depressive psychosis under the label "moral insanity" (197).

In 1878, Gouster presented the first clinical picture of the symptoms found in "moral insanity": long-standing "moral perversion"; a delight in mischief, excitement, and passion; "enfeebled judgment"; and certain abnormal physical proportions (98).

Gouster's early description of the psychopath drew heavily from the more general work of Cesare Lombroso, an Italian doctor. One of Lombroso's categories, the "born criminal," strikingly resembles the modern concept of the psychopath. Lombroso described the "born criminal" as a "moral imbecile"; guiltless, highly aggressive, boastful, impulsive, peculiarly insensitive to social criticism and physical pain. He believed that "born criminals" could be identified by physical stigmata. He depicted such criminals as atavistic throwbacks to a more primitive stage in human evolution. Although much in his well known work—particularly his causative theories—has been disproved, his study has had profound influence.

In the 1870's the concept of "moral insanity" had gained wide popularity and general acceptance within the medical world. Maintaining that a specific faculty, the moral sense, had become diseased, seemed to explain the disturbed behavior of certain highly aggressive patients.

Though medicine accepted the new concept, religion and law rejected it with horror. "Moral insanity," lawyers felt, would destroy the basis for criminal responsibility. Ministers detected a planned attempt to subvert free will and turn the world back to "paganism and license."

As early as 1812, the American psychiatrist Benjamin Rush outlined the problem in this philosophic battle, a battle involving issues beyond the scope of psychopathy alone. After treating cases which we would today call psychopathic, Rush admitted: "How far the persons whose diseases have been mentioned should be considered as responsible to human or divine laws for their actions, and where the line should be drawn that divides free agency from necessity, and vice from disease, I am unable to determine." [2]

Rush's quandary was one which we face today, but the civic leaders of his century had a ready answer: "The only disease to which the moral nature is subject," said Professor Ordronaux, "*is sin*" (185, p. 313). Ordronaux and other defenders of the faith saw a sinister motive behind the idea of moral insanity. Ordronaux believed the concept was "an attempt to return to belief in demon possession of the Middle Ages and a reversion to superstition." [3] A Dr. Elwell expressed common opinion: The idea was fostered by a "class of modern German pagans, who are trying with what help they can get in America to break down all the safeguards of our Christian civilization, by destroying, if possible, all grounds for human responsibility." [4]

The dispute reached its climax in the highly publicized trial of President Garfield's assassin. Guiteau, the murderer, went before the courts in 1881. His defense lawyers called in several psychiatrists who diagnosed Guiteau as morally insane and therefore not responsible for his acts. The prosecution produced other psychiatrists who disagreed and testified that Guiteau, since he "knew the difference between right and wrong," should be executed. Guiteau lost his case. The defenders of righteousness were jubilant, and criminal responsibility had been temporarily upheld. The trial, of course, settled nothing concerning the issue of moral responsibility, which is still very much alive today.

Throughout the nineteenth century, investigation into causes and treatment of psychopathy, as well as other mental disorders, was buried in speculative dispute. Those few who thought about the problem concerned themselves with theoretical, almost theological questions like: "Can the moral sense be diseased and the intellectual faculty remain unimpaired?"

Yet the nineteenth century did witness the first faltering attempts to characterize this highly disturbing personality. Because of loose classification and lack of research, psychiatric pioneers accomplished little, but they stimulated an intellectual movement which, by the early nineteen hundreds, had begun to build a store of observational data.

The turn of the century witnessed an upsurge of research and an important shift of interest. Scientists abandoned theoretical conflicts, turning to observation of the psychopath himself. Because of its unpleasant connotation, the term "moral insanity" was replaced by "psychopathic inferiority," a label invented by Koch in 1888. Koch implied that the disorder was caused by a constitutional predisposition. In time, "constitutional psychopathy" gained wide use.

Careful observers set about refining the concept and giving it a specific meaning. Meyer, in 1912, excluded neurotics from the category. Mercier, in 1913, won official recognition (through the British Mental Deficiency Act) that conduct disorders were one particular variety of insanity. And Birnbaum, in 1914, pointed out that criminal behavior *per se* was not psychopathy, nor did psychopaths necessarily exhibit intellectual defects.

By the end of the first World War, psychiatrists had reached a consensus that psychopathy was a special disorder manifested in "strong vicious or criminal propensities on which punishment has had little or no deterrent effect." [5] Although they agreed on this definition (which today would be rejected as too general), they could not agree on the causes of the disorder. Some, like Mercier, emphasized intellectual deficiency; others, like Birnbaum, pointed to "pathological emotionality"; while still others, like Meyer, continued to postulate a constitutional inferiority.

In America, the first person to initiate an empirical study of the psychopath was Bernard Glueck, a psychiatrist at Sing Sing Prison. Glueck posited that the criminal act, in every instance, is the resultant of the interaction between a particularly constituted personality and a particular environment (82). In 1918, he investigated 608 Sing Sing convicts, 18.9 per cent of whom were psychopaths. Glueck found that the psychopaths had the greatest recidivism, the highest proportion of drunkenness and drug addiction, and the earliest onset of antisocial behavior.

Stimulated by Glueck's study, other scientists examined the psychopath himself. On both sides of the Atlantic, the psychological makeup of the psychopath became an important issue. Cyril Burt in England and Augusta Scott and Alice Johnson in America studied the motives and character of the psychopath. Of these early studies, John Visher's work in 1922 has best withstood the test of time. Visher selected 50 cases of psychopathic personality from a veterans' hospital and subjected them to intensive psychological examination. He found that normal hospital treatment had no effect on the men and that many had neurotic parents. Most importantly, Visher presented an almost modern picture of the psychopath's character traits: extreme impulsivity, lack of concentration, marked egotism, and abnormal projection. The most critical disability of the patients centered around a guiltless, uninhibited social nihilism.

In the 1930's two new intellectual currents redirected the study of psychopathy. One movement had begun with Bolsi's discovery, in 1924, that encephalitis can result in psychopathic symptoms. Biologically-oriented psychiatrists hailed Bolsi's findings as proof that organic malfunctions within the brain accounted for the psychopath's quirks. Accepting this premise, many medical men turned from the study of the psychopath's behavior and personality to a study of his brain. Some of this work uncovered information about the psychopath's neurology which has proved highly useful; but, by assuming that the cause of psychopathy had been discovered, this biological approach hindered the exploration of other possibilities.

The 1930's also marked the spread of the psycho-analytic school. Americans and Europeans, oriented toward Freudian, Adlerian, or Jungian interpretations, felt that the neurological school ignored many facets of the psychopath's character. They proceeded to elaborate their own theories. Coriat depicted the psychopath as a perennial child, a basically immature person who had never resolved the Oedipus conflict. Wittels conceptu-alized the psychopath as "stuck" at the Phallic stage of development. Partridge pushed the psychopath's original maladjustment back even further into childhood; he de-scribed the disorder as a permanently fixated concentra-tion on oral needs.

Of all the psychoanalysts who dealt with the issue, Franz Alexander has had the greatest influence. In 1930, his paper on the "neurotic character" was interpreted by many as relegating psychopathy to a subordinate category, as one among many neuroses. He described neurotic characters as "living out their impulses," as "solving in-tense inner conflict" by "acting out," and as seeking gratification on an "alloplastic" plane (i.e., discharging instinctual tension by changing the environment). For Alexander, the "neurotic character" was a regressed, self-injuring person, dominated by father-hatred and typified by an underdeveloped ego.

Today, most social scientists believe that Alexander's theory depicts the personality of the acting-out neurotic rather than the true psychopath. Alexander's emphasis on inner tension and conflict as dominating motives fails to jibe with the modern acceptance of the psychopath as uncontrolled by conscience, free of anxiety, and driven by a craving for primitive pleasure.

In the 1930's, the neurologists contributed knowledge of the psychopath's brain (see Chapter 4), and the psychoanalysts developed explanatory hypotheses. Mean-while, another group, the "classifiers," confused the issues.

German psychiatry had long delighted in systematized

classification. In 1888, Kraepelin had proposed a "typology" of psychopathy and had divided the disorder into seven subtypes: the excitable, the unstable, the impulsive, the eccentric, the liars and swindlers, the antisocial, and the quarrelsome. Obviously, Kraepelin brought together an uncongenial variety of mental disorders and social deviance. In the context of the nineteenth century, with psychology in its youth, such a mixture was understandable.

But in the 1930's, after years of careful definition and research, little excuse could be made for systems which lumped a bewildering variety of hysterics, compulsives, sex deviants, and borderline psychotics under the title of "psychopathic personality."

Eugene Kahn's book, written in 1931, defined such a potpourri: "By psychopathic personalities we understand those personalities which are characterized by quantitive peculiarities in the impulse, temperament, or character strata" (128, p. 62). Based on this definition (or rather, lack of definition), Kahn launched into a "clinico-descriptive" classification of "Psychopaths." Among them, he included the "nervous," the "anxious," the "sensitive," the "hyperthymic." Only one of his many types, the "cold autists," seems to approximate the modern definition of psychopathy: "They suffer from moral feeblemindedness. . . . They know as a rule what right and wrong is but they do not feel it" (128, p. 348).

As causative factors, Kahn postulated a mysterious "*anlagen*" which corresponded to various "leptosomatic body builds." The very obscurity of the book impressed many. It passed through several editions and exercised a wide influence in psychiatry.

Some writers revolted against the confusion by rejecting the entire concept. "The term psychopathic personality, as commonly understood, is useless in psychiatric research," wrote one psychiatrist in 1944. He continued: "It does not refer to a specific behavioral entity. It serves as a scrap-basket to which is relegated a group of otherwise unclassified personality disorders and problems" (120, p. 933).

Other scientists—Henderson, Cleckly, Karpman, Lindner—argued that psychopathy was a distinct disorder.

For them, the problem was redoing the job that had been started in the early 1900's: investigating, clarifying, and specifically defining psychopathy.

Each attacked the problem in his own way: Henderson, by classifying the clinical symptoms of the psychopath; Cleckly, by gathering case studies; Karpman, by investigating the thought processes and dreams of the psychopath; and Lindner, by analyzing patients under hypnosis. All four developed similar conceptualizations of the disease.

In 1939, Sir David Henderson's book, *Psychopathic States*, was published in England and in America. Henderson's discussion of the "aggressive psychopath" had profound influence, particularly in Britain. He clarified the distinction between the "epileptoid personality" and the psychopath. He analyzed the connection between the psychopath's motives and the dangerous manifestations of the disorder: crime, alcoholism, and drug addiction. And he noted the close connection between the psychopath's asociality and his lack of guilt.

Certain sections of the book created wide controversy and brought sharp criticism. He linked suicide with psychopathy, overlooking the psychopath's lack of depressive tendencies. He maintained that a psychopathic character underlay some psychoses, ignoring contradictions between the psychopathic and psychotic disorders. He postulated an "inadequate" type of psychopath, apparently confusing psychopathy with certain types of neuroses. (See Chapter 3.)

Another of Henderson's theories, his association of genius and psychopathy, provoked further dispute. Henderson felt that a brilliant but erratic person, like Lawrence of Arabia, should be considered a "creative psychopath." He pointed to Lawrence's impulsivity, his erratic mood changes, and his taste for aggressive action as signs of psychopathy. Henderson overlooked Lawrence's undermining shyness, his hatred for the horrors of war, and most importantly his pervading guilt and desire for expiation: "The craving to be famous, and the horror of being known to like being known (disturbed me); I was standing court-martial on myself" (111, p. 99).

Lawrence may have been a neurotic or a saint, or both,

but he does not seem to have been a true psychopath.[6] A towering intelligence can be associated with psychopathy, but the achievements which we usually consider as the signs of genius seem incompatible with the extreme impulsivity, aggression, and guiltlessness of the psychopath.

Much of the German literature on psychopathy has also been devoted to Henderson's contention that a clear link exists between the disorder and creativity. W. Lange-Eichbaum has, for example, argued that some 600 famous men exhibited "psychopathic" traits and, at various times, Rousseau, Shelley, Nietzche, Flaubert, Carlyle, and Schiller have been labeled "psychopathic" (141). Only if one identifies psychopathy with general instability or eccentricity can one safely argue that many (or most) creators are psychopaths. Perhaps a handful of famous men—prominent examples would be Rimbaud and Rousseau—*might*, with more or less legitimacy, be correctly diagnosed as psychopathic. Yet, it would be a flagrant misuse of terms to identify psychopathy with the neurotic traits which are so often exhibited by famous intellectuals or artists.

Henderson and certain German writers tended to overextend the concept; Hervey Cleckly tried to limit it. His book, *The Mask of Sanity* (38), written in 1941, produced the most complete clinical description of the decade. Cleckly, too, emphasized the personality traits of guiltlessness, incapacity for "object love," emotional shallowness, egocentricity, purposelessness, and impulsivity. In addition, he introduced some new observations on psychopathic characteristics. He perceived the charm with which psychopaths sometimes conceal their association; he recognized the psychopath's characteristic inability to learn from experience; and he pointed out the psychopath's tendency to seek external control, sometimes punishment, for his behavior. Cleckly asserted that psychopaths could be found not only in prisons but also in society's most respected positions: as doctors, lawyers, politicians, and even as psychiatrists.

Because "psychopathy" had been widely misused, Cleckly suggested replacing the term with "semantic dementia" (i.e., a disorder characterized by a split between word and action). He pointed out that psychopaths can

understand the strictures of society and parrot them with
skill, but they dissociate what they say from what they
do.

The label "semantic dementia" had merit, yet it
stressed one symptom of the disorder, ignoring other essential elements: aggressiveness and inability to identify
with others. Because most social scientists could not
agree that "semantic dementia" was the fundamental
symptom (and because "psychopathy" had been used
for many years), Cleckly's new concept never gained
wide popularity.

Like Cleckly and Henderson, Benjamin Karpman,
chief psychotherapist of St. Elizabeth's Hospital, devoted
himself to the clarification of the psychopath's personality structure. Karpman described the same general picture, but added material derived from intensive analyses
of the psychopath's dreams, his thought processes, and
his capricious character. In a series of articles published
throughout the third and fourth decades of this century,
Karpman drew upon his clinical experience for fascinating case studies of the psychopath under treatment.

In 1941 Karpman attempted to draw a distinction between two varieties of psychopathy: "idiopathic" and
"symptomatic." With the "idiopathic" psychopath, "psychopathic behavior is the central feature . . . and the
core of his personality . . . it is found impossible to
elicit anything suggestive of psychogenesis" (131). With
the "symptomatic" psychopath, psychogenic causes could
easily be discovered. In its original form, Karpman's di-
vision could have had important practical consequences:
it could have separated those for whom there was a
known treatment (symptomatic) from those for whom
no treatment had been discovered (idiopathic).

In later articles, Karpman postulated that "symptomatic" cases were neurotics "parading" as psychopaths,
and that "true" psychopathy never resulted from emotional causes (132). True psychopathy, according to
Karpman, always came from an unmeasurable "constitutional acquisitiveness and aggression" (133).

Karpman's exclusion of psychogenic causes from psychopathy seemed to many social scientists an unjustifi-
able obstacle to further analysis of both causes and

treatment. Hervey Cleckly, among others, attacked Karpman's classification: "I cannot, however, follow him in the assumption that, when he or any other investigator does not succeed in finding basic conflict and a dynamic pattern behind pathologic behavior, such factors can be regarded as nonexistent." [7]

Robert Lindner observed the same character structure in the patients whom he treated. Lindner's experiments immeasurably broadened knowledge of the psychopath's physiology, childhood, and personality.

While some scientists worked with the definition and theory of psychopathy, others laboriously attacked specific segments of the problem. Throughout the depression, research on causation flourished, and numerous workers produced evidence concerning the psychopath's brain waves, the functions of his cortex, his childhood experiences, the characteristics of his family, and the effects of early social isolation upon his personality.

With the coming of the second World War and the military draft, managing the psychopath assumed new dimensions. In the armed forces the psychopath's behavior soon brought him to the attention of the Medical Corps, the correctional services, and even the General Staff. Numerous articles appeared dealing with the problems of segregation, diagnosis, and treatment.

By the end of the war, social science had come to realize the importance and the danger of the psychopath. The work of Karpman, Henderson, Cleckly, and Lindner laid foundations for the growing research into causation and treatment. At long last the dispute about whether the psychopath really existed had come to rest.

Although a few demurred, most observers felt that the psychopath differed so markedly from the normal criminal, the neurotic, or the psychotic that he must be thought of as having a separate disorder. From those who treated the psychopath came the stoutest defense of the concept. The American psychiatrist Chornyak commented: "Those of us who work in psychiatric clinics and in courts . . . continuously have to deal with this type of abnormal personality" (37, p. 1327). And an English psychiatrist, E. T. O. Slater, said in 1946: "If we were to drop the term altogether, we should be obliged to invent an equivalent or to overlook a whole series of clinically very important phenomenon" (236).

By 1951, the editors of the influential *British Journal of Delinquency* could, without fear of criticism, devote an entire issue to psychopathy and announce: ". . . Psychopathy has now emerged as the most important of the great transitional (borderline) groups of mental disorders . . . it occupies a fixed intermediate position in a hierarchy of developmental disorders. . . ." [8]

At mid-century, social science underwent another shift of emphasis. The problem of definition seemed close to solution, and the issues of causation had been clarified by research; but the treatment of the psychopath remained an obscure field.

Scientists coming from all branches of psychology, psychiatry, and sociology increasingly focused their attention on treatment. Physicians experimented with barbiturates, dilantin sodium, shock therapy, and lobotomy. Social workers called on the techniques of group therapy and psychodrama. A handful of psychoanalysts hesitatingly applied their methods, and psychologists attempted therapy ranging from informal counseling to hypnoanalysis.

Significant findings came from those who worked with maladjusted children. Few of the pioneers in child therapy concerned themselves exclusively with the psychopathic child. Yet, by the 1950's, observers felt that the work of Aichhorn, Bettelheim, Redl, and Papanek offered considerable hope for the psychopathic child. (See Chapter 5.)

Along with the greater emphasis on treatment, the early 1950's marked the emergence of another significant trend: a linking of psychopathy with politics. Nazi concentration camps had stirred the world's interest both in those who directed the horrors and in those who committed them. Although much of the behavior of many storm troopers could be understood as fanatical obedience, some psychologists discerned a psychopathic tone in some of the Nazis.

G. M. Gilbert, chief psychologist at the Nuremberg trials, described Hermann Goering as an "amiable psychopath." Gilbert pointed to Goering's brutal, loveless childhood as typical of the psychopath's background. Goering's father was a stern Prussian official who valued military discipline above all else. Goering's earliest memory was of "bashing his mother in the face with both fists when she came to embrace him after a prolonged absence. . . ." (80).

As a child, Goering loved excitement, the glaring splash of military uniforms, and early exhibited his taste for sadistic brutality. Uncontrolled behavior and vicious attacks on his sisters led his parents to shift Goering from school to school. His mother predicted: "Hermann will either be a great man or a great criminal!" (80, p. 213).

In his youth, Goering's drive for glory, his brutality, his emotional impulsiveness, and his aggressiveness "found its most desirable expression in the military prerogatives of his culture" (80, pp. 213-214). Goering's recklessness earned him the distinction of being one of Germany's top air aces in World War I, but his uncontrolled greed brought him into illegal wartime adventures. He took illicit leaves, accepted bribes, and established a clandestine army supply company.

After the war, he married a rich Swedish countess. Despite his newly found wealth, Goering missed the excitement of war. Attracted by Hitler's militancy, Goering was swept into the Nazi party. He moved from honor to honor as president of the Reichstag, head of Nazi industry, and chief of the Luftwaffe. His objective was expressed in a Reichstag speech: "I am not here to exercise justice, but to wipe out and exterminate!" (80, p. 218).

Goering's spectacular rise to power provided him with the means of satisfying his craving for pleasure. He turned to drug addiction, mistresses, and "Roman" orgies. As Germany collapsed, Goering pranced through his palace, Karinhall, dressed in a toga, with painted fingernails and lips.

With the fall of Germany, Goering, along with the other Nazi leaders, went on trial for his part in the war crimes. Gilbert, who came to know Goering during the trial, noticed a singular lack of guilt. After seeing a documentary film of mutilated bodies from a concentration camp, for example, Goering commented only: "It was such a good afternoon, too, until they showed that film —they were reading my telephone conversations on the Austrian matter and everybody was laughing with me— and then they showed that awful film, and it just spoiled everything" (80, p. 226).

Before ending his life with poison, Goering left this message for the West: "You Americans are making a stupid mistake with your talk of democracy and morality. . . . Don't think that Germans have become more Christian and less nationalistic all of a sudden . . . you can take your morality and your repentance and your democracy and stick it up!" (80, p. 228).

Many features of Goering's personality fit the psychopathic syndrome: his asociality, his impulsive craving for pleasure, and his guiltlessness; but other traits seem atypical (for example, his ability to carry out the long-range plans necessary in administrative tasks). Yet, Hermann Goering illustrates a frightening possibility: with luck, with the right social and political conditions, a psychopath could gain control over a nation's destiny. Robert Lindner has soberly warned: "The psychopath is not only a criminal, he is the embryonic storm trooper" (153).

Other investigators in the early 1950's traced a predilection of criminals for a political ideology centered around ethnocentrism, admiration of power, authoritarianism, and conservatism. The writers of *The Authoritarian Personality* found that convicts were generally more antidemocratic than any other segment of the population (3). Naturally, we do not equate criminality with psychopathy, but it seems probable that the psychopath's aggression, his lack of respect for others, and his intermittent need for outside control of his behavior would predispose him to an authoritarian ideology.

Reviewing the history of "psychopathy" shows that a small group of investigators, with only a few setbacks, have built an impressive ladder of knowledge:

   In the early 1800's, Pinel, Pritchard, and Lombroso first described and labeled the "morally insane."

1878, Gouster presented the first complete delineation of the psychopath's symptoms.

In the early 1900's, Meyer, Birnbaum, and others excluded irrelevant disorders from the concept.

In 1918, Glueck studied the behavior and characteristics of the psychopath in prison.

In the 1920's and 1930's, numerous scientists empirically attacked the problem of causation.

In the 1940's and the 1950's, many investigators experimented with the full-scale studies of the psychopath's psychology and introduced the modern concept of the disorder.

In the 1940's and the 1950's, many investigators experimented with the treatment of the psychopath and connected his disorder with other social and political problems.

By mid-century, no investigator of the psychopathic personality had to begin entirely anew; he could draw upon the accumulated theories and research of 150 years. Perhaps the most important achievement of these investigations has been the establishment of psychopathy as an independent personality syndrome. As the editors of the *British Journal of Delinquency* commented in 1951: "It is no longer possible to maintain without fear of brisk contradiction that the concept of psychopathy is a psychiatric fiction covering inadequacies in clinical classification. . . ."

Yet this research has not solved the problem of causation. The British editors continued: ". . . fifty years of sporadic investigation of the subject have resulted in little more than a profusion of contending generalizations . . . our understanding of psychopathy is still rudimentary and our researches wretchedly inadequate." [9]

The debate on causation continues at a brisk pace. In 1953, G. N. Thompson argued in his *The Psychopathic Delinquent* that psychopathy could, in all cases, be traced to brain damage while, in contrast, Carl Frankenstein, in 1959, interpreted the disorder primarily in psychogenic, Jungian "terms" (256, 69). And, at the same time, British psychiatrist Harold Palmer resurrected the ghosts of the 1930's when he attributed psychopathy to a "cerebral pathophysiology" of a seemingly constitutional, genetically determined variety.[10] The disparate strands of evidence need to be drawn into a unified whole.

Moreover, these years of research have failed to cope with the psychopathic disorder. Therapy awaits further scientific investigation.

The structure of the psychopath's personality needs deeper study. There is some, but not enough, knowledge of what goes on inside the psychopath's mind, how he differs from other deviants, and how he can be correctly diagnosed.

NOTES

1. Quoted in David Henderson (111, p. 11).
2. *Ibid.*, p. 13.
3. Quoted in S. B. Maughs (165, p. 345). Maughs presents a comprehensive review of the history of psychopathy.
4. *Ibid.*
5. This is the description settled upon in the British Mental Deficiency Act of 1913.
6. Although Richard Aldington (5) emphasizes the negative qualities of Lawrence of Arabia, his biography gives little evidence of psychopathy.
7. Quoted in A. Cruvant and Leon Yochelson (48).
8. *British Journal of Delinquency*, 2:77, 1951.
9. *Ibid.*, p. 78.
10. Palmer also returned to the diagnostic confusion of the 1930's by defining psychopaths as "individuals who seem to be more or less permanently awry" (188, p. 1). Admitting that the definition represented a hodgepodge of types, Palmer nevertheless included under the rubric of psychopathy those who suffer from intense anxiety, hysteria, depression, mania, paranoia, and a variety of other conditions.

3

The Problem of Diagnosis

Everyone is forced into a pattern. . . .

JOSEF BORLOV, San Quentin convict

The concept of psychopathy has been greatly clarified during the past hundred years. Unfortunately, however, the studies seldom influenced workers in the field: the police court judges, the wardens, the prison psychologists. Each of these workers used his own definition of the disorder, so the practical task of uniform diagnosis remained.

Conflicting published reports illustrate this diagnostic dilemma. At one Illinois state prison, 98 per cent of the inmates were labeled "psychopathic." At another midwestern prison, psychiatrists diagnosed only 5 per cent as "psychopathic" (239). The diagnosis of sex offenders offers another example of this confusion: 52 per cent at New York's Bellevue Hospital were called "psychopathic," but only 15 per cent who appeared before the New York's courts' psychiatric clinic were so titled (239). Obviously, these institutions meant very different things when they spoke of psychopathy.

This confusion on the practical level simply reflects the "battle of diagnosis" which is fought (and refought) on the theoretical plane. Some contemporary psychiatric schools of thought attempt to redefine the concept of psychopathy as just another variety of neurosis. This tendency may, as Richard Jenkins has argued, come from the desire of some psychiatrists to depict all mental aberrations as the result of internal conflict. As Jenkins has pointed out, ". . . [the] realization that morbid conditions may be due primarily to a *lack* of conflict within the personality represents a readjustment of thinking which is apparently beyond the flexibility of many professional persons" (123, p. 318). Other scientists, particularly in the ranks of American sociology, would prefer to deny the existence of the psychopath altogether. This tendency to reject the concept emerges, at least partially, from the sociologist's belief that all crime is "natural"— in the sense that the criminal, like other men, has been subjected to a process of socialization which leads him to differ from the norms employed by the middle class. Because of the historical connotations of "psychopathy"— that it is a "constitutional," innate, incurable disorder —some sociologists apparently fear that the concept is retrogressive and a burden to scientific research.

This continuing debate has eventuated in a number of books aimed primarily at clarifying the dilemma of diagnosis.[1] Indeed, Carl Frankenstein has described his recent *Psychopathy* as entirely "a study in clinical semantics" (69). Much of the confusion arises from viewing all deviant behavior as psychopathic. Many investigators, particularly those who make unusually high estimates of the incidence of psychopathy, seem to use antisocial behavior as their sole diagnostic criterion.

Deviant behavior alone is, of course, an inadequate standard. It obscures the critical distinction between the psychopath and other deviants, complicates the study of causation, and hinders experimentation in therapy. Both the study and the treatment of psychopathy require clear classification.

Some contemporary psychiatrists have proposed that diagnosis of psychopathy be based entirely on causative factors. Unfortunately, those who advocate such a criterion cannot agree about its causes. Karpman, for example, maintains that the psychopathic label should be applied only when the individual's disorder has "idiopathic" (presumably constitutional) causes. "In the true psychopath," he wrote, "we have instinctive antisocial behavior which is without any motive except that associated with constitutional acquisitiveness and aggression" (133). Karpman never defines "constitutional acquisitiveness," nor does he show how it differs from those drives which he would term "neurotic" (i.e., "the search for security, the satisfaction of the ego, or the struggle for power") (133).

Ralph Rabinovitch, another psychiatrist, apparently agrees with Karpman that the diagnosis of psychopathy should be based on causation. He does not agree, however, that psychopathy is caused by a constitutional predisposition. Just as stoutly as Karpman would limit psychopathy to constitutional causes, Rabinovitch would confine it to psychogenic causes. In direct contrast to Karpman, Rabinovitch believes that the "definitely known cause" of the disorder is childhood emotional deprivation (201).

These two opposing positions present the inadequacy of a causative standard for diagnosis. Despite diagnostic confusion, most researchers agree upon the existence of a distinct psychopathic syndrome. Furthermore, recent studies have shown that psychological tools can successfully distinguish the psychopath from other individuals. These studies have turned to personality structure as the key to diagnosis.

One group of investigators used projective tests, particularly the Rorschach, in an attempt to establish reliable diagnostic tools. Robert Lindner initiated this movement in 1943 with a study of convicts. He administered the Rorschach to 40 "normal" criminals and 40 psychopathic criminals. The psychopathic group had originally been determined by the prison psychiatric staff on the basis of clinical interviews.[2] In their Rorschach protocols, the two groups exhibited profound qualitative differences.[3] The psychopaths showed an intense explosiveness, an almost complete egocentricity, general superficiality, and an avoidance of threatening material (155).

Stimulated by Lindner's discovery, other researchers used the Rorschach in their investigations of the psychopath's personality structure. Heuser, in 1946, found the same qualities (shallowness and violent upheavals) in the responses of 28 psychopathic soldiers. In addition, Heuser's protocols showed the men to be "ruled by basic instinctual and sexual desires," lacking inner controls, and unable to learn from experience (112).

In 1947, Bowlus and Shotwell confirmed the Rorschach findings of Lindner and Heuser in a study of 12 psychopathic girls at the Pacific Colony (27).

While some scientists worked with Rorschach analyses,[4] others investigated the application of the Thematic Apperception Test (T.A.T.) and the Picture Frustration

Test. In 1943, Kutash administered the T.A.T. to 60
psychopathic morons. Their most frequent responses
showed aggression, eroticism, fear of death, an unconscious desire for punishment, "separation anxiety" (fear
of rejection by society or family), and "ambition conflicts." [5]

In 1952, Holzberg and Hahn used the Picture Frustration Test on 17 psychopathic boys and a control group
of normal delinquents in a reform school. Although the
psychopathic boys appeared no more extrapunitive than
other delinquents, they seemed to have much less inhibition of aggression when faced with the disapproval of
authority figures.[6] And Albert Rosen has demonstrated
that another standard test, the MMPI, can successfully
differentiate the psychopathic syndrome (210).

Handwriting analysis, too, has been tried in the search
for diagnostic aids. In 1935, Naegelsbach compared the
handwriting of 59 "aggressive psychopaths" to 30 "inadequate psychopaths" (probably acting-out neurotics).
He believed that the powerful, free, and large writing of
the aggressive cases reflected their overstimulation, excitability, and force (177). Naegelsbach's provocative
paper did not cite his methods for selecting psychopathic
cases. Consequently, it has had little practical influence
in clarifying the problem.

One of the most challenging attempts to differentiate
the psychopath from the normal person was initiated by
Simon, Holzberg, and Unger. In 1951, these scientists
investigated Cleckly's hypothesis that psychopaths learn
social values but do not act in accord with them when
conflict arises between primitive desires and social restrictions. They administered a completion test to 22
psychopathic women and 22 student nurses at the Long
Lane School.[7] The psychopathic women significantly
more frequently chose responses which disregarded the
wishes of others.

Social science in the last decade has been concerned
not only with showing which personality traits characterize the psychopathic syndrome, but also with finding
which traits do not.

Intelligence has frequently been proposed as a standard for diagnosis. Observers in the early 1900's (e.g.,

Mercier) believed that the psychopath was mentally defective. More recently, scientists (e.g., Henderson) have emphasized intellectual brilliance as typical of the syndrome. In 1947, Milton Gurvitz laid the dispute to rest by proving that the psychopath is neither a dullard nor a genius. In a comprehensive examination of 3,649 inmates of a federal prison, Gurvitz found that the 851 psychopaths had the same I.Q. distribution as the non-psychopathic convicts. Moreover, neither group significantly differed from the intelligence range of normal Americans (105). And Lewis Sherman's recent study has demonstrated that the memories of psychopaths are actually more retentive than those of either neurotic or normal subjects (221, p. 25).

Some psychiatrists have used "incurability" as a major criterion of psychopathy (132). This "diagnostic" standard has obstructed therapeutic experimentation in psychopathy as it did in "dementia praecox." [8] When dementia praecox was assumed incurable, research stagnated. Gradually, a few studies showed that the disease could be successfully treated. The "incurable" connotation of dementia praecox was abandoned, but, in its time, it did great harm. Recent research indicates that the judgment of "incurability" is just as inapplicable in the study of psychopathy. The psychopath, though difficult to treat, is not incurable. (See Chapter 5.)

Although the postwar period has witnessed a flurry of new discoveries about diagnosis, the problem has not been completely solved. Michael Craft, after reviewing contemporary diagnostic standards, arrived at the conclusion—an unduly pessimistic one, we believe—that no existing "ancillary methods" can aid in diagnosing the psychopathic personality (46). The psychological tests applied during the last decade should be of considerable value, but tests are needed which tap the psychopath's basic symptoms: his apparent guiltlessness and his difficulty in relating to others.[9]

Impulsivity, aggressiveness, egocentricity, though symptomatic of the psychopath, do not distinguish him from other deviants. The paranoid can be ruthlessly aggressive, the neurotic can be narcissistic, and a manic-depressive psychotic can be purposelessly impulsive. The psycho-

path's underdeveloped conscience and his inability to
identify with others differentiate him from other deviants.

The next decades will probably produce adequate tests
of guilt and relational ability, but until that development,
clinical judgment must carry the major burden in diagnosis. Tests can help, but the scientist's perception of
the over-all personality structure provides the most dependable criterion. Again, we should emphasize that
total personality, rather than a single behavioral feature,
is the key to diagnosis.

Such a "gestalt" approach to diagnosis requires that
the observer should possess more than the usual amount
of knowledge concerning the past actions and attitudes
of his patient; he cannot depend, as with many other
disorders, on the overt behavior, symptoms, or complaints
of the subject at the time of contact. Nevertheless, the
task is not impossible, for a consensus seems to have
been reached empirically on the "clinical signs" which
distinguish the psychopathic syndrome. Craft, for example, reviewed some 200 clinical and scientific references
on the psychopathic personality and found that seven
traits—most prominently, "affectionlessness," antisocial
behavior, and guiltlessness—were commonly used in describing the psychopathic pattern.[10] A comparison of the
psychopath with other deviants should highlight the
unique pattern of his personality.

The psychopath certainly differs from the *psychotic*.
Yet, at times, the two disorders have been confused. Not
only have psychopaths been misdiagnosed as psychotic
(178), but, as a recent study by Bernard Glueck, Jr., has
shown, psychotics have been mislabeled as psychopaths
(84). Glueck, director of the Sex Research Project at
Sing Sing, subjected 200 sex offenders to a thorough psychological examination. Most of the men had been diagnosed (at some period in their lives) as psychopathic personalities. Deeper analysis indicated, however, that the
convicts actually suffered from a type of schizophrenia.
Under well-developed defenses, the sex offenders had
subtle delusions, mild depression, and anxiety arising
from basic conflict. In addition, most of these sex "psychopaths" felt guilty about their crimes.[11]

As Glueck's study illustrates, psychotics have a variety of symptoms. They share, however, a serious loss of contact with reality (269). The psychotic withdraws from frustration and creates a private delusional world. Self-reference pervades his thinking, and hallucinations surround him. Sometimes the psychotic undergoes extreme depression (involutional melancholia), sometimes an exalted grandiosity (hebephrenic schizophrenia). Often, he has delusions of persecution (paranoia). In some psychotic varieties, he alternates torpor with frenzy (manic-depressive psychosis).

A recent longitudinal study of psychotics has indicated that in childhood, long before the appearance of overt symptoms, psychotics were withdrawn, introverted, and plagued by unrealistic fears and feelings of inferiority— a pattern which clearly differentiates them from the typical psychopath's history of impulsive antisocial behavior (171).

Whatever the form, psychosis differs from psychopathy in that the psychotic generally withdraws from reality, but the psychopath attacks;[12] the psychotic usually creates a world of hallucinations, but the psychopath does not; and the psychotic often feels intense guilt (or at least intense anxiety), but the psychopath never does.

One type of psychosis, that of *paranoia*, has proved particularly difficult to distinguish from the psychopathic syndrome—and indeed, as Norman Cameron observed, ". . . in actual clinical practice," the task of differentiating the paranoid states from other varieties of disorder, ". . . often seems hardly worth the effort" (34, p. 508). Some paranoids, of course, exhibit persistent, complex, and highly logical delusional systems which set them apart from the usual run of psychopaths. Others, officially described in the American Psychiatric Association's classification as suffering from a "paranoid state," have persecutory or grandiose delusions of an unsystematized and often transitory nature; they are not subject to the hallucinations characteristic of schizophrenics. In such cases, if certain psychopathic traits are present, diagnostic distinctions become blurred and often impossible. The notorious case of Charles Starkweather, murderer of 11 people, demonstrates the difficulty.

In a period of 59 days, between 1957 and 1958, Charles Starkweather, a 19-year-old Nebraskan, went on an orgy of murder. Included among his 11 victims were the family of his paramour, Caril Fugate, who accompanied him in the rampage. When intensively interviewed in his death cell by James Reinhardt, Starkweather exhibited an almost classic picture of psychopathy. "In approximately thirty hours of interviewing," Reinhardt commented, "I never witnessed a sign of genuine remorse. Once, when he was telling me about how Jesus came to him in his cell, I asked, 'How do you feel about killing the little girl?' He retorted: 'What could we do with the kid? Do you think we could take her with us?' " (205, p. 16). His fundamental guiltlessness was illustrated in the fact that he and Caril celebrated a sexual orgy in the same house with the three bodies of her family. From childhood onwards, Starkweather had been plagued by unsatisfied desires for power, by feelings that everyone hated him, and by the desire to kill. Before the murders, he would often practice with a gun in front of a mirror: 'If I'd a killed as many people as I've shot at myself I'd a killed a thousand" (205, p. 99). He always felt lonely, cut off from other people. Caril Fugate's presence temporarily helped Starkweather overcome his aloneness. However, her erotic stimulation provided the match which exploded his emotions: "Caril stirred up somethin' in me . . . guess it wuz already there 'cause it came easy and seemed like it wuz somethin' I'de been waiting fer" (205, p. 69). Guns and knives came to symbolize power for him, and finally he used them with horrible effect.

Yet, along with his psychopathic characteristics, Starkweather showed pronounced persecutory symptoms and certain delusions which might lead some diagnosticians to call him paranoid. At night, for example, he believed that "Death"—a tangible figure to Starkweather, one which he could even draw for Reinhardt—visited him in his home or his cell. Psychiatrists for both prosecution and defense seemed equally confused about the proper label for him. Psychiatrists for the state declared that Starkweather suffered from a "personality disorder" but that he was neither "medically nor legally insane." Defense psychiatrists testified that Starkweather was incapable of premeditation (in the legal sense) and that "Pumping bullets into a human is no different to Starkweather than pumping bullets into a rabbit" (205, p. 11). Both sides agreed, therefore, on the essentially psychopathic nature of the criminal, but Reinhardt, after his investigation, tended to describe the killer as "paranoid" and psychotic. It would be fruitless to continue the controversy, for Starkweather falls in that shadowy borderline area between psychopathy and psychosis.

The distinction between the usual run of *neurotics* and psychopaths seems reasonably clear. The neurotic, like the psychotic, feels intense anxiety and inner conflict. He is continually under tension, chronically dissatisfied, and often (although not always) rigid and inhibited. The neurotic attempts to solve this conflict in a variety of ways: by repression, by regression, or by other protective mechanisms. He may develop a phobia (an unreasoning fear of certain symbols), an obsession (a persistent idea oppressing his thoughts), an hysteric symptom (paralysis, anesthesia), or he may revert to severe anxiety attacks if all defenses fail.

The neurotic tries to assuage his inner disturbance with unrealistic means. He does not, like the psychotic, sever his contacts with reality. He can still function in society and can still take care of himself. The degree of social adjustment best marks the hazy dividing line between "insanity" and neurosis.

The personality of the psychopath differs greatly from that of the neurotic: the neurotic feels intense inner anxiety, but the psychopath feels little; the neurotic is often oppressed by guilt, but the psychopath apparently feels no guilt at all; the neurotic can usually maintain bonds of love, but the psychopath seldom can; the neurotic usually represses his hostility, but the psychopath rarely does. In fact, psychopathy is almost the antithesis of neurosis. In terms of emotional sensitivity, the neurotic is "thin-skinned," and the psychopath is "thick-skinned."

Recent research (148) has indicated the incompatibility of the two disorders.[13] In 1944, Mason studied 636 military criminals and discovered that the psychopathic criminals had the least neurotic characteristics. From the

Army's point of view, Mason concluded, the neurotic was the better risk (164).

Although the psychopath is radically different from the average neurotic, he is not so easily distinguished from the *"acting-out neurotic."* [14] Like other neurotics, the "acting-out neurotic" feels chronic inner conflict. Instead of repressing his feelings, the acting-out neurotic tries to resolve the conflict through antisocial behavior. Usually such behavior runs in episodic spurts. For a time he maintains a sullen, depressed demeanor, but when anxiety and tension increase unbearably, he explodes into aggressive attacks.[15] In an analysis of some 5,000 child guidance clinic cases, Richard Jenkins and Sylvia Glickman (124) demonstrated that both psychopathic children and "socialized delinquents" differ strikingly from the neurotic cases. The "syndrome of internal conflict" which they noted among the neurotics included such traits as inferiority feelings, depression, undue worries, and extreme sensitivity—characteristics which clearly distinguish such patients from the psychopathic character.[16]

Many so-called "sex-psychopaths" are really acting-out neurotics. Their behavior stems from compulsion, hysteria, and depression, which can be appeased only through action (134). The psychopath is often sexually deviant, but he seldom becomes fixated on a particular object. He is sometimes homosexual, sometimes heterosexual. He is willing to try anything, but no compulsion drives him to do so. Unlike the typical sex offender, he does not concentrate on one bizarre form of gratification.

Similarly, alcoholics are often labeled as psychopathic when they would be more correctly described as acting-out neurotics. Although some psychopaths may be diagnosed as alcoholics, the typical alcoholic craves satisfaction of his dependency needs and tends to express this craving either while drunk or sober (170), and, unlike the psychopath, the alcoholic generally exhibits signs of extreme guilt.

This confusion between the psychopath and the acting-out neurotic is understandable since (superficially) their symptoms are so similar.[17] The case history of a neurotic San Quentin convict, who shall be called "Jack

Baker," should help to differentiate between acting-out neurosis and psychopathy.

Jack Baker was born in a rural community in New York. Because of his parents' harsh treatment, Baker ran away from home when he was 12. Police captured him and returned him to his parents, who committed him to a reform school. Although the school had no walls, Baker refused to run away because he had given his word that he would remain.

At the age of 15, he began "hoboing" around the nation, supporting himself by farm work and burglaries. During this period, he "rolled" drunks, robbed apartments, and was continually in fist fights. He drifted to California and began stealing cars which he then sold to a "fence." In 1949, he was strolling on the Long Beach "Pike" looking for pickpocket prospects. He stopped before a "hell-fire and brimstone" preacher whose eloquence convinced him that he should reform.

Baker turned himself in to the Los Angeles police. They telegraphed his parents, offering to return the boy to New York, but the parents refused to accept him. At 19, Baker was too old for reform school. Therefore, he was sent to San Quentin for burglary and theft.

Baker recorded his impressions of San Quentin:[18]

> When you arrive, you are dazed and sort of numb to any feeling. You are led into the inside of the towering grey walls, then out a gate into a lovely garden. "Ah," you sigh, "this isn't bad after all." But you are soon stripped of clothes and assigned to the West Block as a "fish.". . . You have a cell partner. He's a nice guy. He shows you how to pick locks. You are alone with your dreams and no one pays any attention to you.
>
> Some of the men get to ridiculing you. They call you "Punk.". . . That night, your cell-mate gives you a knife. You thank him and think he is trying to act like a movie character. Your cell-mate asks you why you don't line up with so and so, so you do. Now you are happy. Self-consciousness flees when you are with your new friends. You can face those guys who call you "Punk." Up to now, you have been quiet and never in trouble, always a good worker. . . .
>
> But now you must impress your new friends and prove to

yourself that you are afraid of nothing. So you begin robbing cells, staying out of school, refusing to work, getting smart with the guards, sneaking in the show, getting up for seconds. And your friends went with you.

Now you've been caught. You stand naked with the loot before you. (Everything you do in here seems to be an occasion for disrobing you.) So, up to the shelf you went. After that, you go to the Hole. Finally, you are sent to the South Block Segregation. There, a big Negro tries to con you. He has a knife. You cry with shame. You ask Smith to send you back to Old Prison Segregation.[19] He tells you to go fight the Negro. You can't believe it. The man must know that you could be killed. The next morning you did fight the nigger, but you couldn't seem to hurt him and he kept backing you up. . . .

As Baker's story indicates, he became one of the prison "tough guys." But his toughness did not come from guiltlessness or from callous disregard for others. Baker is not a psychopath. He feels tremendous guilt, he is "self-conscious," and he "cries with shame." A further excerpt shows Baker's confusion and anxiety:

Ever since I can remember, everything concerning sex has been embarrassing to me. Why this is so I have never been able to learn. As I grew older, I began to desire relations with women, but because of my acute embarrassment, those relationships I did have with them were unsatisfactory. I hate myself for these thoughts. I feel the desire to gratify my sex impulses, while at the same time, I feel disgust for such things and at myself for being so weak.

Baker has the neurotic symptoms of permeating anxiety and intense inner conflict; yet he reacts with aggression rather than repression. This characteristic marks him as an acting-out neurotic.

The acting-out neurotic has, in common with the psychopath, the behavioral symptoms of aggressiveness and asociality. But, unlike the psychopath, the acting-out neurotic possesses strong guilt feelings and is plagued by intense anxiety.

Psychotics and neurotics, acting-out neurotics and psychopaths are all psychologically disordered people. In one way or another their personalities have become maladjusted. Often they come into conflict with the demands of society. Yet not all personality maladjustment results in behavioral deviance (a degree of compulsiveness, for example, is almost a prerequisite for the successful scholar).

Not all deviance, on the other hand, results from a disordered personality. Many *criminals and delinquents*, though socially maladjusted, are psychologically healthy people. In one study of delinquents, in fact, Sheldon and Eleanor Glueck found that 48.6 per cent had no conspicuous mental pathology (92).

Increasingly, social scientists have recognized that criminality cannot be equated with psychopathy. In 1951, British investigators compared psychopathic and nonpsychopathic convicts, using clinical interviews, E.E.G. examinations, and psychological tests. The psychopaths exhibited much greater resentment of parents (particularly of fathers), insensitivity to moral appeals, inability to profit from punishment, and a complete lack of long-range goals. They revealed more neurological difficulties, more abnormal E.E.G. patterns, and greater proclivity for serious crimes. The psychopaths differed so significantly from the other criminals that the investigators concluded: "The psychopath in prison is a clinical entity distinct from other prisoners." (237).[20] In the study of child guidance cases by Richard Jenkins and Sylvia Glickman, they noted a "syndrome of socialized delinquency" which clearly differed from the psychopathic syndrome (124).

The total pattern of the psychopath's personality differentiates him from the normal criminal. His aggression is more intense, his impulsivity more pronounced, his emotional relations more shallow. His guiltlessness, however, is the critical distinguishing trait. The normal criminal has an internalized, albeit warped, set of values. If he violates these standards, he feels guilt. The words of a professional criminal, reported by a psychologist at San Quentin, portray these subcultural mores:

> I befriended this man, gave him money. He was down and out and I helped him get on his feet. I introduced him to my friends. I taught him the trade. I always insisted that he get a good-sized cut of the proceeds. He was quite happy. He was now well off. In one of the jobs, he was caught to-

gether with several others. I escaped. All the others kept
their peace. He squealed on me. . . . Such an action is
almost incomprehensible to me (41, p. 114).

Thus, any study of delinquents or criminals must distinguish between three varieties of offenders:

(1) the "socialized delinquent" who has, partly, been
formed by a deviant subculture and who adheres to the
values of his group;

(2) the "neurotic delinquent," whose behavior springs
from the anxiety created by unresolved, unconscious conflicts; and

(3) the "psychopathic delinquent" who commits a
wide gamut of aggressive acts without anxiety, without
guilt, and without attachment to any other human being.
Fortunately, certain groups, such as the research branch
of the California Youth Authority, are undertaking systematic diagnostic research aimed toward providing the
proper treatment for each type. On the adult level, the
efforts of J. D. Grant and M. Q. Grant in the development of a "maturity scale" for diagnosing different types
of criminals should soon furnish social science with systematic techniques for measuring the differences among
delinquents (99).

Accurate diagnoses often facilitate the development of
curative measures. Results of psychological testing and the
contributions of comparative studies have illustrated the
gulf which separates the psychopath from other criminals,
from the neurotic, and from the psychotic. Admittedly,
the proliferation of definitions, the tendency to expand the
concept to include all deviant behavior, the discrepancies
in judgment between different observers—these pitfalls
in the history of the concept—are enough to make a
systematic diagnostician weep. Yet, under whatever term
—"*manie sans délire*," "affectionless character," "aneto-
path," "idiopath," "born criminal," "sociopath"—the
psychopath has made his existence known for 150 years.
The fact that observers have been forced to utilize the
concept in every Western country from Ecuador to Israel
suggests its indispensability. The idea of the psychopath
". . . has the important virtue that, as a result of long
usage and much observation and argument, it is now a

realistically descriptive term based on experience, rather than a theoretical term based on a deduction from preconceived premises" (123, p. 318).

In order to cure his disorder, the psychopath must be recognized as having a unique personality syndrome of aggressiveness, guiltlessness, affectional shallowness, and extreme impulsivity. Techniques which help the psychotic or the neurotic do not work equally well with the psychopath.[21] Nor do causal explanations which have fitted other disorders apply to psychopathy.

Some of the same men who have clarified the concept of psychopathy have addressed themselves to the challenging problem of causation. The last 30 years have marked a proliferation of theories and a smaller, but still impressive, amount of evidence concerning the cause of psychopathy. It is with this issue that the next chapter deals.

NOTES

1. See Schneider (216) and Palmer (187).

2. Lindner, Heuser, Bowlus, and Shotwell used approximately the same definition of psychopathy as that presented in Chapter 1.

3. Although Lindner found marked qualitative differences in the protocols, he did not find quantitative differences between the answers of the two groups.

4. Sheldon and Eleanor Glueck in their significant study of causation, *Unraveling Juvenile Delinquency* (92), also used the Rorschach as a diagnostic tool for differentiating various forms of mental pathology. Since their study concerned other problems, they have not as yet published an analysis of the psychopathic delinquents' responses.

5. Kutash, (140) selected his cases primarily on the basis of intense antisocial behavior and egocentricity. He probably included acting-out neurotics in the sample.

6. Holzberg and Hahn (118) used intense behavioral aggression as the major standard for selection.

7. Simon, Holzberg, and Unger (233) selected the psychopathic women in accord with Cleckly's "clinical profile," one which closely agrees with the description of the psychopath in Chapter 1.

8. The unfortunate connotation of "constitutional incurabil-

ity" adhering to the label "psychopathy" was one of the major
reasons why the American Psychiatric Association replaced the
term with "sociopathy" in 1952 (108).

Many psychologists are reluctant to prejudice a child's future
by labeling him a psychopath. If the standard of incurability
is abandoned, the term is no more opprobrious than "neurotic,"
"behavior disorder," or "psychotic."

9. The Picture Frustration Test and the completion test
described above have potential value in diagnosing the psychopath's guiltlessness. Research in this area has been sporadic,
and the usefulness of the tests has not been established. In
Chapter 6 of the previous edition of this book, we described
a test of guilt feelings which can be applied to child psychopaths and may help to solve this diagnostic problem.

In testing "affectional ability," structured situations have
sometimes been used. Such a method is cumbersome, and
other methods need to be devised.

10. Craft's description of the psychopath (46, pp. 237-238)
corresponds to that used in this book, with one exception. As
the seventh trait of the psychopath, Craft noted that some
authors mentioned an "undue dependence on others," a characteristic which we would not commonly associate with psychopathy.

11. Dr. Glueck, in a later article (83), apparently extends
his findings with sex offenders into a general criticism of the
concept of psychopathy: "The classical hallmarks of the psychopath, his lack of anxiety and guilt, are no longer valid diagnostic criteria, since we have been able to demonstrate a great
anxiety and guilt in individuals so diagnosed." Glueck ably
demonstrates the inapplicability of the psychopathic label to his
group of sex offenders, but his evidence does not seem to con-
tradict the numerous studies which indicate the *true* psychopath's guiltlessness.

12. The paranoid psychotic is often aggressive, but at the
same time, he withdraws from reality.

13. Sheldon and Eleanor Glueck, in their study of delinquency causation (92, p. 240), found a significantly higher proportion of neuroticism in non-delinquent boys than in delinquent boys.

14. The category of acting-out neurosis has recently gained
recognition among such prominent investigators as Karpman
(134), Alexander (6), and Weinberg (266).

15. Acting-out neurotics and psychopaths have sometimes
been confused with brain-damaged patients. Brain damage can
result in aggressive, impulsive, irritable behavior; but, alone,
it does not result in the peculiar guiltlessness or emotional
callousness of the psychopath. Differential diagnosis is actually

relatively simple in the case of brain-damaged patients. Advances in psychological testing and E.E.G. analysis have provided techniques for separating the brain-damaged person from other personalities.

16. In subsequent clinical studies, Jenkins (123) has noted that both neurotic and psychopathic traits can appear in the same individual.

17. The causative studies of both Levy (146) and Greenacre (102) seem to be dealing with acting-out neurotics rather than psychopaths.

18. Quotations are from personal communications.

19. South Block Segregation was used for trouble-makers. Old Prison Segregation was used in the attempt to isolate homosexuals.

20. Prison psychiatrists selected the psychopathic cases on the basis of Henderson's definition of the psychopath. Henderson emphasized recurrent asocial conduct, lack of guilt, and unresponsiveness to treatment. Therefore, it is not surprising that the investigators discovered repeated convictions and rejection of the "lessons of punishment" in their psychopaths. Other differences cannot, however, be explained as due to the selection of cases. Resentment of fathers, ill-defined goals, and impulsiveness have no necessary correlation with antisocial conduct.

21. In recent years, substantial progress has been made in differentiating the psychotic, the neurotic, and the psychopath. In 1955, for example, Paul L. Crawford (47) reported that the LAIS, the WAIS, and the Porteus Maze significantly distinguished psychopathic from psychotic patients. The psychopaths consistently scored lower, particularly in the nonverbal sections.

In 1958, P. Pichot (192) noted that a new test, the "PNP" showed promise of significantly differentiating psychopathic disorders from other types of mental illness. In 1960, G. A. Goulds (96) showed that psychopaths have a more positive self-conception than do neurotics.

4

The Causes of Psychopathy

The child is father of the man. . . .

WORDSWORTH

"We are all born psychopaths," Harry Lipton recently observed; ". . . we are born without repressions." The newborn child has no inhibitions. He expresses anger with complete freedom. No inner control moderates his impulsivity. Certainly, the new baby has no guilt feelings. In these traits at least, all men *are* born psychopaths.

Yet almost immediately the normal baby moves out of his "psychopathic stage." The baby soon shows a need for love and perhaps a need to give love. The baby learns to control his impulses and to adjust himself to the demands of his environment. Within six months he begins to react to his environment with more effective means than sheer fury. In time, after developing inner controls, the normal baby acquires "human nature."

Why do a few children (the psychopaths) never make this transition into "humanness"? Why have they such inadequate internalized controls? Why can they not form "loving" relations? Why, as adults, do they continue to react to frustration with infantile aggression?

A great many attempts have been made to answer these questions. Some scientists have looked at reflexes, others at brain formations, others at electroencephalographic patterns, others at ancestral history, and still others at parental treatment. With these approaches, and many others, science has tried to solve the mystery of psychopathy.

Why does one man develop a psychopathic character while another man does not? We do not yet have a definitive answer, but the past decades of research have not been altogether fruitless. We know a great deal more about the psychopath than we did 25 years ago: We know something about the electrical impulses within the psy-

chopath's brain; we know more about his early family
life; and we know a great deal about the general results
of affectional isolation.

Theoretical bickering has often obscured the goal of
research. Many of those who have studied the psychopath have insisted that only their particular line of investigation could furnish a satisfactory answer to the
problem. Often, "studies" of psychopathic causation
have been circular arguments which eventually prove the
a priori judgments of the authors. There has been little
exchange of information among the various theoretical
"schools" and no synthesis of their discoveries. Since the
psychopath, like all men, is both a biological and a social
organism, many approaches must be used in studying his
disorder. In this chapter, we will attempt to bring together the various sorts of evidence into a more coherent
pattern of causation.

I. THE HEREDITARY APPROACH

Some scientists have sought the causes of psychopathy
in hereditary factors. In various ways they have attempted
to prove that the disorder results from an inherent predisposition. Such "Victorian" psychiatrists as Pritchard,
Pinel, and Kraepelin postulated that an inborn defect, an
hereditary lack of "moral sense," caused "moral insanity." Is there any evidence for this belief?

Some investigators hoped that genealogical research
would link psychopathy and heredity. G. E. Partridge, in
1928, meticulously traced the lineage of 50 psychopathic
personalities. He discovered that 24 of the cases had
ancestors "in a direct line" who showed psychopathic
traits (190).

Other investigators tried this same type of study. In
1939, an Ecuadorean psychiatrist investigated psychopathic personalities in the Quito Prison and found a
high incidence of epilepsy and alcoholism in their parents (49). In 1946, a team of American scientists discovered that 54 per cent of their psychopathic patients
had ancestral histories involving epilepsy, "maladjusted
personality," or alcoholism (95). And, in 1947, Dr. Peter
Mohr examined the case histories of 226 psychopaths ad-

mitted to the Swiss Königsfelden asylum and found that
68 per cent had maladjusted ancestors (176). In a recent
summary on the problem, P. R. Newkirk declared that
"psychopathic traits are inheritable" (180).

Many modern observers, impressed with these findings, insist that psychopathy must be an hereditary disorder. Yet, the figures give only meager support to such
a generalization.

The "hereditary" studies characteristically defined
their "psychopathic" subjects in vague terms ("erratic,
antisocial, eccentric"). Consequently, various disorders
were confused under the amorphous label of psychopathy. Their analyses did not provide for comparative
standards. In fact, the same proportion of normal people
seem to have "hereditary defects" as do psychopaths
(20). A recent study of normal people revealed that
57 per cent had a "positive family history of neuropathic
taint" (174). Finally, they have not isolated the relative
influence of heredity from that of environment. The
child raised by maladjusted parents may become psychopathic. This fact alone does not show whether heredity
or an insecure home life causes the disorder.

Franz Kallman's study, in 1930, produced provocative
findings concerning heredity versus environment. Kallman showed that the children of psychopaths have a
higher percentage of psychopathy than the siblings of psychopaths. Apparently, the incidence of the disorder does
not follow the closest lines of blood kinship, and other
factors must play the dominant role. Kallman believed
that the children of institutionalized psychopaths fell
prey to the disorder because their family status declined
when the parents were incarcerated (129).

In the 1930's other investigators attempted to ap-
praise the influence of nature and nurture by comparing
the life histories of twins. The most prominent of these
scientists, Johannes Lange and A. J. Rosanoff, hoped to
demonstrate the dominant influence of heredity by proving that identical twins had more similar personalities
than fraternal twins.[1] At least one in each pair was
known to have a criminal record. Lange discovered that
77 per cent of the identical twins and only 12 per cent
of the fraternal pairs had similar prison histories (142).

During the same year, in America, A. J. Rosanoff analyzed the criminality of 400 pairs of twins. Rosanoff also noted a greater incidence of both identical twins being delinquent than of both fraternal twins. Rosanoff found the similarity in identical twins 1.4 times that of fraternal twins—as compared to Lange's 6.4 ratio (209).

Neither Lange nor Rosanoff, however, adequately established the identical relation of the "identical" twins.[2] Critics of their work believe they had no valid basis for their conclusions. Even more importantly, both relied upon numerous agencies (of dubious reliability) for information regarding their subjects. Furthermore, analysis of Rosanoff's study reveals that the "identical" twins who had been raised in separate families had less similar criminal records.

Thus, neither study convincingly demonstrates heredity's influence on criminality. Even if identical twins do behave more similarly, this may be due (as Edwin Sutherland has pointed out) to the very similar treatment that they receive as children.

More recently, scientists have applied the "twin" method specifically to the study of psychopathic causation and have discovered no definite connection between heredity and psychopathy. Slater thoroughly studied the life histories of nine pairs of twins. Some were psychopathic, some neurotic. He found that only two of the pairs possessed similar personality traits.[3] Yet, other scientists have observed twins raised in separate environments and have found a close resemblance in the incidence of psychopathy and even the date of antisocial actions (181). This suggestion that genetic factors or perhaps early experiences in infancy plays a role led Slater to conclude that the disorder emerges from a genetic basis, but that specific symptoms were precipitated by environmental influences (234, 235).

Historically, the hereditary approach has been closely associated with the "constitutional school." Hooton, Kretchmer, and Sheldon have attempted to demonstrate a relation between physique and character. Although their work does not necessarily presuppose hereditary causation, most of the constitutionalists have postulated an hereditary basis for both physique and character.

The constitutionalists have been concerned with criminality in general, rather than with the specific problem of psychopathy.[4] Lombroso's work with Italian criminals pioneered this approach to criminal causation. Hooton's *Crime and the Man* (119) and Sheldon's *Varieties of Delinquent Youth* (220) carried it on with more sophisticated techniques. Their attempts to establish a typical criminal body-type have exerted little influence in criminology, primarily because their findings were contradictory. Hooton, for example, concluded that the criminal was physically inferior to the "normal" man. Sheldon maintained that the delinquent has a "mesomorphic" (muscular, athletic, tightly-knit) body and was, therefore, physically *superior* to the average boy.

The recent work of Sheldon and Eleanor Glueck represents the most rigorous attempt to relate bodily constitution to delinquency causation. The Gluecks compared the body types of 500 juvenile delinquents with 500 nondelinquents. They report that delinquents were generally superior in gross body size, exhibited a more homogeneous build, and (following an initial lag) develops rapidly after the fourteenth year. The Gluecks found 60.1 per cent mesomorphs among the delinquents.

Unlike other scholars, the Gluecks did not assume a necessary relation between constitution and heredity. Nor did they portray the bodily physique as the dominant cause of delinquency. Rather, they pictured bodily constitution as one factor among many dynamisms which influence behavior (92, 93).

Although the Gluecks' analysis shed light on delinquency causation, it was not designed as an investigation of psychopathy. As yet, no research shows a specific relationship between physique and the psychopathic personality.

It would appear, therefore, that the research on the constitutional or genetic basis of psychopathy is inconclusive and contradictory. Studies of twins reared in different environments hint at a constitutional predisposition, yet other research has produced evidence which contravenes this belief. The work of Kallman and the Royal Medico-Psychological Association has (tentatively) shown:

Psychopathy does not follow the lines of closest blood kinship: the children of psychopaths have a higher incidence of developing the disorder than do the siblings of psychopaths.

The ancestors of psychopaths apparently have the same incidence of hereditary "taint" as the ancestors of normal people.

In a recent study of the psychopath's ancestors, Hervey Cleckly concluded: ". . . any consistent or even suggestive history of familial inferiority is notably lacking in the present series" (38). Consequently, this facet of the disorder remains a mystery.

Heredity cannot yet be excluded as a causal factor. With more adequate delineation,[5] with more rigidly controlled experiments, and with more sensitive measurement, an hereditary link may possibly be established. Given our current knowledge, however, the extravagant claims of the geneticists must be questioned.

II. THE NEUROLOGICAL APPROACH

For more than a century, medicine has known that injuries to the brain can result in antisocial behavior. For more than three decades, some scientists have hoped to trace psychopathy to a defective brain.

In the famous "crowbar case" of 1848, a man who had been hit on the head changed from a law-abiding citizen to a "childish kind of crook: profane, obstinate, and given to outbursts of temper" (111, p. 29). Often, in the history of medicine, damaged brains have caused striking transformations in behavior.

Reports of surgical operations on the brain include similar changes in behavior. The current fashion of excising the frontal lobes sometimes turns patients into egocentric, aggressive misfits. The controversial operations of Walter Freeman and James Watts first demonstrated that prefrontal lobotomy caused certain patients to shed their social controls, their inhibitions, and their long-range goals (70). Other clinicians, such as A. Kennedy, have frequently reported the appearance of a psychopathic syndrome as a result of brain damage (136, p. 873), and a few scientists, like G. N. Thompson, have stretched these findings to the interpretation that psychopathy can *always* be correlated with cerebral injury (256).

Brain operations or other forms of injury do not always have the same results. Sometimes people become more inhibited, or intellectually retarded, or greatly depressed. Recent experiments have shown that the aggressive pattern occurs in almost every case when one specific area of the brain is damaged—the hypothalamus.

In 1944, after studying cases of verified lesions of the hypothalamic area, B. Alpers concluded that the aggressive behavior of his patients had markedly increased. In addition, "obvious antisocial tendencies and partial or complete loss of insight" occurred (11).

Experimental operations on animals further pointed to hypothalamic damage as a cause for "antisociality." Fulton and Ingraham, for example, made surgical incisions injuring the hypothalamic region of healthy, friendly cats. Immediately after the operation, the cats' behavior changed from playfulness to violent, impulsive, "sham" rage. Patting their backs produced snarling aggressiveness (74). A similar experiment with dogs, involving removal of the entire thalamic area, brought about a condition of chronic anger (60).

Disease, as well as injury, can cause an increase in antisocial conduct. In 1939, British neurologist David Henderson reported that victims of encephalitis, chorea, and epilepsy, sometimes "became transformed; those who, previously, were models of virtue and good behavior are changed into libertines and ne'er do wells" (111, p. 30). In 1942, after analyzing a great many postencephalitic children, Lauretta Bender concluded that the disease increased aggressiveness and decreased the patients' anxiety concerning his uninhibited behavior (17). The relationship is by no means invariable. F. Puntigam, in 1950, reported that not one of 15 persons who had suffered postvaccinial encephalitis developed a psychopathic pattern in the 30 years which followed their disease (199). And, in 1956, Essen-Moller (65) failed to find any psychopaths in a group of 64 adults who had undergone childhood meningitis and encephalitis.[6]

The similarity between the behavior of a brain-damaged person and the psychopath—in aggressiveness, impulsivity, and lack of inhibition—suggested a path for new investigation. The analogous behavior might be indicative of deeper similarities. In fact, many scientists believed that early brain damage might prove to be the cause of psychopathy.

The rapid development of electroencephalography permitted a partial test of this hypothesis. The new instrument made possible the tracing of electrical impulses within the brain. Early experiments soon demonstrated that brain-damaged individuals had a high incidence of abnormal waves: sharp spikes or unusually slow undulations. If the psychopath exhibited an aberrant pattern, this might indicate that he, too, suffered from a defective brain.

D. Hill and D. Watterson were the first to measure the electrical pattern of the psychopath's brain. In 1942 they tested 104 patients in a mental hospital, dividing them into "aggressive psychopaths" (aggressive, antisocial, guiltless, impulsive) and "inadequate psychopaths" (egocentric, immoral, but nonaggressive). Sixty-five per cent of the "aggressive psychopaths" evidenced abnormal E.E.G. patterns, in contrast to 32 per cent among the "inadequate psychopaths" (116).

In the same year G. Bradley measured the brain waves of child "behavior disorders." Some of these children exhibited the psychopathic traits of aggressiveness, guiltlessness, and inability to relate to others. Bradley, too, found that 65 per cent had abnormal tracings (28).

Using the same method, Silverman examined 75 "psychopaths" in a federal prison. He found that 53 per cent had definitely abnormal patterns. An additional 26 per cent had "borderline" tracings.[7] A year later, and using a larger sample of criminal subjects, Silverman repeated the experiment and obtained approximately the same results: 75 per cent of his cases had either borderline or definitely abnormal brain waves (229).

Three additional studies seemed to corroborate the assumption that brain disorder played a prominent role in psychopathy. In 1945 the British psychiatrist Sessions-Hodges examined 70 "psychopaths"; he declared that all had abnormal E.E.G. tracings.[8] In 1946 a team of American scientists (Gottlieb, Ashley, and Knott) reported that 58 of 100 "psychopaths" had abnormal patterns.[9] And in 1947 Rockwell and Simmons reported their study of 10 "psychopaths," all of whom exhibited abnormal brain waves.[10]

A comprehensive analysis of 1,000 normal individuals, in 1943, showed that only 15 per cent had abnormal patterns (77). Therefore, the studies which found that over 50 per cent of the psychopathic subjects had abnormal tracings greatly encouraged many to believe that a cause for the disorder—a defective brain—had been discovered.

Other research tempered the original enthusiasm. Simmons and Diethelm, in 1946, studied 69 criminal "psychopaths and concluded that only 27 per cent showed definitely abnormal brain waves.[11] In 1947 another research team compared a group of "constitutional psychopaths" to a group of normal individuals. They found no appreciable difference between the E.E.G. patterns of the two groups.[12] And Milton Greenblatt, in 1950, reviewed 380 cases of "psychopathy" at the Boston Psychopathic Hospital. He reported an incidence of 30 per cent aberrancy.[13]

These varied findings reflected the researchers' vague standards in selecting their cases. Many personality types had been commingled, and the research lost much of its value. If neurologists give careful, specific descriptions of their subjects' personalities, the E.E.G. examinations could clarify the issue of causation.

One early study of the psychopath's brain waves adhered to a clearly delineated standard in establishing psychopathy. Carried out in 1946, this research by Ostrow and Ostrow involved the E.E.G. analysis of 440 inmates of the Federal Prison Bureau's Medical Center (186). Sixty-nine convicts were extraordinarily impulsive, unable to accept social limitations, and showed seriously warped empathetic abilities. Only these were labeled psychopathic. The Ostrows compared the E.E.G. patterns of the psychopaths with those of homosexuals, epileptics, schizophrenics, and imprisoned conscientious objectors. The findings are summarized in Table 4-1:

TABLE 4-1

Diagnosis	Percentage of Abnormal Patterns
Psychopathy	50
Homosexuality	56
Epilepsy	98
Schizophrenia	80
Conscientious Objectors	65

Careful diagnosis, made after thorough review of case histories and intensive clinical interviews, adds weight to the Ostrows' findings. Their tests indicate a high degree of abnormality not only among psychopaths, but also among other imprisoned deviants.[14] Perhaps the most interesting implication of their work is that the type of personality abnormality could not be deduced from the E.E.G. pattern. Certainly the conscientious objector's personality differs from that of the psychopath, just as the psychopath's differs from the schizophrenic's. Yet, many men in each of the groups seem to have damaged neural structures.

Although not conclusive, the Ostrows' research stands as one of the most rigorous of the neurological studies. More recent studies, also utilizing clear definitions of psychopathy, have further substantiated the opinion that psychopathy can be partially traced to some form of cerebral dysfunction. R. J. Ellingson, in a comprehensive review of the literature up to 1954, concluded that "with remarkable regularity" research has shown that some 47 per cent to 58 per cent of psychopaths exhibit E.E.G. abnormality (64). And, in 1956, S. K. Ehrlich and R. P. Keogh reported that 80 per cent of a sample of Canadian psychopaths had E.E.G. abnormalities. They noted that a high proportion of their subjects exhibited theta waves —rhythms commonly associated with aggressive behavior (62).

Despite confusion, the past years of E.E.G. examinations have removed some of the mystery surrounding the psychopath's neurological processes. Although often failing to differentiate psychopathy from other disorders, the research nevertheless indicates the strong probability of a greater proportion of abnormal E.E.G. patterns among psychopaths than among the normal population. The exact incidents or nature of abnormality has not yet been established. Obviously, the highly tentative E.E.G. studies fall short of proving that all psychopathy is caused by defective brain.

Seeking further evidence of physical abnormality in psychopaths, neurologists looked for those abnormal reflexes, tics, and tremors which often signal the existence of neural disorder. Silverman, in 1943, was the first scientist to examine psychopaths for external signs of brain disorder. Silverman found that 21 of 75 criminal "psychopaths" had pathological reflexes and severe tremors.[15]

In 1945, after investigating 70 criminal "psychopaths," Sessions-Hodges noted that 76 per cent had dysfunctional signs, in contrast to only 9 per cent in a control group of 50. The psychopaths exhibited a flickering movement of fingers and an equivocal plantar response.[16]

In 1951 a group of British prison psychiatrists compared criminal "psychopaths" (prisoners who seemed unresponsive to treatment) with nonpsychopathic convicts. They divided the psychopaths into three groups: those who had a history of epilepsy, those who had a history of head injury, and those who had neither disorder in their background (237). Surprisingly, the psychopaths who were free from epilepsy and brain injury had the highest proportion of neurological symptoms. (See Table 4-2).

Yet, after their study of 69 psychopaths, Simons and

TABLE 4-2

Diagnosis	Percentage Exhibiting Neurological "Signs"
Nonpsychopathic criminals	25
Psychopaths with epileptic history	36
Psychopaths with head-injury history	46
Psychopaths without epilepsy or head injury	52

Diethelm had concluded: "No defects in the function of the nervous system were found. There was no evidence of any structural change in the patients' brains" (230).

Like the E.E.G. studies, the examination of physical symptoms suffered from inadequate diagnosis of psychopathy. The investigators almost certainly included non-psychopaths in their samples, thus preventing a reliable gauging of abnormal symptoms.

One study of the psychopath's physiology was based on more satisfactory criteria. In 1943 Robert Lindner experimented with criminals in an attempt to detect the reactional differences of psychopaths. Lindner compared 103 nonpsychopathic, first term prisoners in a federal institution to 105 psychopathic inmates. Diagnosed after clinical interviews, the psychopaths were egocentric, rejected authority, lacked insight, and had knowledge of —but did not internalize—social regulations.

Lindner used an electric shock as the basis of his experiment. One minute before the shock, a bell gave warning. From the sounding of the tone until two minutes after the shock, instruments recorded galvanic and respiratory reactions, as well as dorsal pedis pulse. Only the galvanic response significantly distinguished the psychopathic from the nonpsychopathic criminals. Before the shock, the psychopaths showed less tenseness; during and shortly after the shock, they exhibited greater anxiety. Yet the psychopaths more quickly reverted to their normal physiological functioning (150).

Lindner believed that psychopathic impulsiveness could be traced to his discovery that they are "poised more delicately and are more responsive to alterations in the situation." Perhaps, too, the lack of continued anxiety in this test situation might help explain why psychopaths fail to internalize social controls: physiologically, they do not protract the tenseness induced by a punishing situation.[17]

Although Lindner's study portrayed a new facet of the psychopath's physical structure, it furnished no evidence of organic brain disorder. Still seeking indications of neurological defect, some psychiatrists examined psychopaths' medical histories for possible causative factors.

Silverman's study, in 1943, had noted that 36 per

cent of the psychopathic cases showed medical histories indicative of cerebral lesions. His cases had had such diseases as dystocia, tumors, birth trauma, and childhood head injury (227). Gottlieb, Ashley, and Knott found that 38 per cent of their psychopathic subjects had, as children, experienced anoxia, convulsions, or head injury (95). The Stafford-Clark team discovered that 45 per cent of their criminal psychopaths had a history of epilepsy or head injury (237). A. M. Shotwell, on the other hand, examined 22 "psychopaths" at the Pacific Colony and found no history of early brain damage.[18]

Like other attempts to relate psychopathy to brain damage, inadequate diagnosis hampered these studies. The incidence of early brain disease among psychopaths cannot be determined if many disorders are indiscriminately included in the sample.

Though recognizing the inadequacies of the neurological studies, a few provisional generalizations seem justified:

> Psychopaths more often exhibit E.E.G. abnormalities than do normal people.
> Compared with normal people, a greater proportion of psychopaths exhibit signs of neurological disorder (tremors, exaggerated reflexes, tics).
> Psychopaths are probably more physiologically responsive to physical changes in their environment.
> Compared with normal people, a greater proportion of psychopaths have a history of early diseases which damage the brain.

Few scientists maintain that brain damage invariably causes psychopathy. Yet, from this cursory evidence, some theorists have concluded that all psychopathy is caused by neural disorder. Most frequently, they have indicated encephalitis, subclinical epilepsy, or a defective hypothalamus as the precipitating cause.

Those who champion encephalitis present the weakest case. Some investigations have, of course, revealed a relatively high incidence of chronic encephalitis in the history of psychopaths, but other studies, as we have previously mentioned, have failed to indicate any causal relation. In 1950, after the most extensive review of the lives of 154 individuals who had undergone postvaccination encephalitis, a German research group found no evidence for believing that psychopathic, or even criminogenic, consequences resulted from the disease (199).

The belief that epilepsy causes psychopathy rests on a dubious analogy. Both epileptics and psychopaths exhibit "unstable emotionality" and "aggression resembling psychic seizures." In addition, abnormal E.E.G.'s appear in both psychopaths and epileptics. Similarities undoubtedly exist; but these causal theorists have still to explain why so few psychopaths have a verified history of epilepsy, why so many psychopaths have normal E.E.G. patterns, and why so few epileptics develop psychopathic personalities.

Citing recent experiments with Dilantin Sodium, some psychiatrists maintain that the psychopath must have a "subclinical" variety of epilepsy (144). Epileptic seizures of some types can be reduced through dosages of Dilantin Sodium, and two recent studies have tentatively indicated that the psychopath may also respond favorably to the drug (228). Therefore, these theorists reason, epilepsy and psychopathy are two forms of the same disorder. This reasoning (from treatment to cause) is tenuous, particularly since experiments using Dilantin Sodium with psychopaths are inconclusive.

Although there seems little justification for blaming either encephalitis or epilepsy for psychopathy, more substantial evidence connects the disorder with a defective hypothalamus. Modern neurological research has shown that the hypothalamus governs various internal mechanisms within the human body. In addition, the hypothalamus (along with cortical areas) plays an important part in the establishment of normal associational patterns, and—together with the limbic system, the temporal lobes, and the medial frontal cortex—governs emotional expression and behavior. When the hypothalamus is damaged, the patient almost invariably becomes unstable, aggressive, and "antisocial." Consequently, several scientists have suggested that the hypothalamus is the brain area responsible for inhibition: that if it is damaged, or "inherently" defective, a psychopathic character results.[19]

Since a history of hypothalamic injury has been discerned in only a minority of psychopaths, the theory must postulate that brain damage occurred in the intrauterine stage, or that the hypothalamus was hereditarily defective. The theory rests on the behavioral similarity between the psychopath and the brain-injured person. The apparently higher incidence of E.E.G. abnormality, of physical symptoms of brain disorder, and of histories of head injury lend it credence. Yet the few autopsies known to have been performed on psychopaths do not confirm the theory (218). Before being accepted as an explanation of psychopathy, the hypothalamic theory must be subjected to further research. There is evidence that the hypothalamic area does control inhibition and, therefore, damage to this area may contribute to psychopathy.

Because of a confused interpretation of psychopathy, neurological research has been somewhat unsatisfactory. Epileptics, neurotics, and psychotics have been included in several of the studies and may account for much of the neural abnormality attributed to psychopaths. Indeed, some environmentalists dismiss all the neurological evidence by arguing that psychopaths, in the course of their aggressive explosions, inevitably incur some brain damage, but that the injury itself plays no causative role. Nevertheless, more psychopaths seem to have defective neural structures than would be expected in a normal population, and it seems likely that such defects have some causative importance.

III. THE ENVIRONMENTAL APPROACH

An ancient German legend tells of a brutal experiment performed by Emperor Frederick II. In the 1400's the Emperor ordered that a group of babies be raised at his court. The infants received everything they wished—except love. Frederick forbade any demonstrations of affection. The children, so the legend says, all died.

Perhaps lack of love can kill. Today, most social scientists would view early emotional deprivation as at least a seriously warping experience. The research in psychoanalysis and social psychology has shown that childhood relationships play a paramount role in the formation of adult personality.

An increasing number of social scientists have applied the philosophy and methods of dynamic psychology to the study of psychopathy. The last two decades of research have amassed an impressive fund of knowledge about the psychopath's early social relations. In the search for the causes of psychopathy, social science has tapped two major sources of information: the study of psychopaths' childhood experiences, and the examination of rejected or isolated children. In this twofold approach, some investigators look to the psychopath himself and attempt to distinguish the environmental factors which caused his unique character syndrome. Others analyze the love-starved child and try to ascertain whether early emotional deprivation leads to a psychopathic personality.

A reform school psychotherapist, G. E. Partridge, was the first scientist to study the early environmental influence on psychopaths. In 1928 Partridge thoroughly examined 12 psychopathic delinquents. All the boys hated their parents, but more importantly, all of the boys had been rejected as young children (190).

Five years later, Elizabeth Knight, a social worker, noticed similar rejection in her study of aggressive boys. Knight compared the family backgrounds of nine extremely aggressive children with those of nine very submissive children. The mothers of all the aggressive boys rejected their children; the mothers of the submissive lads appeared overprotective. An overtly punitive atmosphere dominated the homes of the aggressive cases; the homes of the submissive children, on the other hand, were "harmonious." [20]

In 1940 Minna Field turned up further provocative evidence about environmental causation. After rigorous analysis of 25 children at the State Psychiatric Institute, Field found that 23 had been rejected by their parents. Field traced the children's aggressive and destructive behavior to the influence of their maladjusted parents, particularly the mothers. None of the mothers were "well integrated," and none had been loved by their parents (68).

B. L. Haller's research, in 1942, also pegged rejection
as a causative factor. Haller demonstrated that a majority of 52 "psychopaths" paroled from a mental hospital had either been neglected or rejected as children.[21]
Haller concluded, after interviewing the psychopathic
patients, that they had a subconscious overattachment
to their mothers. Although his findings have not been
confirmed, there is reason to expect that the severely
rejected child wants (even more than the normal child)
to have his mother's affection.

Other studies in the 1940's appeared to find a dis-
tinctly different familial constellation in the background
of psychopaths. Due, perhaps, to some differences in the
use of the term "psychopath," S. A. Szurek, W. L.
Heaver, and Phyllis Greenacre found that the "psychopath" was rejected, if at all, only by his father. His
mother, on the other hand, was highly indulgent and
subconsciously approved of the child's deviant behavior.

Szurek, in 1942, initiated this theory when he reported
his experience with the treatment of "psychopathic"
children. Szurek cited one of his cases, a highly aggressive
six-year-old, as evidence. The little boy kicked his play-
mates, struck his cousin with a hammer, chased other
children with a knife, and attacked his teachers. Interviews with the boy's mother showed her to be emotionally involved with the child, extremely anxious, and
overprotective. Szurek found that the mother got "deep
pleasure from martyr-like submission to his whims and
her smothering impulses towards him (243). Separation
from the mother caused a noticeable improvement in the
boy's behavior. From this evidence, Szurek concluded
that the unconscious encouragement of the mother
caused "psychopathic" traits in the child.

The work of Heaver and Greenacre tended to confirm,
at least in part, the conclusions of Szurek. In 1943
Heaver studied 40 patients at a New York hospital and
discovered that the majority had neglectful, but materi-
ally indulgent, mothers. The fathers were stern authori-
tarians, unconcerned with their children (109). In 1945
Phyllis Greenacre reported her analysis of nine "psychopaths." All the psychopaths had "stern, respected,
and often obsessional fathers . . . remote, preoccupied,

and fear-inspiring." The patients' mothers were frivolous, pleasure-loving, and continually seeking adulation from their contemporaries (102).

In terms of the standards proposed earlier in this book, Szurek, Heaver, and Greenacre may have mislabeled acting-out neurotics as "psychopaths." [22] Their patients were aggressive and antisocial. They did not, however, exhibit the psychopathic traits of guiltlessness and warped emotions. Though provocative as analyses of causative factors in neurosis, the findings shed little light on true psychopathy.

More accurate diagnosis marked the work of Robert Lindner. In 1944 Lindner hypnoanalyzed eight criminal psychopaths. After many hours of treatment, the patients revealed an "abrupt cessation of psychosexual development before the successful resolution of the Oedipus conflict." All had experienced brutal parental treatment.[23] Lindner hypothesized that the psychopathic child develops a deep hatred for his father. Instead of resolving the Oedipus complex (as do normal children) through identification with the father, the psychopathic child turns bitterly against his father. Lindner believed that his patients, deprived of parental identification and a stable superego, had transplanted their hatred to a symbol: society.

Subsequent studies substantiated the belief that psychopathy flourishes in an atmosphere of rejection. In 1944, for example, R. L. Jenkins and L. Hewitt compared the backgrounds of 52 psychopathic children with a group of 500 unselected cases from a child guidance clinic. Among other notable differences, they remarked that the psychopathic children were raised by parents who did not want the child, who were in perpetual conflict with each other, and who violently abused their children. Jenkins later stated that "the product of this background is a child of bottomless hostilities and endless bitterness, who feels cheated in life, views himself as the victim . . . and is grossly lacking in guilt sense over his misconduct" (123, p. 326). In 1947, after examining the familial records of "antisocial characters," British psychoanalyst Kate Friedlander found that severe emotional deprivation precipitated their behavior (73).

Three years later, American psychiatrist R. D. Rabinovitch reviewed his therapeutic experience with child
psychopaths and concluded that a "gross limitation of
mothering" caused the disorder (202). In 1952 John
Bowlby reported that his research with "affectionless
characters" showed a high incidence of familial rejection
in their backgrounds (25). Michael Craft, in 1959, reported a control series study where he noted a strong
relationship between emotional deprivation and adult
psychopathy (45) while Richard Jenkins, researching the
backgrounds of war veterans again found, in 1960, that
psychopaths tended to come from backgrounds characterized by paternal and maternal rejection, strict discipline, and parental conflict (123). Although using different labels, Jenkins, Friedlander, Rabinovitch, Bowlby,
and Craft dealt with the guiltless, affectionless, asocial
psychopath.

Hence, the last decade of British and American research spun a consistent web of psychopathic causation.
In study after study, emotional deprivation appeared to
have precipitated a psychopathic personality structure.[24]
The validity of this research has not passed entirely un-
challenged. From long clinical experience, for example,
Hervey Cleckly has commented, "I have not regularly
encountered any specific type of error in parent-child
relation in the early history of my cases . . . I am increasingly impressed with the difficulty in obtaining objective and reliable evidence of what was felt twenty or
thirty years ago. . . . Assumptions about infantile, and
even intrauterine, experience are sometimes made solely
on the basis of analogy and symbolism. These methods
can be used with such elasticity that it is not difficult to
'discover' in the unconscious virtually anything the investigator chooses to seek" (39, p. 584).

Although Cleckly's criticism is logically sound, our
recent longitudinal study of crime—based on information gathered in *childhood* before the onset of delinquent
behavior—adds confirmatory evidence to the earlier studies (173). The research, conducted over a period from
the end of the 1930's until 1956, indicated a strong link
between early emotional deprivation (parental conflict,

cruelty, erratic punishment, and particularly, parental neglect) and the emergence of a psychopathic syndrome. Albert Bandura and Richard Walters' recently published *Adolescent Aggression*, a most carefully controlled study, again demonstrated a relation between frustration of dependency longings in the child and the appearance, in adolescence, of unsocialized aggressive tendencies (15).

Among the most definitive works was that done by Lauretta Bender. In her clinical work at New York's Bellevue Hospital, Bender examined hundreds of child psychopaths. She found similar personality symptoms in all: diffuse impulsiveness, and inability to feel guilt, manipulation of morality without emotional meaning, and an "inability to identify themselves in a relationship with other people." Furthermore, her study indicated that all the psychopathic children had experienced emotional deprivation, neglect, or discontinuous affectional relationships. Bender believed that early emotional starvation, particularly during the first three years, leads to psychopathy. "We know that the critical time," she wrote, "is the first three years, especially the first year; any significant break in parent relationships or any period of deprivation under five years may be sufficient to produce this personality defect" (18).

Although more recent research gives evidence that the theory of identification may be erroneous and that early changes in family structure may be beneficial (167), Bender's clinical approach served as an additional substantiation of environmental causation. Bender and other investigators attributed the psychopath's inability to maintain close relations with others to early rejection. Bender found that the psychopath, as a child, had little experience with normal relationships, little opportunity for identification, and virtually no satisfaction of his craving for love.

Without affection, most social theorists believe, no child can evolve a mature conscience. One theory is that the normal child internalizes his parents' values because he fears the loss of their love. When his parents have no love to offer, the child does not fear its withdrawal. The unloved child becomes the unsocialized adult because he was not rewarded with affection. Physical punishment may bring temporary obedience, but when the threat of punishment no longer exists, no residue of conscience remains.

Although theoretically compact, the case for environmental causation is inconclusive. Much of the research confounds psychopathy with other disorders, thus weakening the evidence. In the more rigorous studies, the number of cases was not extensive. Nevertheless, the careful work of Lindner, Friedlander, Rabinovitch, Bowlby, Jenkins, and Bender has consistently shown that psychopaths, as children, were either neglected or rejected by their parents.[25]

While some scientists studied the psychopath himself, others investigated a related problem of great significance. It seems appropriate to ask: "Does rejection *necessarily* result in psychopathy? If not, what other factors make the critical difference?" Analyses of emotionally deprived children help to answer these questions.

Psychologist H. W. Newell, in 1934, examined 33 rejected children from the Cleveland Public Schools. He found the children extraordinarily aggressive, and their aggression seemed to be proportionate to the amount of overt rejection shown by the parents.

Two years later Newell added 42 cases to the original 33 and included a control group of 82 children (every pupil in one of the third grades and one of the fifth grades in a Baltimore public school). After prolonged observation Newell categorized the children in terms of their behavior: aggressive, submissive, mixed, or stable. Again, he observed a high proportion of aggression in the rejected children. His results gave the pattern[26] shown in Table 4-3.

TABLE 4-3

Behavior	Percentage of Rejected Children	Percentage of Control Children
Aggressive	29	5
Submissive	29	29
Mixed	41	11
Stable	0	55

In 1937 psychiatrist David Levy sought further verification of the effects of affectional deprivation. Levy studied rejected children undergoing treatment at New York's Institute for Child Guidance. He, too, found a high incidence of aggression. In addition, he discovered that the children lacked emotional depth and were severely handicapped in their ability to learn from experience—characteristics important in the development of psychopathy" (147).

Research by Percival Symonds, in 1939, confirmed the earlier findings. Symonds matched 31 pairs of children by age, sex, grade in school, social background, and intelligence. One of each pair was rejected by one or both parents; the other was accepted by both. Symonds' staff recorded information concerning the children's behavior, personality, and attitudes. Tabulation uncovered significant differences between the two groups: accepted children seemed "stable, well socialized, calm"; but "rejected children . . . showed much emotional instability, an excess of activity and restlessness, are generally antagonistic toward society and its institutions, and show apathy and indifference." [27]

The early studies of rejected children indicated that rejection causes socially destructive traits: aggression, inability to learn from experience, lack of emotional response, and antagonism toward society. Mildred Burgum, in 1940, set herself the task of determining constructive traits which might be traced to rejection. She studied 25 rejected children who had developed such admirable personality traits as self-assurance, self-reliance, and "independence." This unusual reaction to rejection might, she believed, be due to several factors: high intelligence, the child's desire to escape from the home, or possibly the child's experience that "independence" brought him some approval.

Despite the fact that Mrs. Burgum specifically selected subjects who exhibited constructive characteristics, she found only eight who responded to affection, and but five who could be considered "responsible." The majority reacted "with destructive aggression, defensive escapes, or personality and conduct disorder" (32).

Lewis Wolberg, in 1943, gleaned further evidence of the effects of rejection. He examined 33 children being treated for extreme emotional disorders. Although not initially selected as rejected children, he found they had all been rejected by their parents. Some of the children showed a desperate need to cling, to be reassured and fondled. Others desired complete seclusion and avoided all interpersonal relations. Twenty-eight of the children manifested extreme aggression, temper tantrums, and destructiveness (even homicidal attempts). Of even greater significance in the study of psychopathic causation, Wolberg found that "most of the rejected children seemed never to have developed the capacity of delaying immediate gratification for future pleasures; and the experience of deprivation mobilized tensions of an almost uncontrollable nature" (272).

In 1945 the Fels Research Institute sponsored an extensive analysis of parent-child relations. Over a period of 2½ years, Fels' observers visited the homes of 124 families. After long analyses, they classified parents as acceptant, casual, or rejectant. Among the 31 rejectant homes, they found two distinct varieties: nonchalant disinterest in the child's welfare and actively hostile dominance of the child. All of the rejecting parents were hostile, unaffectionate, and disapproving. Conflict, quarrels, and resentment pervaded the atmosphere.

The Fels Institute's research demonstrated a high correlation between parental treatment and child behavior. Children raised in the rejectant environment usually showed extreme hostility, a "highly emotional nonconformism," and a marked resistance to adults. Although the rejected children usually reacted with aggression, some of them turned to other types of behavior: overdependence, withdrawal, or precocious self-sufficiency. The severity of rejection seemed to make the difference: the "actively" rejected children responded with the most severe symptoms, the greatest emotionality, and the least inner control (13).

Also in 1945, Schactel and Levi administered Rorschach tests to 50 nursery school children who had been brutally treated by their parents (212). They, too, found that rejected children responded sometimes with positive self-reliance, but more frequently with hostile truculence. Some of these very young children seemed definitely psychopathic:

> Johnny is extremely scattered, disorganized, and excitable . . . although he longs for expansion and adventure, he is quickly bored. He has virtually no fear, guilt, or conscience; rather, he is daring, incalculable.

Schactel and Levi noted that rejection molded the child's attitude, even at this early age, toward all human beings: "They accept the fact that they are not loved . . . [and] view all relations in terms of getting something from others. . . ." [28]

By mid-century, studies of the rejected child had clearly demonstrated the relation between rejection and behavior disorder. In recent years the Harvard Laboratory of Human Development has carried out a comprehensive examination of the effects of child training on personality. The researchers interviewed 379 mothers and observed their nursery-age children in various play situations. They concluded that rejection significantly increases both aggression and dependency (217). The Harvard Laboratory admitted the difficulty of measuring rejection; yet, in cases where *any* signs of rejection could be discovered, the children were more aggressive toward their parents, as well as more clinging and demanding of attention.

The Harvard research emphasized the fact that rejection usually, but not always, increases aggression. Frequently the rejected child exhibits the psychopath's syndrome of uncontrolled hostility, excessive impulsivity, low guilt, and apparent incapacity for love. Some rejected children respond differently, exhibiting no hostility, isolating themselves, and withdrawing from reality. Contemporary studies in England have lent further credence to this variability. Hilda Lewis, in her important investigations on emotionally deprived children found, in 1954, a statistically strong—although not inevitable—association between overt rejection and psychopathy (145). And in 1956 John Bowlby followed up 57 children who had been subjected to intense deprivation and noted that many (though not a majority) had developed a psychopathic pattern (26).

Studies of unloved children temper the claims that rejection, by itself and in every case, results in a psychopathic personality. Certainly, analysis of psychopaths has demonstrated almost overwhelming rejection in their childhood backgrounds. Yet studies of rejected children have clearly shown that lack of love does not *inevitably* cause psychopathy. Psychopaths were rejected as children, but not all rejected children become psychopaths.[29]

The severity of rejection may be the key *differentia specifica*. Several studies of the rejected child (e.g., the Fels' investigation) indicated that aggression and guiltlessness increase with greater parental rejection. The greater the deprivation of love, the more psychopathic the child's personality. Aggression increased with more pronounced rejection in the Newell studies, as well.

Several recent investigations of isolated children—children raised away from normal human love or social control—support such an interpretation.

In the past few years investigators have examined the effect of institutional isolation on personality. Between 1935 and 1945 William Goldfarb published a series of reports on this problem. In 1945 he compared 70 children who had been reared in institutions for their first three years with 70 children who had lived in foster homes from infancy through childhood. Goldfarb found decided distortions in the institutionalized children: a serious lack of inhibition, an insatiable longing for love, and an "incomprehensible cruelty to other children, foster parents, and animals." Goldfarb believed that institutionalization had "primitivized" the children: "This tendency to meagerness of feeling for other humans is complemented by the absence of normal anxiety following acts of hostility, cruelty, or unprovoked aggression" (94, p. 253).

Institutionalized children attracted the attention of another psychiatrist, Lawson Lowrey. In 1940 Lowrey analyzed 28 children who had lived in an institution for the first three years of their lives. These children, too, showed an inability to relate to others, hostile aggressiveness, infantile behavior, and "unsocial" attitudes. Sur-

prisingly, Lowrey discovered that this "isolation personality" occurred only when the children had been institutionalized before the age of two years (159).

In England, Anna Freud and Dorothy Burlingham
examined these "infants without families." The children,
observed in a wartime nursery, were isolated from their
parents and deprived of familial love. Freud and Burlingham noticed antisocial tendencies and stunted inner controls in their cases. They theorized that the children's
consciences failed to develop because they lacked the
ability to identify with adult love objects. Without emotional attachment, the children could not internalize
adult demands or restriction (71).

John Bowlby's more recent work closely linked affectional isolation and psychopathy (26). Bowlby analyzed
cases of early deprivation and concluded that "isolated"
children are seriously handicapped in the later formation
of affectional bonds. Due to this defect, the child develops other socially maladjusted traits. Bowlby's studies
led him to conclude: "Certainly it would appear that
the more complete the deprivation in the early years, the
more isolated and asocial the child . . ." (26, p. 4).

There have been few cases of *total* infant isolation
which might serve to check such conclusions. One of
the most extreme cases was discovered, in 1940, by child
welfare officials. A child of five had spent her short life
tied to a chair with her arms locked above her head. The
girl was the illegitimate progeny of a young woman who
lived with her stern, fundamentalist parents. The grand-
father secluded the baby in a closed room. After the
child's discovery, sociologist Kingsley Davis attempted
to trace the influence of isolation upon the child's personality.

In any usual sense of the word, the child had no personality. Five years old, she could not walk, talk, or feed
herself, and she just barely responded to loud noises
made near her. After transfer to an institution, the girl
showed little improvement. But after being moved into
a foster home, where she was given affection, she began
to walk upstairs, talk, and feed herself. She remained
wild, unable to form relations, and extremely retarded
(56).

Other children raised away from human contact—Sanichar, Kamida, and the "girl of Songi"—showed the same symptoms as Davis's case. These extraordinary individuals never became "human." Their isolation was so complete that even the "socialization" necessary for psychopathy did not occur.

The social isolation of the institutionalized child, although severe, is not absolute, and many institutionalized children resemble the adult psychopath.[30] Apparently, severe affectional isolation predisposes a child to psychopathy, but absolute isolation results in total retardation.

Factors other than severity of rejection undoubtedly play a part in molding the person into a psychopathic pattern. In the authors' recent longitudinal studies of several kinds of personality disorders—psychotics, homosexuals, sexual perverts, and alcoholics—such influences as parental values, the parental model, and the form of discipline emerged as important variables. Although almost all deviants had been subjected to parental conflict and emotional deprivation, these other elements in their environments directed the choice of symptoms. Unlike typical psychopaths, for example, homosexuals were exposed to sexually anxious, authoritarian mothers (172); psychotics were submitted to a regime of unrelenting domination and control (171); sexual perverts were reared by promiscuous fathers and sexually stimulating mothers (172); and alcoholics were raised by ambivalent, escapist parents (170). Such evidence would indicate that the effects of parental rejection and deprivation can be channeled into very different paths—quite often into psychopathy, but even more frequently into other forms of disorder.

IV. A NEUROSOCIAL THEORY OF CAUSATION

"If we cannot see clearly," Freud once said, "at least we can see the obscurities clearly." His dictum describes contemporary knowledge of psychopathic causation. Twenty-five years of research have resulted in disparate, often conflicting, explanations. Yet, beneath theoretical disputes lie some established facts and a few probable hypotheses.

The "hereditarians," the neurologists, and the "environmentalists" have each contributed a share to this growing pool of knowledge. Although they failed to establish a congenital cause for psychopathy, the hereditary "school" has shown that:

Psychopaths apparently have the same proportion of "tainted" ancestors as do normal people.

Psychopathy does not follow the lines of closest blood kinship and thus is probably caused by nonhereditary factors.

Through analyses of brain waves, reflexes, and medical histories, the neurologists have tentatively established that:

Injury to the frontal lobe region or the hypothalamus results in aggression and antisociality.

Many psychopaths exhibit physical signs of brain disorder.

Proportionally, more psychopaths than normal people have a history of early brain diseases.

The psychopath's physiology responds more quickly to physical changes in the environment.

The environmentalist research has contributed many important insights. Through their analyses of rejection and affectional isolation, as well as their studies of the psychopath himself, the environmentalists have indicated that:

The vast majority of psychopaths have been rejected in childhood.

Aggression is the dominant reaction to rejection.

Rejected or institutionalized children often, but not invariably exhibit the psychopathic syndrome. They lack normal guilt feelings; they are impulsive, aggressive, pleasure-seeking, and they seem incapable of relating to other people.

Each of the three schools has, in general, conducted its research and defended its theories without regard to other findings, but none of the theories has satisfactorily shown a cause for psychopathy.

In the 1930's the "hereditarians" insisted that psychopathy resulted from genetic defects. Yet, psychopathy does not follow the Mendelian law; psychopaths do not have a higher incidence of "queer" ancestors; and "twin studies" failed to establish an hereditary base for the disorder.

In the late 1930's and early 1940's the neurologists proclaimed that organic brain damage caused psychopathy. Yet only a minority of psychopaths reveal abnormal brain waves, only a few psychopaths have a history of head injury or early brain disease, and only some psychopaths show physical symptoms of brain disorder. Furthermore, abnormal brain waves appeared equally frequently in certain other types of deviants.

By mid-century, the environmentalists' theory reigned supreme. Psychopathy, they maintained, resulted from childhood rejection. Yet, not all rejected children developed into psychopathic personalities.

Each causal theory, alone, has fundamental defects which invalidate its claims. Some observers have, therefore, concluded that the causes of psychopathy can never be known. Such pessimism, however, is unjustified. The last 20 years of research indicate that a combination of neurological and social insights can produce a plausible, if not definitive, explanation of the disorder.

Because all psychopaths have been at least mildly rejected, rejection seems to be prerequisite in the development of the syndrome. But not all rejected children become psychopaths. Thus rejection, while necessary, is not a sufficient cause. Either a particular type of rejection or some additional factor must tip the balance toward psychopathy. Studies of rejected and institutionalized children have shown a correlation between severity of rejection and psychopathy. Severe rejection, though not complete isolation, seems to account for many cases of psychopathy.

The evidence of neural defect in some psychopaths probably warrants the conclusion that brain damage plays a causative role. Injury to the forebrain sometimes deletes restraints, increasing impulsive and aggressive actions. But brain damage alone does not result in the distinctive characteristics of the psychopath: guiltlessness and lovelessness. Neural malfunction seems to be the catalyst which, in some cases, turns a rejected child into a psychopath. The proclivity for psychopathy found even in mildly rejected individuals, if aggravated by a neural system incompatible with inhibition, develops into the psychopathic syndrome.

Thus, there seem to be three causal patterns:

(1) *Severe rejection, by itself, can cause psychopathy;*

(2) *Mild rejection, in combination with damage to the brain area* (possibly the hypothalamus) *which normally inhibits behavior, causes psychopathy;*

(3) *Mild rejection, in the absence of neural disorder, can result in psychopathy if certain other influences in the environment fail to provide alternatives.*

Specifically, in this third case, we would hypothesize that an environment characterized by mild rejection and, in addition, by a psychopathic parental model, by erratically punitive discipline, and by an absence of adult supervision results in a psychopathic pattern. This theory, we believe, reasonably synthesizes the superficially conflicting discoveries about the psychopath.[31] Rejection, sometimes severe and sometimes complemented by neural or environmental defects, plays the paramount role. The psychopathic syndrome evolves from this rejection.

The psychopath's *inability to maintain close relations* seems due to his inexperience with affectional bonds. As a child, the psychopath was consistently rebuffed. He did not experience the satisfactions which accompany emotional attachment. Since he never developed ties of affection, he never acquired the ability to "empathize."[32] Because he early learned that the world offered him no love, the psychopath reacts to other human beings with suspicious indifference. He doubts the sincerity of those who may seek to establish close relations. Though the psychopath might wish to develop an emotional attachment, he lacks the necessary techniques. His erratic, uninhibited, and aggressive behavior drives people from him.

Failure to develop a conscience flows logically from the psychopath's lovelessness. Almost all social scientists believe that the internalization of moral controls takes place primarily through the child's acceptance of his parents. The child and the parents strike an unconscious bargain: in return for the child's conformity to social restrictions, the parents give the child love. If the child fails to conform, disapproval follows.[33] In time, the child looks ahead to the consequences of his acts. If he is about to misbehave, a gnawing fear warns that his parents might stop loving him. Thus, the inner anxiety eventually results in internalization of the parent's morality. The child has developed a rudimentary conscience.[34]

There is, of course, a more positive aspect in this development of inner controls: not only does the child fear withdrawal of love, he also identifies with his parents. He loves them, and he wishes to emulate them. As Gordon Allport has pointed out, children who fear the loss of love develop the concept of "must," but the "ought" of behavior comes only through identification with parents and other moral symbols.[35]

In a rejectant environment, love, the central element, is missing. Because the rejected child does not love his parents and they do not love him, no identification takes place. Nor does the rejected child fear the loss of love— a love which he never had—when he violates moral restrictions. Without love, the socializing agent, the psychopath remains *asocial*. And if love is too weak to countermand brain lesions which make socialization difficult, the child becomes a psychopath.

Since there is no real conscience in the psychopath, he allows uninhibited expression to whatever aggressive urges he has. *Aggression* seems intensified in the psychopath, although recent research with psychopathic children indicates that their aggressive drives may be no more pressing than the normal person's. (See Chapter 5.) Since he does not have strong emotional ties, the psychopath does not understand the effects of his aggression on other people.[36]

Impulsivity is also intimately connected with early rejection. As a child, parental love did not compensate the psychopath for moderating his behavior and, in at least some cases, neurological dysfunctioning weakened his inhibitory faculties. Thus, as an adult, his impulsivity is unchecked.

Although inconsistent and purposeless behavior is a product of impulsivity, it may also be due to a deficiency in the psychopath's ego. Harrison Gough (among many others) believes that the normal person's self-concept arises through emotional interaction with other people (97). The child records the evaluations of those around him and gradually absorbs these into his feeling toward himself. If these early evaluations are missing or are inconsistent, the child is unable to develop a coherent attitude about himself. Absence of long-range goals and erratic impulsivity may be due to the psychopath's underdeveloped attitude toward his "self." [37]

The psychopath's *pleasure seeking,* like his other traits, seems primarily due to his early experiences. His emotional frustration, in all probability, increased the intensity of his desires. Because he so seldom experienced it, the psychopath craves pleasure with heightened intensity. Uninhibited by either conscience or attachment to others, the psychopath seeks immediate satisfaction for his whims.

Aggression, pleasure seeking, and impulsivity cause the psychopath to violate society's rules. These traits, in turn, come from deeper deficiencies: warped ability to form relations and consequent lack of conscience.

Thus, the psychopathic syndrome can be traced to early deficiency in affectional relations. Extreme emotional deprivation or moderate rejection coupled with other environmental conditions or with neural damage to inhibitive centers, best account for the development of psychopathy. Although this position obviously requires the confirmation of empirical research,[38] the theory reconciles the two major discoveries: that all psychopaths are, in some degree, rejected, and that many psychopaths have a neural disorder.

V. THE EFFECTS OF SOCIAL
AND CULTURAL FORCES

In addition to individual causative factors, consideration should be given to the cultural forces that may contribute to psychopathy. Unfortunately, less research attention has been given to this important area of consideration. The scanty research of the past few years indicates that four social factors influence psychopathy: social crisis, class structure, technological-social complexity, and cultural attitudes toward children.

Insofar as emotional deprivation causes psychopathy, social crises (e.g., war and depression) can be expected to increase the incidence of the disorder. At such times social functions, including child rearing, are impeded.

Families often separate, depriving children of their normal quota of love. Even in united families, pressures on adults often disrupt relations.

Studies of children isolated from their parents during wartime tentatively support the interpretation. Freud and Burlingham examined English nursery school children who had been separated from their parents. The children showed a great deal of antisocial behavior, a seriously underdeveloped conscience, and a lack of identification with adults (71).

Rosemary Pritchard and Saul Rosensweig also investigated the effects of war stress on London's children. The children usually reacted with aggression, pilfering, truancy, and disorganized behavior. The researchers also found that the war led to an increase in neurotic and psychosomatic difficulties (198).

Tracing the effects of war, Szondi analyzed refugee children who had lived in concentration camps. He too noted intolerance for frustration, increased aggression, hypomania, and impulsivity.[39]

These few pieces of research certainly do not prove that war directly increases psychopathy. They do, however, suggest that the effects of social crises, particularly those which precipitate separation at an early age, predispose the victims to a psychopathic character.

Other research indicates that class structure, at least in America, may have some influence on the incidence of psychopathy. The Fels Research Institute and the Harvard Laboratory of Human Development have attempted to relate parental attitudes to social class. The Fels group discovered that rejectant parents came primarily from lower economic levels and lacked education.[40]

The Harvard study, too, showed a correspondence between rejection and socioeconomic class. After interviewing 379 mothers about their childrearing attitudes, the researchers found that "upper-lower" class women more often rejected their children than did the "upper-middle" class. The lower-class mothers were significantly less demonstrative of their affection, cooler in relations with their children, and more overtly rejecting. Lower-class fathers had significantly less warm relations with their children (217).

Hollingshead and Redlich's analysis of social class and mental disorder also suggests a relation between class position and psychopathy. Although their intensive study did not specifically focus on psychopathy, their findings concerning the incidence of "antisocial" reactive disorders (which presumably included some true psychopaths) indicated that these forms of deviance reached their height in the lowest social class (117).

The lower-class attitude seems to be a result of economic position. A family barely "making ends meet" probably does not welcome the birth of new babies. Although these three studies did not attempt to link psychopathy with social class, a possible implication of their findings is that psychopathy has a higher incidence in the lower class. If rejection causes psychopathy and lower-class mothers more often reject their children, there should be a correspondingly higher incidence of the disorder.[41] The greater disorganization, poorer housing, and the other social penalties of lower-class position quite probably, too, take their toll in increasing familial disorder.

Over 20 years ago Mandel Sherman and Thomas R. Henry conducted a cultural analysis which tentatively indicated that psychopathy, unlike other mental disorders, is less prevalent in technologically complex societies. They compared four communities in the Blue Ridge Mountains. Two of them, Oakton and Rigby, were undergoing rapid social change and increasing technological complexity. Two others, Colvin and Needles, were static, simple societies. Sherman and Henry found a higher incidence of "psychopathy" in the simple societies. The people of Colvin and Needles "accepted sexual indulgence, stealing and lying; they had slight guilt feelings and shallow emotional relations. In general, they revealed a stunted emotional development" (222).

Most social scientists believe, however, that the stresses of modern society disrupt the family and thereby promote psychopathy. Sherman and Henry concentrated on the investigation of other types of mental disorder, and their finding pertaining to psychopathy has not been confirmed. Indeed, more recent research implicitly contradicts the conclusions of Sherman and Henry. Joseph Eaton and Robert Weil in their intensive analysis of a Hutterite community found, for example, a strikingly low incidence of various forms of behavior—crime, alcoholism, "behavior disorders"—which might reasonably be considered as signs of psychopathy (61). The homogeneity, tight social organization, and simplicity of the Hutterite group apparently served to decrease all forms of social deviance (including, unfortunately, creativity). The evidence, therefore, remains contradictory, but the trend of research tentatively suggests that the incidence of psychopathy remains low in the more stable, simple, and rigidly organized communities.

Other anthropologists have investigated issues which indirectly relate to psychopathic causation. One important study analyzed the connection between guilt and cultural methods of socialization. In 1953 John Whiting and Irwin Child compared the child training patterns of a number of cultures, relating "nurturance" and discipline to guilt. For their study, they measured guilt in terms of the individual's feelings of responsibility for the sicknesses which befell him. A "guilty" culture was one in which invalids blamed themselves for their illnesses.

After computing correlations, the anthropologists concluded that cultures which punish by withdrawal of love create significantly more guilt than those which punish by physical means (although the amount of initial "nurturance" did not correlate with guilt) (270).

The work of Whiting and Child adds substances to the belief that the "socialization anxiety" created by withdrawal of love leads to the internalization of guilt. Psychological research has shown that psychopaths, lacking the reward of love, do not internalize social restrictions. The anthropological findings tend to show that cultural patterns may furrow the ground for the growth of psychopathy.

Another cultural study, Cora DuBois' analysis of the Alorese, produced some suggestive evidence concerning the relation between methods of socialization and psychopathic traits. The Alorese are reared in a changing, inconsistent, rejective atmosphere. Two weeks after birth, the Alorese mother returns to work in the fields. Her baby is left to the sporadic care of other children. Parents tease, ridicule, and deceive their children, and the infants have little opportunity for continuous identification with an adult.

Such child training, in DuBois' view, leads to an adult personality characterized by shallow guilt feelings, fearfulness, temper tantrums, a vague self-image, competitiveness, power seeking, and ambivalence. Although they have a subconscious desire for dependency, the Alorese maintain only tenuous, hostile relations with others (59). Thus, in many respects, the typical Alorese resembles what we call the psychopathic personality. Although they are not completely denied love, their identification with others is hampered, and they do not have the opportunity for developing internalized social standards.

Anthropologists and sociologists use techniques which should be applied to the study of psychopathy. Such problems as the internalization of guilt, the effects of culture on psychopathy, the relation between social change and personality, and the impact of crises on character demand deeper examination than they have yet received.

Before the process by which a baby develops into a psychopath can be fully understood, all the varied resources of psychological, social, and medical science must be utilized. Nevertheless, the achievements of the past decades should not be esteemed too lightly. Although knowledge of the genetic, neurological, and cultural background of psychopathy remains somewhat skimpy and contradictory, there is rather substantial knowledge of the early familial factors which are most likely to produce a psychopathic syndrome.

The history of John Straub illustrates one of the ways in which these deficiencies occur.[42] John Straub might be considered a prototype of the psychopath. At the age of 19, he was standing trial for his life when I began to piece together his history. What had attracted my attention was the newspaper story which headlined: "Son of wealthy family goes awry." The story reported that John had held up a bar not far from the suburban town in which he lived. While making his getaway, he shot over his shoulder into the crowd, killing one of the customers. Neither the papers nor the police could make sense of the killing. John had cleaned out the cash register, and several witnesses were equally able to identify him should he be apprehended. In prison, John expressed no guilt for his crime and explained only that he didn't know why he had shot. Since the town in which he lived had relatively few crimes, this one became an important topic of local gossip. The many friends of his family seemed to be united in the opinion that the boy had had everything he needed. I heard only one dissenting voice: a former neighbor of the Straubs, knowing that I was interested in the case, told me that John, when he was three, had often been left all day in a large wooded area near his family home, watched only by his five-year-old brother, while both parents continued their careers.

While looking up the newspaper files on the boy (11 previous arrests, sometimes convictions, for crimes ranging from petty theft to larceny) I discovered that the file clerk had known John in school. She was more than willing to talk about him and repeated again and again, "He was so charming; he could have done anything." I learned from her that he had been quite well liked in school, thought of as happy-go-lucky, and that he kept shifting from group to group, never seeming satisfied with one set of friends.

I wanted very much to meet the family, to help if I could. At first, my telephone inquiry was greeted with rebuff: "I'm a professional lecturer, you know, and I plan to discuss the case in one of my lectures," said the mother. But finally, I was invited to the Straub home for an evening. I had not anticipated the charm of the home nor the warmth of the reception that I was given. We talked about the house and about the military career of Colonel Straub. After 10 or 15 minutes, I broached the subject of John, thinking it might be tactful to repeat that I had heard he had started a promising career in architecture. Mrs. Straub's face hardened and her voice became harsh as she said, "He fooled everyone. He was really no good at architecture, he only used that false charm of his." Again and again through the evening, when she spoke about John, the same hard features and harsh voice involuntarily revealed the revulsion she felt for her son.

A flow of stories followed my question, "What was he like as a child?" The stories emphasized such words as "stubborn," "untrainable." They included tales of calling the police because the boy refused to come down from a treetop for dinner, being told to pack up and leave home at the age of 11 when he refused to attend a party given by his parents, being sent to reform school as "incorrigible" at 14. ("The only thing that ever really did him any good, but he's never quite forgiven me.")

Mrs. Straub talked about how she had been sure each day before leaving for work that there was enough food for the boys to eat at lunch and that she had taken particular care to insure that they received one hot meal a day. When she and her husband traveled, they rented the house to young couples who promised to provide the hot meal. Mrs. Straub frequently compared her two sons: how much more cooperative and obedient and less troublesome Bill, the older boy, had always been. How Bill had gotten into "the usual boyhood difficulties with police" but had never been in serious trouble. (At 21, he was divorced and couldn't hold a job.) Letters shown to me from John, written in a childish scrawl, dealt with money matters primarily. There was no note of remorse, although he included some mention of various "angles" for the trial. When Colonel Straub was called to the phone, Mrs. Straub told me that her husband had no use for children, that this might be part of the reason John had turned out so badly. She explained that the only time she had thought John really "cute" [sic] was when John, at the age of five, had stood up to his father during a whipping with his riding crop, saying: "I'll use that on you one of these days!" Mrs. Straub said she did not believe in whippings because one is apt to lose control as her husband did. When Mrs. Straub was on the phone, her husband, who remained silent when the two were together, told me that, in fact, he was sure that John would have turned out better had his wife been willing to give up her career to care for the children. Both parents were truly bewildered by what had happened. They searched the past, they almost convinced themselves that John's difficult birth (forceps, twilight sleep) was responsible for his personality. But then, with a pathos that was hard to believe possible, Mrs. Straub sighed, "If only I had known it could be so important, I would have done better."

John Straub, like all psychopaths, suffered from some rather striking deficiencies in socialization. In the next chapter, we will examine some of the varied attempts to "resocialize" the psychopath—those forms of treatment which have aimed at enrolling people like Straub, often for the first time, as members of the human community.

NOTES

1. Although the research of both Lange and Rosanoff dealt with delinquents in general, their findings bear on the problem of psychopathy. Some psychopaths were presumably included in their samples.

2. Lange used physical resemblance, photographs, and fingerprints as his criteria. Rosanoff did not state his standards.

3. Cited in Wheelan (267).

4. Although Sheldon uses the terms "first and second order psychopathy," this category includes a variety of personality types.

5. Inadequate diagnosis is one of the most critical defects in all research on the heredity of psychopathy. With few exceptions, the investigators either gave no description of their cases, or defined psychopathy in vague terms.

6. Richard Jenkins in his review of an earlier edition of this work in the *American Journal of Orthopsychiatry* (122), made the valuable correction that a distinction should be drawn between chronic encephalitis lethargica, "with its progressive pathology of basal ganglion cells and its bizarre effects on impulse, and the toxic encephalitis, which affect chiefly the white matter." Such a distinction may well explain the contradictory results in the literature on psychopathy and encephalitis.

7. Used extreme anti-social behavior as the criterion for his selection of psychopaths (227).

8. Used extreme antisocial behavior as the criterion for his selection of psychopaths (218).

9. Their standard of selection was not reported (95).

10. Used extreme antisocial behavior as the criterion for selection of psychopaths (231).

11. Selection based on "unsatisfactory functioning of self-

reliance or adjustment to the group in which they live." "Psy-chopathic" cases were divided into the "neurotic type," the "cyclothymic type," those with "poor ethics," "immature," and "inadequate psychopaths" (230).

12. Selection based on extreme antisocial behavior. The team did, however, find a higher proportion of F-2 and S-2 waves in the psychopathic cases (232).

13. His standard for selection was not reported (103).

14. The Ostrows also noted an exceptionally high proportion of slow paroxysmal waves (especially indicative of sub-cortical dysfunction).

15. Silverman used extreme antisocial behavior as his criterion for selection of psychopaths (229).

16. His standard for selection was not reported (218).

17. Lindner's test could be used as a diagnostic measure. Lindner administered it to 25 prisoners whom the prison psy-chiatrists had independently diagnosed as psychopathic or non-psychopathic. The judgments agreed 96 per cent.

18. Shotwell selected his cases on the basis of severe anti-social behavior (223).

19. See Henderson (111) and Sessions-Hodges (218).

J. J. Michaels, the Boston psychiatrist, has found a high in-cidence of enuresis among the psychopaths. This may be con-nected with neural damage (175).

20. Knight did not distinguish the psychopath from the ag-gressive child. Her descriptions show that some of her cases were psychopaths (138).

21. Haller selected his cases on the basis of severe antisocial behavior (107).

22. A more recent study by Johnson and Szurek recognized this criticism. In an article published in 1952, they added that this familial background was found only in cases where there was "no generalized weakness of the superego" (125).

23. Lindner's definition of psychopathy resembled the syn-drome presented in the first chapter. Lindner's position on guilt, however, is not clear. He intimates that the psychopath may have deeply repressed guilt concerning his attacks on society (and, in a symbolic way, on his father). See *Rebel Without a Cause* (153).

24. In 1948 Terry Rodgers studied 50 "psychopaths" at the Portsmouth Naval Prison. He loosely defined psychopathy in terms of behavior and found that 70 per cent of his cases came from rejecting families, 96 per cent from "abnormal" families. Rodgers felt that there was a close relation between neurosis and psychopathy: "Anxiety is the *vis a tergo* of each" (208).

25. David Levy cites a few cases in which he believes over-

protection resulted in psychopathy. From his brief descriptions of these children, it seems more probable that they are acting-out neurotics. Although uninhibited, they felt guilt; although selfish, they formed affectional relations (146).

26. Statements by a mother that her child was unwelcome at birth were used in the selection of cases (179).

27. In spite of Symond's careful tabulations, there were deficiencies in the study (241). Conversation with parents accounted for most of the data and, in all likelihood, rejectant parents would indicate negative personality traits of their offspring and acceptant parents would report more positive personality traits.

28. Some of the children, however, could maintain intimate relations with other people (212, p. 221).

29. Sheldon and Eleanor Glueck (92) found a much higher proportion of rejected children among the delinquents than among the nondelinquents. The Gluecks' work showed that a fairly large proportion of delinquents were rejected, yet only a minority (7.3 per cent) became psychopathic. They found that 16.9 per cent of fathers of delinquent boys rejected their sons, and 1 per cent of the nondelinquents' mothers did so. Only 32.5 per cent of the delinquents' fathers seemed emotionally attached to their boys, but 65.1 per cent of the nondelinquents' fathers maintained close ties. The study showed 64.9 per cent of the delinquents' mothers were emotionally attached to their children, though 89.8 per cent of the nondelinquents' mothers had strong emotional ties (92, pp. 125-127).

30. Institutionalization does not appear prominently in the histories of psychopaths. Lauretta Bender, however, in her studies of psychopathic children at Bellevue Hospital, found that most of the children had undergone critical breaks from their families (18).

31. Possibly, entirely different factors can result in psychopathy. The psychopathic syndrome may be a "pheno-type, that is, a complex of symptoms (like fever) which can be caused by numerous factors. Nevertheless, it seems more likely that either severe rejection or rejection in combination with neural damage accounts for the phenomenon of psychopathy. Neither mild rejection nor brain damage alone seems to cause psychopathy.

32. Perhaps, as Maslow believes, the constant early frustration of the psychopath's need for love extinguishes the need.

33. The Laboratory of Human Development at Harvard has been studying the relationship between identification and guilt and between guilt and methods of discipline. Their evidence tends to confirm this hypothesis.

34. Recent experimental evidence tends to confirm this theory. Christopher Heinecke studied parental attitudes of a group of families. Then he watched the behavior of their children in doll-play. In the experiment, the doll violated a moral rule. Heinecke observed the children's reactions and later questioned them about their concepts of evil, confession, etc. He concluded that the children with the greatest guilt received the greatest "nurturance," and that their parents disciplined them primarily by withdrawal of "nurturance." Also, the children with the greatest guilt more often identified with the parent of like sex, more often identified with the adult role, and less often evidenced overt aggression (110).

35. See Allport (8) for a discussion of different "levels" of conscience.

36. Many observers believe that the psychopath uses aggressive behavior to get attention and recognition. In any case, all psychopaths are subject to aggressive explosions. While some can temporarily maintain a sociable exterior, frustration almost invariably produces an aggressive reaction.

37. Gough conceptualized the psychopath's weak conscience in similar terms. The psychopath has no early social interaction. He therefore never learns to take "the role of the other" and to evaluate his actions through the eyes of other people. Thus he never develops an image of the "generalized other," society (97).

38. Probably the most critical test of its validity would be a combined neurological-environmental study. If psychopathy is caused both by severe rejection and by mild rejection plus neural damage, then all psycopaths who have been only mildly rejected should show signs of brain damage.

39. Cited by Bowlby (25).

40. The upper-class parents in the Fels research were primarily college teachers. The unique attitudes and superior education of this group may have affected their attitudes toward children and thus biased the Fels sample (13).

41. Studies of psychopathy specifically in relation to social class have not been made.

42. This is an actual case history, although identifying information has been removed.

5

The Treatment of Psychopathy

This disease is beyond my practice . . .

Doctor, in *Macbeth*

"As a probation or parole risk the psychopath's chances of failure are 100 per cent," a psychologist recently said. He added gloomily, "There is no evidence to my knowledge that any psychopath has ever been cured by imprisonment—or by anything else" (166). Such pessimism is by no means unique; almost every prison administrator would agree. After reviewing his experiences and the conclusions of others, a prison psychiatrist observed: ". . . the disease is of lifelong duration in almost every case" (52). A psychotherapist who personally dealt with many psychopaths reached the typical conclusion: " 'We must learn to face the fact . . .' that psychopathy is untreatable" (37). And, in 1959, Hervey Cleckly, the psychiatrist who has had perhaps the most extensive experience in the treatment of psychopaths, acknowledging the general failure of psychoanalysis, concluded, "All other methods available today have been similarly disappointing in well-defined adult cases of this disorder with which I am directly acquainted" (39, p. 586).

Prisons have done little to reform the criminal, be he nonpsychopathic or psychopathic.[1] Yet incarceration has been society's major response to crime. In prison, the psychopaths lead most of the riots, pass most of the drugs, and indoctrinate most of the young newcomers (41). The psychopaths commit the greatest number of prison offenses (150) and spend the most time in solitary confinement (237). In prison and out of prison, the psychopath contaminates society.

The well-publicized story of Earl Ward illustrates the

effect of prison on the psychopath—and the effect of the psychopath in prison.

On Sunday evening, April 20, 1952, a young convict at the Jackson Prison shoved a knife into the stomach of a guard and forced him into a cell. The convict opened the doors of other prisoners' cells in Jackson's block 15, its "hole." Picking up crowbars and knives, the men went on a rampage, beating all those who opposed them. Convicts smashed and burned furniture, started fires in the vocational shops, and flooded the cells.

Unable to stop the riot, the warden called in 200 state troopers who subdued all the prisoners except those in block 15. There, the toughest convicts locked themselves in, holding 15 terrorized guards as hostages. The leader of the block: Earl Ward, psychopath.

Ward and his partner, "Crazy Jack" Hyatt, presented a list of demands to the prison authorities as their price for ending the battle. Mercilessly, Ward and Hyatt beat up those prisoners who wanted to surrender. One burglar was beaten with a blackjack, kicked in the head, and thrown into the prison yard.

After days of negotiation, the governor consented to Ward's petition and the block surrendered.[2] The riot cost millions of dollars in physical damage. In human terms, the riot took a toll of 15 wounded men, one dead convict, and the nervous breakdown of a hostage.

In childhood, Earl Ward hated his parents, fought with his teachers, and revolted against every form of authority. At 15, he tried to join the army, but his father refused to grant permission. Earl ran away from home, was arrested several times, and chose reform school rather than return to his parents.

Ward was sent from one reform school to another. Always, he fought, ran away, and caused "trouble." After each release Ward attacked his family or stole. Extensive analysis in a state hospital resulted in Ward's diagnosis as a psychopath.

During early adulthood Ward posed as a doctor, stole drugs, and performed illegal abortions. In 1949 a charge of burglary sent him to Jackson Prison. The prison's administrators, intimidated by hints of past murders and anxious to rid themselves of a potential menace, trans-

ferred Ward to smaller Marquette. There Ward joined
a group planning to kidnap the governor when he visited
the prison. The plot failed; but Ward's part in it (plus
a death warning to a Marquette official) brought Ward's
return to Jackson's maximum security section. The official whom Ward threatened to kill said: "In my fifteen
years in this business I have heard many threats. This
one, however, I take as no idle jest" (162, p. 78).

Back at Jackson, Ward threatened to kill a guard who
had searched his cell. Everyone in the prison feared
Ward. Yet the disciplinary committee was impressed by
his "sincerity" and "understanding." Though he appeared before them three times in one year, Ward's demeanor could be convincingly contrite.

During the 1952 riot, Ward assumed leadership:
"They had no more idea what the hell they wanted than
flying in the air. That's why I took control" (162, p. 83).
He conducted negotiations skillfully, won all his demands, and, after surrendering, was put on trial.

The Jackson riot brought to public attention many of
the inadequacies of the American prison system. For a
time, the publicity given Ward's case dramatically pin-
pointed the psychopath's menace to society. Yet memories are short, and there are many Wards in prisons
from Sing Sing to Alcatraz.

Though tempted to say—like the doctor in *Macbeth*
—"This disease is beyond my practice," a few intrepid
therapists have tried to cure the psychopath. Their experiments have approached the problem with a variety of
techniques: group therapy, prison counseling, psychodrama, psychoanalysis, drugs, electroshock therapy, and
even lobotomy.

Some of these experiments have required courage not
usually demanded of the therapist. The psychopath is
like a chow dog who may turn and bite the hand that
pats him. The psychopath's hard emotional shell, his
disturbing aggression, and his complete irresponsibility
make therapy a thankless task. Nevertheless, a few determined men have accepted the challenge which society
has long ignored.

I. THE TREATMENT OF ADULT PSYCHOPATHY

Institutionalization has failed to cure the psychopath. Few objective studies have been made, but those few indicate that the chances of success are slim.

From Switzerland, Peter Mohr reported that the well-equipped Königsfelden asylum failed to cure most "psychopaths." Although Königsfelden was ostensibly an asylum for psychopaths, it treated many cases of sex deviance, neurotic criminalism, and other types of psychiatric disorder. Only 40 per cent of the patients had not committed a crime within two years of release (176).

American institutions have had no greater success.[3] The most optimistic estimate, by W. L. Heaver, places the proportion of success with psychopaths treated in a hospital at 40 per cent.[4] Other follow-up studies have shown more disappointing rates of reformation. B. L. Haller, investigating 52 psychopaths six months after their release from a mental hospital, found that only 13 per cent had made a "satisfactory adjustment." [5]

Punishment seems useless. A British research team found, in 1951, that the average psychopathic convict had already served seven sentences: twice the number of convictions of the ordinary British criminal (237). In other words, double the usual punishment had not deterred these psychopaths. In a later follow-up study, the team reported that 76 per cent of the psychopaths had subsequently been convicted for two or more crimes (79).

Isolation offers but limited protection to society. Under our contemporary system of justice, the imprisoned psychopath will some day be set free to continue his depredations, and new generations of psychopaths constantly appear. Society's best hope for protection lies not in imprisonment, but rather in curing the disorder.

Some therapists believe that this cure might be effected within the prison, but only if special techniques are used. Group therapy has often been advocated as a treatment for psychopathy. During the last war, the Army met the costly problem of criminality by establishing "rehabilitation centers." According to Army claims, these institutions had amazing success, particularly with their group therapy programs. Imprisoned soldiers (30 per cent of them psychopaths) participated in discussions of alcoholism, personality development, relations to authority, and "levels of loyalty." [6] The leader maintained a permissive, nonauthoritarian attitude.

The convict-soldiers were divided into separate groups according to personality traits. The psychopaths were placed in the "aggressive" section. During typical sessions in this group, the leader tried to get the men to identify with him as a friendly figure, and with his goals as both reasonable and right. This approach—and the leader's skillful way of deflecting hostile attacks—is illustrated in the following exchange (1):

> One soldier grumbled, "I don't like the way Sergeant . . . treated K." Approving comments swept the group.
> "The Sergeant is always doing things to K," the first soldier continued. "They are all the same, making us unhappy." The other group members nodded in agreement.
> The leader, who had kept quiet until then, asked: "How do you like me?"
> "You are like all the rest. I hate you too!" said the soldier. The remark antagonized the group. They began to shift their allegiance to the leader:
> "He never done anything to us."
> "He is our friend."
> The first soldier answered, "You're just hand-shaking."

Gradually, with group support, the leader questioned the soldier. Why did he feel the way he did? Eventually, the soldier concluded that he might have transplanted his attitude toward his father to officers. With this insight, the soldier began to form different, warmer relations with the leader.

Supervisors of the group therapy program believed that it held unusual promise in the treatment of psychopaths: reportedly, most psychopaths achieved some form of identification with the leader. Unfortunately, no study assessed the long-term effects of this method on the psychopathic personality.[7]

After the war, other institutions initiated group treatment. Chillicothe Reformatory set up a segregated unit for habitual offenders, a unit which soon became known as "Little Alcatraz." Inmates were forbidden visitors, movies, and trips to the canteen. Stern punishment kept the segregated block under control.

Treatment consisted in vocational classes, occasional well-disciplined discussion groups, and brief conferences with a psychologist. An official committee reviewed each man's progress periodically, giving him greater privileges if his behavior merited them. Chillicothe officials called their system "demonstro-therapy" because of its emphasis on achievement (81).

According to prison diagnosis, only 12 per cent of the "Little Alcatraz" convicts were "fully developed, mature psychopathic personalities." [8] Probably the proportion of psychopathy was higher. Most of the habitual offenders were described as egocentric, unable to learn from experience, highly aggressive, and unable to form close ties.

Chillicothe officials felt enthusiastic about their "demonstro-therapy." Tests showed some gains in the convicts' school achievement, personality adjustment, and a marked improvement in their behavior within the prison.[9] However, because no control group was established, it is hard to assess the effects of the therapy itself.

San Quentin prison, too, has utilized group methods in attempting to curb psychopathy. In addition to regular group discussions in a permissive atmosphere, the prison psychologists used psychodrama (43). Small groups of volunteers met several times a week to act out their problems and their pasts in spontaneous plays. After some initial shyness, the men participated in role-playing with enthusiasm. The story of one psychopathic convict demonstrates the method.

"B.E.," a 21-year-old burglar, had spent his childhood in foster homes. As a boy, he wandered from job to job, farm to farm. During the war, he joined the Navy. Because of drinking sprees, gambling, and extensive A.W.O.L., he spent 18 months in a Navy prison. "The Navy," he later summarized, "was mean to me."

Following a series of burglaries, he landed in San Quentin prison. In regular group therapy, the young convict remained aloof. In psychodrama, however, he slowly dropped his shell of emotional hardness. After observing the group for several weeks, he suddenly volun-

teered to reenact his belligerence toward the Navy and
his attempted escape from prison. His attitude became
more cooperative. He gradually admitted the futility of
his conduct, and later he volunteered to take the part
of obnoxious, aggressive people in other plays. During the sessions, B.E. formed a "big-brotherly" attachment to another convict. By the end of treatment, the
psychologist noticed definite changes in B.E.'s personality: ". . . he had a sincere belief concerning the futility of his conduct. The dramatizations afforded an
abreaction of any doubt" (43).

Unfortunately, San Quentin, like the Army and Chillicothe, has made no systematic study of the treatment's
effect on psychopaths. Harrison Gough, nevertheless, believes that psychodrama is uniquely beneficial for the
psychopath. Because the psychopath is seriously deficient
in his ability to relate to other people, role-playing might
help in showing him the feeling of others. Recent reports
of the successful use of psychodrama with individual
cases lend some credence to this view (42). Although
in the last few years a number of prisons have experimented with group treatment of psychopathy, none has
made a complete evaluation of its impact (193).

The effects of individual counseling have, however,
been more thoroughly analyzed, and the results have not
been as discouraging as many social scientists believe.

Harry R. Lipton, a prison psychotherapist, noted remarkable improvement in a psychopath who received
only sporadic counseling from a chaplain and a psychiatrist. Lipton's case underwent the typically harsh treatment in childhood that seems conducive to psychopathy.
Raised by a brutal uncle, he began his asocial career at
the age of nine. Many crimes followed: burglaries at 13,
manslaughter at 19, robbery at 20, assault and robbery
at 25. Society retaliated with reform school and prison
terms. In prison, the cynical young man bragged, fought,
and led violent disorders. Psychological examinations uncovered the psychopathic syndrome and an aggressive
father-hatred.

Equipped with this information, the prison psychiatrist and the chaplain began patient counseling of the
convict. After seven years, the man's behavior changed

radically. He became editor of the paper, sponsored better inmate-guard relations, and established strong ties with his mentors. In 1944, after his release from prison, he began a successful career as copy writer for an advertising company (158).

Louis Weber, also, developed rapport with a psychopath. "B.T.," Weber's patient, had witnessed his father's suicide. At eight, he began stealing from his grandmother, who had taken care of the abandoned child. He stole throughout adolescence, but still he graduated from high school. During service with the navy, B.T. rolled drunks, picked up homosexuals, and smoked "reefers." Following his discharge, B.T. passed from job to job, forging checks and staying with relatives until he stole from them. Once, after robbing his grandmother, he borrowed $300 from her and skipped town. At his mother's request, he was brought to jail.

After setting fire to his cell, he was transferred to a state hospital for observation. There, psychologist Weber began his counseling, but not soon enough to prevent B.T.'s escape. B.T. stole a horse, soon abandoning it for a stolen airplane. Although he had not studied flying, B.T. somehow got the plane off the ground and later landed it.

Returned to the State Hospital, B.T. boasted of his exploits, while Weber tried to reach him through counseling interviews. B.T. turned every friendly overture to his own advantage. When the psychologist—upon the patient's request—gave him a model airplane kit, B.T. secretly poured the kit's glue into "cokes" to make his own bootlegged liquor. Gradually, however, Weber made progress with the case. Under Sodium Amytal B.T. spoke about hatred of his parents and shock over his father's suicide.

After release from the prison hospital as legally "sane," B.T. went to the counselor's home three times each week. At the counselor's urging, the patient went to work and began to repay the airplane damage. Although he lost his first job, B.T. did well as a clerk in a grocery store.

The months passed and Weber noted an increasing attachment. The patient accepted almost all suggestions.

He joined the Y.M.C.A. and signed up with the Naval Reserve. Worried because of his record, B.T. asked his counselor whether he should inform the grocery store about his escapades. Weber agreed that he should. The store owner already knew about them, B.T. discovered; but B.T.'s concern over the matter was remarkable because of his former absence of remorse.

The interviews tapered off as B.T. assumed more control over his life. Suddenly, the interviews stopped altogether. B.T. lost his job and left without a word—for California.

Did the long counseling process fail completely? Probably not. B.T.'s mother reported that the young man was leading a normal, successful life in California and, for a year, had not gotten into trouble. The psychologist cautiously assessed the result: "Although [I] would hesitate to conclude that there was definite and lasting improvement, it does appear that some improvement took place" (265).

The psychopath's disorder, Robert Lindner felt, lies too deep for ordinary methods to affect it. In an attempt to cure psychopathy, Lindner tried the unusual instrument of hypnoanalysis. After an hypnotic trance had been induced, Lindner used free association and dream analysis, supplementing these psychoanalytic techniques with hypnotic suggestion.

In *Rebel Without A Cause*, Lindner reported his experience with criminal psychopaths. He reproduced tape-recorded transcripts of his interviews with one patient. Harold, the psychopathic subject, was a federal convict boasting a long court record. In addition, he had an eye disability approaching blindness.

Harold first came to Lindner's office for treatment of his blindness. Medical tests indicated a psychological, rather than organic, cause. Slowly, Lindner led the patient into discussion of his antisocial behavior. Harold agreed to undergo hypnoanalytic treatments, ostensibly for his blindness.

During the first hours, Harold evidenced stubborn resistance: "I feel as if I am in a daze or up against a big cliff. It seems somehow as if my path is blocked" (153, p. 35). Gradually, the convict unveiled a picture of his earlier years: the harsh authority of his father, his sexual attachment to his mother, and lurid erotic experiences. In talking of "Perry," his homosexual friend in the prison, Harold showed the beginnings of an attachment to his therapist: "He is the first one besides you who ever took any interest in me" (153, p. 63).

As the therapy progressed, Harold's hatred of his father emerged. The boy's thefts began with the stealing of his father's penknife and razor. This act he committed in reaction to the father's threat of castration: "My sister was a tomboy and he would say things about cutting off my penis and giving it to her" (153, p. 46).

Conflict with the father began because of intense jealousy: "Well—I—I—ever since I can remember—because—these things—my mother. . . . Well, because ever since I can remember I wanted to possess—my mother—more than anyone else . . ." (153, p. 283). This maternal attachment and the resultant father-hatred culminated in the attempted murder of a criminal who had jokingly taunted Harold about his love for his mother.

Under deep hypnosis, Harold recalled watching his mother and father having intercourse. Lindner believed that Harold associated the traumatic experience with an early movie in which his eyes had been blinded by the movie projector. The lustful glint in his father's eyes became attached to the momentary experience of blindness. Harold had "seen things that were forbidden" and had permanently blinded himself as punishment.

By the end of therapy, Harold accepted the connection between his blindness and the early traumatic experience. Furthermore, according to Lindner, Harold recognized that his criminality was an attempt to prove his manliness. Both were manifestations of his hatred for his father. "He was stronger than me, I was afraid of him." Lindner believed that the father's brutality caused distrust in Harold and a blind drive to express his aggressive feelings.

Although Harold may not have been a true psychopath, Lindner felt that Harold's new insight caused a startling reorientation of character. Realizing that his clashes with the law came from father-hatred, Harold was better able to control his hostile urges. Harold's highly repressed "guilt" about incestuous desires—perhaps existent in all psychopaths—became conscious.[10] Lindner reported success with the method in seven other cases of psychopathy. Hypnotherapy seems to provide the patient with an opportunity for working out youthful hatreds and for gaining deeper insight into behavior.

Terry Rodgers, a naval psychologist, found that hypnotherapy improved a passive, emotionally-starved marine in a mental hospital. The marine gained insight, and many of his painful symptoms disappeared. Although Rodgers' patient was not a psychopath (as Lindner's may not have been), his family had been highly rejectant. Rodgers believes that hypnotherapy can be particularly valuable for those who have been raised in a loveless environment (207). Possibly it breaks through the hostile, suspicious barriers which ordinarily make relationships so difficult. Hypnotherapy, as yet scarcely tested, may prove to be one of the most valuable instruments for the treatment of psychopathy.

Psychoanalysis, unsupplemented by hypnosis, has also been used with psychopaths. The earliest experiments had dismal outcomes. In 1924 Mary O'Malley reviewed the reports on psychoanalysis and concluded: "Psychoanalysis as a therapeutic measure for the psychopathic personality . . . has proven a failure. . . ."[11]

In Germany, only 1 of 23 psychopaths treated at the Berlin Psychoanalytic Institute "improved greatly." Eighteen patients had discontinued treatment, and 4 had shown no improvements under analysis.[12]

In 1948 Walter Bromberg psychoanalyzed a psychopath in a naval prison. Bromberg's 19-year-old patient had been raised by his grandmother. His parents were divorced, and his father, a criminal alcoholic, persistently beat the boy. The patient's record of fights, knifings, and riot leadership within the prison made him a dangerous challenge.

In the first analytic sessions (which the prisoner was forced to attend) the boy refused to talk with his analyst. Once the psychopath drew a knife on Bromberg. Eventually, however, the boy's extreme resistance gave way under the therapist's patient prodding. The boy

related the story of his love-impoverished life. His first
dreams dealt with killing: killing guards, killing convicts,
and killing his therapist. Later, the the theme shifted to
fear of the analyst.

Bromberg's nondemanding friendliness, coupled with
firm consistency, impressed the convict—and partial
identification took place. Unfortunately, the analysis
ended abruptly when Bromberg returned to civilian life
(30).

Melitta Schmideberg reported a high degree of success
in her use of psychoanalysis with psychopathic personalities. Schmideberg analyzed 11 major criminals: "habitual, hardened, callous" offenders (213). In addition to their antisocial attitudes, most of her patients
had meager guilt feelings and impoverished relational
abilities. Schmideberg diagnosed the majority as true
psychopaths. Surprisingly, Schmideberg reported substantial improvement in every case. Two of her cases
illustrate the startling transformations:

One man, an American "tough guy," had committed
32 armed holdups. "He claimed that there is no crime
that he did not commit with the exception of murder,
counterfeiting, and cheating at cards." He had never
held a job, earning money instead through constant
criminal activity. One of the patient's favorite techniques
was luring homosexuals to his room and, while the victims slept, smashing them over the head with a bottle
and stealing their money.

Immigrant parents had deserted the patient in early
childhood. At 13, convicted for 20 minor offenses, he
entered a reformatory. After discharge he lived the life
of a vagrant gangster. At 21, with a long record of robberies, he was sentenced to prison.

Paroled from prison six and one-half years later, the
patient was sent to Schmideberg for analysis. With
patience, with repeated demonstrations of her confidence
in him, and with permissive acceptance, Schmideberg
slowly established rapport. The treatment, more than 60
sessions, stretched over a long period.

As therapy progressed, the man disclosed profound
feelings of inferiority and rejection. The causes of his
behavior, Schmideberg reported, became clear to him.

By the end of treatment, his personality had undergone a striking change. Perhaps most importantly, his ability to form emotional relations developed to a mature level. The analyst's last check on him showed that he had married, had children, and had turned into a "settled, contented, good father and husband" (214, p. 175).

Another of Schmideberg's patients, a middle-aged English woman, had served 15 sentences for misrepresentation and theft. Her father, a clergyman, was an alcoholic. Her relatives protected their social prestige by paying 5,000 pounds to cover the woman's crimes. In her twenties several psychiatrists had examined her. Finding her a psychopath, each refused to treat her.

She married an irresponsible man and gave birth to two children. Abortions prevented the birth of other children who had been sired by lovers.

Released from one of her many prison sojourns, the patient went to the Institute for the Scientific Treatment of Delinquency. Schmideberg accepted the case. At first, therapy achieved nothing. The patient continued to steal and returned to prison. Undiscouraged, Schmideberg visited her in prison. Assured of the analyst's support, the patient gained new emotional security.

Again paroled, she showed improvement. Suddenly, however, she renewed her thieving. Only later did the analyst discover the reason for the relapse: blackmail. A former lover had been extorting money from the woman because she had killed their illegitimate baby years before. Again the analyst came to her aid and saved her from a return to prison.

Prolonged therapy apparently developed new values and inner stability. The therapist's last examination showed that the woman had adjusted to society and its demands.

One of Schmideberg's therapeutic problems was getting the psychopaths "to endure kindness." Suspicious of all human beings, and inexperienced in maintaining emotional relations, the psychopaths rejected friendship. Only through persistent permissiveness could the therapist develop the patients' trust. Love, permissiveness, loyalty, and great patience seemed to ameliorate the symptoms of psychopathy. Schmideberg commented: " 'Standing by,' showing forbearance again and again helps the patient gradually to acquire the love and security he missed in childhood, and enables him to gain a social attitude by identification" (214, p. 187).

Fortunately, the techniques used by Schmideberg are not exclusively the prerogative of psychoanalysis. Love, patience, and permissiveness can be used by any therapist who treats psychopathy and, if Schmideberg's cases are any indication, can be used successfully.

Nevertheless, the transformations through psychoanalysis, reported by Schmideberg, and through hypnoanalysis, reported by Lindner, are exceptional.[13] Other therapists have experienced more failures than successes. Even when there has been improvement, as psychoanalyst Phyllis Greenacre points out, success may be illusory: "[Psychopaths] very often . . . make quick dramatic improvements which are soon revealed to be only 'skin deep' or to disappear as dramatically as they were instituted; it is then apparent that the fundamentally unsound organization of the personality of the psychopath has not been much influenced or even touched" (101, p. 378). Thus, the impact of therapy requires careful and complete study.

Because the psychopath's capacity for identification is so limited and his sense of responsibility so meager, psychotherapy has been difficult. Drugs, of one variety or another, have often been used to wedge the psychopath's resistance (55).

Carl Adatto, for one, found barbiturates helpful in establishing initial rapport. From the Mendocino State Hospital, Adatto (2) selected 14 "psychopathic" inmates and subjected them to narcoanalysis. He administered Pentothal Sodium intravenously and, while the patient relaxed, asked personal questions. Many of the patients had strong hatred for their fathers but also unexpectedly strong attachments to their mothers.

"Tell me about your mother," the interviewer asked.

"Mother? She could have every last cent I got!" the patient began to cry.

"I had the best mother in the world. I would lay down and die for her; but she is gone, she is gone."

George Train, a psychologist at Lewisburg Prison, also used Pentothal Sodium on convicts (260, pp. 542-557). Again the drug proved useful as an adjunct to psychotherapy. One of Train's psychopathic patients had a record of juvenile crimes, an unstable work history, and unsatisfactory emotional relationships. During a pentothal interview, the patient described the "primal scene" he had witnessed, which he had interpreted as a chastisement of his mother and remembered vividly. Train deduced that this memory resulted in antagonism toward the patient's father and all authority. Other interviews followed, and the therapy caused a slight improvement in the patient's behavior. He was sent to a mental hospital. Four months later he was reported as "adjusted satisfactorily."

F. A. Freyhan, a hospital psychiatrist, used drugs as a therapeutic aid (72). Freyhan selected two "psychopaths" and gave them Sodium Amytal. One man did not change; the other showed a greater willingness to talk and a more friendly attitude. He became more accessible to psychotherapy.[14] Unfortunately, Freyhan did not record the eventual outcome of his therapeutic sessions.

In their search for a cure, some scientists used drugs alone. In general, these investigators believed in a constitutional cause of psychopathy, an organic condition which could be entirely corrected by physical means.

In 1944 Daniel Silverman (228) studied the effects of a variety of drugs on 64 psychopathic inmates of a federal prison.[15] Some patients were given Dilantin Sodium, others phenobarbital, Benzedrine sulphate, or a combined dosage of Amytal and Benzedrine. A control group received placebos of sugar and water resembling the narcotic tablets. Silverman traced the E.E.G. patterns of the subjects before and after treatment. In addition, he secured reports from the prison officials concerning the men's institutional behavior.

Only Dilantin Sodium seemed to bring any improvement. Prisoners who had taken the drug became less antagonistic and more reliable. They reported a greater feeling of well-being and contentment. Their E.E.G. patterns normalized. The other drugs brought no be-

havioral improvement and little change in the E.E.G.
tracings. Benzedrine sulphate actually caused more abnormality in the brain waves. The placebos induced a
feeling of "well-being" in some of the prisoners.

Silverman did not follow the subsequent behavior of
the men, nor did he measure the impact on basic personality structure.[16]

Dennis Hill (113), in 1947, found that amphetamine
sulphate, too, improved the behavior of "psychopaths."
Hill administered the drug to aggressive, "bad-tempered"
patients. After taking the narcotic, the patients' personalities appeared "more integrated," and they had a "more
mature expression of the primary appetitive drives."
The drug, Hill hypothesized, exerted an oxidating influence on the associational areas of cerebral cortex. Unfortunately, Hill did not report what happened once the
drug was removed.

Also in 1947, J. J. Shovron (224) reported from England on the effects of Benzedrine. Using three adult
"psychopaths," Shovron found that the drug had only
temporary usefulness. The patients' aggression lessened
for a period, but the drug's effect was short-lived.[17]

In 1959, J. Tong studied aggressive psychopaths at
Rampton in terms of their autonomic response to a
stressor agent. His findings suggested the existence of
two types of psychopaths: the "affectionless schizoid"
and the "emotionally unstable." He predicted that the
first group might best be treated with amphetamine,
while the second might respond to the drugs composing
the promazine group (259). M. Craft's experiments lent
credence to this opinion when he discovered that benac-
tyzine created a statistically significant improvement in
the behavior of "emotionally unstable" personalities
(44).

Nevertheless, the general results of narcotherapy have
been disappointing. For some patients, particularly those
with an epileptic history, Dilantin Sodium and some
barbiturates may have a temporarily soothing, euphoric
effect. Possibly such drugs will prove a useful supplement
to psychotherapy. By calming the psychopath's aggression the drugs should help to "lubricate" the therapeutic

relationship, but science has yet to develop a miraculous pill which can transform the psychopath.

Electric shock and lobotomy, the "last resort" instruments of modern psychiatry, have been tried on psychopaths. The first and the only thorough measure of the impact of shock treatment on psychopaths was made in 1944 by Eugene Green, George Geil, and Daniel Silverman (100). These prison psychiatrists selected 24 psychopathic convicts and subjected them to electric shock.[18] Before the experiment, the researchers took E.E.G. tracings and compiled reports on the prisoners' behavior.

Six months after treatment, the psychiatrists found that most of the men had not noticeably changed. The behavior of 4 subjects improved, 7 others showed slight improvement, and 13 convicts were unchanged by the experiment. When questioned about their feelings, six convicts said they felt better, two said they felt worse.

Remeasurement of brain waves showed that the E.E.G. patterns of two men had improved, but those of six others had become more abnormal. Fortunately, the latter eventually returned to their original patterns.

The research team attempted to assess the psychological effects of shock treatment. Eight men from the experimental group took the Wechsler-Bellevue intelligence test before and ten months after the shock treatment. Their I.Q. scores increased an average of 9.8 points. The mean score of a control group of eight other convicts increased 4.2 points during the same period. The researchers admitted that the treated convicts, because of the attention given them, may have tried harder.

"Before and after" Rorschach tests of four of these psychopaths revealed that their productivity (the number of responses to the pictures) had significantly increased. Once again, the motivation rather than the treatment may account for the difference. The Rorschach protocols reflected no changes in the character of the psychopathic convicts.

In other experiments with shock treatment, diagnoses were confused, and varied disorders were labeled "psychopathic." The results, at first glance, appeared slightly more impressive.

H. F. Darling found that shock treatment benefited two "psychopaths" and did not help another (53).[19] Golden found that three out of four "psychopaths" improved under shock treatment.[20] And Banay, the most optimistic researcher, reported "beneficial reactions" in all but 12 of 51 cases.[21]

Lobotomy, the incision of a small rotating blade into the prefrontal lobes, has been practiced in the attempt to cure psychopathy. In 1938 Walter Freeman and James Watts first tried this drastic technique on a case "which bears a family resemblance" to the psychopathic personality. Following the operation, the patient, an adult criminal, seemed less aggressive.[22]

In 1942 R. S. Banay and L. Davidoff subjected a middle-aged "sex psychopath" to lobotomy (14). Afterwards, the patient seemed to gain insight, his sense of responsibility appeared to increase and, as far as the authors knew, he had "socially recovered." His eventual adjustment was not reported; nor was his personality thoroughly analyzed.

In 1949 a Swedish psychiatrist, Lennart Nilson, performed the operation on an antisocial patient with a long criminal record. The man, loosely tabbed a psychopath, seemed to improve, but no full study was made (182).

The most enthusiastic advocates of lobotomy, H. F. Darling and J. W. Sandall, tried surgery on 18 severely antisocial inmates of a mental hospital. Seventeen of the patients "improved," and nine were released from the hospital. The researchers believed that psychopathy—although triggered by environmental causes—resulted primarily from inherited weaknesses. Only a change in organic structure, they believed, could cure the psychopath. "If psychopathy were a deficiency in the social interaction of the individual," they reasoned, ". . . the great improvement following the operation would be an impossibility. . . . Certainly, the environment of the patients in the series was not changed by means of a leucotome" (54). Such reasoning, from "cure" to cause, is dubious. Many types of disorders, both functional and organic, respond to lobotomy. Indeed, recent empirical evidence indicates that the original enthusiasm concerning the use of leucotomy should be tempered. A. A. Robin, in a controlled follow-up study done in 1958, found no reason to believe that psychopathy can be eradicated by a leucotomy (206).

Similar recent experiments devoted to an analysis of anterior temporal lobectomy have produced variable results. Although D. Hill and his colleagues reported that the operation typically brought a decrease in aggression and impulsiveness and an increase in friendliness and warmth (115), M. A. Falconer and P. Shurr, in their comprehensive review of recent experiments (66), suggests that any generalization concerning the operation should be reserved until long-term follow-up studies can be conducted.[23]

The label of "psychopathy," often abused, was particularly misused in these studies. Often the patient's only "psychopathic" trait was his antisociality. Furthermore, the ultimate effects of these operations were seldom examined.

The use of lobotomy with any patient is hazardous—and with psychopaths, particularly so. Lobotomy has been successful in decreasing the oppressive anxiety of some psychotics. But psychopaths have little or no anxiety. Indeed, one of the most important tasks of therapy is to increase their anxiety. Postoperative studies have found a striking increase of aggression in some patients, though in others aggression has decreased. For the psychopath—already an overly aggressive person—such unpredictability adds to the danger of lobotomy.

In summary, therapeutic experiments with the adult psychopath have shown:

> Incarceration in prisons or mental hospitals temporarily isolates psychopaths from the larger society. While one cannot be certain, it seems probable that imprisonment is even less effective in reforming these offenders than in reforming nonpsychopathic delinquents.
>
> The effects of "group therapy," whether in the form of discussion groups, "demonstro-therapy," or psychodrama, have not been conclusively ascertained. In some cases, such methods seem to make the psychopath better able to maintain affectional relations.

Psychotherapy has, in isolated cases, resulted in marked changes. Usually, however, even prolonged psychotherapy has not altered the psychopathic character.

Hypnoanalysis, successful with a small number of cases, holds promise of usefulness. Its lasting effects on personality have not, however, been traced.

Certain drugs, particularly Pentothal Sodium and Dilantin Sodium, are potentially useful for easing the problems of individual counseling. They help to make the psychopath amenable to psychotherapy.

Drugs, unsupplemented by other treatment, probably fail to bring lasting improvements in psychopaths.

The effects of electric shock treatment have not been fully measured. Tentatively, results indicate that shock does not alter the psychopath's personality structure.

The results of lobotomy on psychopaths are also unknown. Diagnoses have frequently been inexact, and subsequent behavior has not been thoroughly traced.

Unfortunately, many therapeutic experiments have commingled several disorders under the label "psychopathy." Disappointingly, too, few therapists incorporate personality analysis in their assessment of results. Without careful diagnosis and complete examination of personality changes, we cannot know what, if any, impact the methods have on psychopaths.

The prospect for successful treatment, while gloomy, is not altogether discouraging. Although inadequately assessed, psychotherapy seems to hold the most promise. In one of its forms, hypnoanalysis, Robert Lindner found an effective means of treating several "psychopaths." Hypnosis apparently helped to establish rapport and to uncover repressed memories. The relationship itself offered the patients an opportunity for identification, which they had lacked. Though few in number and questionable in diagnosis, Lindner's successes justify further trial of hypnoanalysis in the treatment of psychopathy.

Psychotherapy, without resort to hypnosis, has at times been successful. If the resistance of the psychopath can be overcome, and if the therapist has great patience, an emotional bond can sometimes be developed. Lipton, Weber, Schmideberg, and Bromberg have apparently utilized rapport for the inculcation of new values and a more acceptable "life style."

This process, however, is unpredictable. Many psychopaths seem incapable of establishing rapport. Moreover, psychotherapy requires an expenditure of energy and time which few psychologists can afford. Possibly such drugs as Dilantin Sodium, Pentothal Sodium, or Sodium Amytal could shorten the process of developing rapport. Here again, there is a need for more experiments and thorough evaluation of results.

One exciting approach—the "therapeutic community" initiated by Maxwell Jones—combines several of the more promising types of treatment (126 and 127). For a number of years, Jones and his colleagues have experimented with autonomous treatment units established in mental hospitals or prisons.[24] These therapeutic communities involve intensive group therapy in which staff members participate equally with patients. Various follow-up studies indicate that Jones' approach reduces some of the more violent tendencies of the patients and results in a lower rate of recidivism (211 and 225).

Although there are some tantalizing hints that the adult psychopath may prove curable, the typical psychopathic personality seems singularly resistant to change. He lacks the desire for change and the anxiety over his condition which most therapists believe is the prerequisite for treatment. Most psychopaths see nothing wrong with themselves and, therefore, no reason to change.

Since rapport is basic to all psychotherapy, the psychopath's deficiencies in this area represent a serious handicap. Without experience in emotional relationships, the psychopath resists the complex patient-therapist bond.

Finally, the psychopath has little guilt. He feels no compunction about breaking appointments, about attacking the therapist (usually verbally, sometimes physically), or about stopping treatment altogether. These three traits—lack of anxiety, lack of "identifying ability," and lack of guilt—make the psychopath a poor prospect for successful therapy.

Thus psychotherapy offers a little hope, but no assurance, of success. Other approaches to the problem seem even less promising: incarceration alone, while temporarily protecting society, does not seem to change basic personality trends; organic treatment (with drugs, shock, or lobotomy) has shown few, if any, beneficial results.[25]

In short, treatment of the adult psychopath, while not hopeless, is far from hopeful. Therefore, attention should be given to the prevention of adult psychopathy. Our best hope lies in the successful treatment of child psychopathy: in changing youths before they mature into hardened psychopaths.

II. THE TREATMENT OF CHILD PSYCHOPATHY

The child psychopath has the embryonic personality traits of the adult psychopath. His tantrums and delinquencies betray his aggressiveness. His truancies reflect his impulsivity. His cruelties to animals and children reveal his asociality. The child psychopath has little, if any, remorse for his diffuse, brutal, usually purposeless activities, and he seems unable to affiliate with other human beings.[26]

Many of the techniques used with adult psychopaths have been tried with the child. Most frequently, the juvenile psychopath has been incarcerated with other delinquents. Although we know that the usual reform school leaves few beneficial imprints on its charges (169), there are unfortunately no studies specifically concerned with the adjustment of the psychopathic child.

Some social scientists, though not generally advocating the severity of the reform school, believe that the child psychopath must be treated in a disciplined environment (200). Only strict regimentation and forced conformity, they contend, can inculcate values into the child psychopath. An experiment at the Hawthorne Cedar-Knolls School put this theory into practice.

The school officials decided that permissive methods would not help "Bernard," a highly aggressive boy. Immature, self-centered, and "affectless," Bernard had insulted his teachers, attacked other children, run away from home, gotten into "sex trouble," and frequently stolen. Hawthorne Cedar-Knolls placed the boy under a special regime of authoritarian control and strict limitations. He was forced to conform to a routine. At all

times, even when they punished him, the school officials tried to act without malice.

Bernard formed a limited attachment to a house
mother, and his behavior became a little more moderate
and self-controlled. He seemed to improve, but the
change was not striking. After release, a follow-up report
indicated that Bernard was "doing well" in the army
(238).

In another study, B. M. Wolfe found that institutional conformity apparently had beneficial results with
only a handful of psychopathic boys. Wolfe examined
16 psychopathic children who had been incarcerated in
the children's group of a mental hospital. Their treatment consisted primarily in disciplined, patterned supervision. Of those cases which could be traced, 11 made
an unsatisfactory adjustment, 3 made a "moderately satisfactory" adjustment, and only 2 seemed to have recovered—and on closer analysis, it was decided that these 2
boys were cases of "adolescent upset" rather than of true
psychopathy (273).

On the basis of admittedly slight evidence, it appears
that forced conformity teaches the child psychopath little
more than it does the adult psychopath. The cure, if
there is one, probably lies elsewhere.

Hoping to find a surer solution to the psychopathic
dilemma, some psychiatrists experimented with narcotics.
Phenobarbital proved useless when tried with aggressive
children in the 1940's (51 and 156). Work with Benzedrine sulphate, however, hinted at the exciting possibility
that this drug might prove the answer to child psychopathy.

In 1941 K. K. Cutts and H. H. Jasper reported that
Benzedrine markedly improved six children who exhibited "behavior disorders." The boys apparently had
epileptoid conditions, and the drug soothed and inhibited
them. The narcotic did not seem to affect six other
"asocial" boys (51). In 1942 D. B. Lindsley and C. E.
Henry administered Benzedrine to aggressive children
and noted beneficial effects on all (156). In the same
year, D. Davidoff and G. L. Goodstone used Benzedrine
and Sodium Amytal on psychopathic boys. They too

found a startling increase in the children's behavioral control (55).

Other experiments, however, dampened the initial enthusiasm for Benzedrine as a cure for psychopathy. In one of these later studies, S. R. Korey selected 11 severely delinquent boys from the National Training School and gave them the drug. Of these boys, four were neurotic; the other seven were psychopathic.[27] Benzedrine induced a feeling of well-being in all the boys, and the behavior of two of the psychopaths markedly improved. One other psychopath improved "moderately," another improved "subjectively," and three boys did not change. After the drug was removed, the "improved" boys reverted to their former states. None of the psychopaths changed permanently in personality structure (139).

Benzedrine had even more disappointing results in cases treated by Lauretta Bender and Frances Cottington. These researchers had found that the drug made neurotics calmer, more secure, and more eager to learn. Yet, when the drug was given to four psychopathic children, an unfavorable reaction ensued.

Two of the children had been in foster homes. The other two had been severely rejected by their parents. All four had caused serious trouble in school. They were self-centered, quarrelsome, and apparently without affection.

The use of Benzedrine on the four children increased their inner tension, instability, and excitability. The children gave way to disorganized fantasies and seemed baffled. Bender and Cottington believed that the drug made the psychopaths aware of emotions which they could not combat. As soon as the drug was withdrawn, its effects disappeared (19).

Dilantin Sodium may offer some hope in the treatment of child psychopathy. The drug has not been tried on known psychopaths, but it has been extensively used on aggressive children (some of whom may have been psychopaths). Lindsley and Henry found that Dilantin Sodium temporarily calmed behaviorally disturbed children (156). In 1947 C. Walker and B. Kirkpatrick enthusiastically reported dramatic improvement in aggressive children who had undergone Dilantin Sodium treatment. Unfortunately, the improvement disappeared with removal of the drug (263).

At least at the present time, there seems to be no "injection" which can cure child psychopathy. There is, however, reasonable hope that some drug (possibly Dilantin) or newly discovered tranquilizers will prove useful in establishing therapeutic relations with psychopaths.

Patient therapists have attempted to bring forth less dramatic, but perhaps more permanent, changes through individual psychotherapy. Assuming that psychopathy is caused (at least primarily) by deficient affection, then emotional attachment should ameliorate the disorder. The psychotherapist tries to establish the rapport which the child psychopath does not have with his parents. If an attachment can be formed, the child identifies with the adult and begins to develop feelings of responsibility and internalized standards.

Dr. Stanley King's remarkable success with one case, as reported by Lippman (157), testifies to the efficacy of individual therapy. Retiring from the Institute for Child Guidance, King and his wife decided to bring severely delinquent boys into their own home. One of these boys, a 14-year-old, had been rejected by his family and had been aggressively destructive for many years.

When the boy first came to the Kings' home he was defiant, abusive, and refused to speak with them. Although given his food with the family, he ate in a corner by himself. Primitive and uncontrolled, he frequently stole from the Kings. They never punished him, but instead tried to win him through friendliness and understanding.

Once Dr. King passed the boy on a street corner and heard him lying about his treatment in the foster home. The boy described horrible beatings and deprivations, but King did not mention the incident.

After many months, the lad began eating with the Kings. Then one day he broke his silence by asking to drive to town with his foster father. From that time on, the boy eagerly sought the Kings' affection. He soon recounted with bitterness his past life and his frustrations. Eventually, the boy followed Dr. King "like a shadow."

He continued to live with the family. His stealing, both at home and in the community, stopped. The Kings legally adopted him, and the boy went to college (157).

Few psychopathic children can receive such encompassing treatment. Even within an institution, however, psychotherapy offers an opportunity for emotional attachment. Two cases reported from a New York school indicate the success in some cases with this technique.

One of the children, a 16-year-old girl, came from a disorganized, brutal home. Small and attractive, she had been the girl friend of a gangster. At the school, she was raucous, vulgar, and defiant. She had a long history of stealing, sex offenses, and other delinquencies. Not only did she seem guiltless about her past, she boasted of her "accomplishments."

E. A. Eisner, the school psychologist, selected the girl for psychotherapy and, much against her will, forced her to attend counseling interviews.

The therapist's persistent and patient kindliness gradually broke through the girl's resistance. As the interviews progressed, she began to laugh at herself and her earlier antagonism.

She became attached to two boys within the school. Both were younger than she. One was babyish and dependent; the other acted older than his age. Although she had promised the therapist that she would "reform," she ran away from the school and lived with one of her two young "lovers."

After her recapture, continued therapy helped the girl realize that her relation to the two boys was a manifestation of her desire for security and love. The girl abandoned the younger boys and turned instead to an older staff member. She "fell in love," but this time she seemed truly concerned about the man's welfare.

In further interviews, she expressed antagonism toward her mother. She seemed to gain security and insight. She gave up her superficial, sexually-tinged relations with men and abandoned much of her antisocial behavior (63).

Also at Hawthorne Cedar-Knolls, another case showed

great progress under psychotherapy. "Robert," an 8-year-old boy, was an uncontrollable, aggressive delinquent.[28] In addition to school trouble, Robert had been involved in arson and stealing. He too had been rejected by his parents.

During his first months in school, Robert formed no close attachments. He tried to use adults for his own purposes, but he seemed unable to develop friendships with them. His behavior disturbed the whole institution. Once he almost blew up the gas tank of the school truck.

After a year within the school, Robert became friendly with a cottage "father." The counselor had long talks with the boy and maintained a consistently warm attitude. He "deprived" the child only sparingly. After two years the boy began to change. He became less irresponsible and aggressive. Near the end of treatment, Robert quipped, "Pop will make a man out of me if it kills us both" (238).

The most intensive form of psychotherapy, psychoanalysis, has been tried only on a few child psychopaths. Kate Friedlander found the treatment a useful, but imperfect, instrument. Over a two-year period, Friedlander psychoanalyzed an eight-year-old, "Billy," who was defiant, "vicious," and impulsive. The boy could stand no interference with his desires. He was a constant truant and stole purposelessly. Friedlander commented: "The most striking factor in this behavior was his absolute lack of feeling of guilt."

During the first therapeutic sessions, Billy set fire to curtains, destroying toys, was constantly late, and refused to talk about himself. Later, he disclosed hatred for his mother who, in turn, hated the little boy. She had wanted a girl, and Billy proved a serious disappointment to her. Underneath this hostility, Friedlander noted that the boy longed for his mother's love.

The analysis uncovered no signs of conscience. Billy's instinctive urges appeared very powerful, unmodified by either a strong ego or an independent superego. The "pleasure principle" dominated his behavior, and he gave full reign to "the onrush of demands arising in the id."

Although the first year of treatment disclosed the

mechanisms of Billy's character, it led to no improvement in his behavior. After 18 months, however, incipient signs of character change appeared. One day Billy remarked that he "should not have stayed out late the night before, as then he would not have to stay in today." This represented, for Billy, the first indication of developing foresight and superego control.

Billy's school behavior improved, his interest increased, and his truancy ended. His penchant for fighting decreased, and a positive relation began with a friend of the mother. Billy formed friendships with other children of his age, and he dropped his former bullying attitude. "He was still not a model boy when treatment ended," Friedlander admitted, "but he had succeeded in . . . developing an independent super-ego" (73, p. 217).

S. A. Szurek, a San Francisco psychiatrist with long experience in the treatment of delinquency, found that psychoanalysis did not work with the child psychopaths handled in his clinic.[29] Because their relations with other people were characterized by "impulsive self-gratification," and their loyalties "showed a relatively poor integration," the psychopathic child was a poor therapeutic risk (244). Moreover, Szurek believes the method is theoretically unsuited to the psychopath because while analysis aims at uncovering unconscious impulses, the psychopath already has insufficient inhibition. Szurek's criticism applies to conventional psychoanalysis, but Friedlander's long-term treatment—a process by which affectional relations are built—seems to create the necessary inhibitive qualities.[30]

Even less encouraging has been the work of Lauretta Bender. A psychiatrist at the Bellevue Hospital, Bender has faced hundreds of cases of the disorder and has tried a great many approaches in attempting to cure it. The children had such a pathogenic lack of love that therapy based on emotional attachment never reached them. "Once the defect is created," she felt forced to conclude, "it cannot be corrected" (18).

Hyman Lippman of the New York Institute for Child Guidance also found that psychotherapy failed to help many of the chronic delinquents whom he treated (157). C. A. Whitaker, another psychiatrist with wide thera-

peutic experience, concurs that the disorder is virtually
hopeless. Whitaker, using "forced psychotherapy" at
Ormsby Village, found that only one of his psychopathic
children recovered (268).

Thus, the impact of psychotherapy on psychopaths
remains uncertain. A minority of such children—possibly
a distinct minority—benefit from the treatment.[31]

The Cambridge-Somerville experiment, a controlled
study of delinquents, attempted a rigorous evaluation of
individual counseling. Dr. Richard Clarke Cabot, the
distinguished physician and social philosopher, initiated
the experiment in 1935. He sought to test the premise
that an intimate, friendly relationship could deflect a
boy from antisocial behavior.

Cabot's original sample of 650 boys was divided into a
control and an experimental group. Within each group
were equal numbers of "predelinquent" and "normal"
boys. The control group received only the usual community and school attention. The experimental group
was given extensive community aid plus the advice and
support of a special counselor. The experiment was to
run over a 10-year period, the same counselors remaining
with the boys throughout the project.

Cabot's plan, simple in origin but complex in fulfillment, met several obstacles. The war intervened. Counselors (and boys) were called into service. Even with
counselor replacements, no boy was treated longer than
eight years, and most boys received about five years of
intermittent counseling.

The counseling itself was not uniform. Some counselors emphasized friendship and warmth; others leaned
toward rather firm guidance of the child's behavior. Some
counselors depended mainly on verbal advice; others
adhered to modern casework techniques. All of the
counselors, however, called upon community resources
for aid: school tutoring, medical aid, camps, and settle-
ment houses.

In evaluating the results of the treatment, varied
methods were used: statistics of delinquency, personality
tests, an impartial observer's rating of terminal adjustment, and analyses of case records. These measures
pointed to a disillusioning conclusion: such treatment
did not in general prevent delinquency. Actually a few

more of the treated boys than the control boys were convicted of crimes, and with approximately the same frequency (195).

Analysis of the case records by an independent observer, Dr. Helen Witmer, indicated that 20 per cent of the boys had received substantial benefits from the treatment. In another 42 per cent, however, the counselor's work seemed "clearly ineffectual."

Witmer concluded that the home situation seemed the major determining factor for success or failure. Counseling could accomplish little when contravened by a rejecting, disrupted home. Moreover, the nature of the child's problems affected the outcome of treatment. The more emotionally disturbed the child, the less he appeared to benefit from treatment.

The research team did not make a specific evaluation of the project's effects on psychopathic children. They did, however, describe a group of "extremely maladjusted" boys—boys who had been rejected by their parents, who were "unable to form close relationships with anybody," and who derived very little benefit from the treatment. Some of these cases, they pointed out, closely resembled the psychopathic syndrome:

"Wilbur," a 10-year-old boy, was one of three illegitimate children. His mother and grandmother led promiscuous lives. The mother, a weak and indecisive person, cared little for Wilbur. His stepfather intensely disliked the boy. The grandmother continuously disparaged him. Only an aunt had the slightest affection for Wilbur, and it was to her the boy turned when "things got too bad elsewhere." Wilbur was a "sullen, moody boy, resentful of everybody." He was described as "having a shell around him that the counselors could not penetrate" (195, p. 558).

"Tony," too, came from a disturbed family. His father, an egocentric man, felt no affection for Tony and deserted him whenever the boy got in trouble. The boy's mother, although fond of him, was apathetic and ineffectual. A description of Tony's character conveys his psychopathic traits:

Temporarily he could adapt to any person or situation very well but, though jealous, he could not form a close relation-

ship with anybody. He stole continuously, derived great
pleasure from doing so, lied about it with no sense of guilt,
and boasted of deeds that had escaped police attention. He
was always demanding material evidence of people's affection
for him (195, p. 559).

With boys like Wilbur and Tony, the counseling had
little effect. Although the counselors devoted a great
deal of attention to them, they could not break through
the boys' emotional indifference. "The whole personality
was organized against interpersonal relationship; to have
been beneficial, the counselors would have had to effect
a complete personality change in these boys," Witmer
concluded (195, p. 559).

In 1956 we followed up the Cambridge-Somerville
boys in the hope that treatment might have had a de-
layed effect, a suggestion made by Gordon Allport. Unfortunately, in terms of court convictions for major
crimes, we could find no evidence that the general program had deterred adult criminality (173). Nevertheless,
the evidence suggested that only a few children had received the intensive, deep counseling which Dr. Cabot
had advocated. This small group of children did, in fact,
have a lower rate of adult crime. Statistical analyses of
the project hinted that intensive counseling, commenced
at an early age, might well have a beneficial effect—even
on highly aggressive boys who exhibited psychopathic
tendencies (173).

As Helen Witmer observed, the "cure" of psychopathy
may well require a complete transformation of the child's
personality—an effect which individual counseling, un-
aided by radical changes in the child's environment, cannot easily achieve. Some therapists believe that the best
way of accomplishing this radical change is through mo-
bilizing the child's total environment for therapeutic
purposes. A transformation of personality, they believe,
demands a reorientation of environment. Every part of
the child's life, from breakfast to bedtime, must be
geared to therapeutic purposes. Increasingly, during the
last 25 years, social scientists have looked to such "total
push" or "milieu" therapy for the cure of a variety of
emotional disorders and social maladjustments.[32]

The story of milieu therapy is intimately linked with

the life and work of the Viennese psychoanalyst, August
Aichhorn. Born of an unexceptional family in 1878,
Aichhorn's background held no hint of his future destiny.
Conventional training led Aichhorn into the comfortable
life of a Victorian educator. In 1907, however, the
young teacher fought the establishment of military
homes for orphaned and maladjusted boys by organizing
his own homes for the children.

The end of the war in 1918, with Austria's defeat, left
the nation with a mass of disillusioned, rebellious youth.
To meet the surge of crime, Aichhorn founded, in Ober-
hollabrunn, a home for delinquents—a home that was to
become so famous that it was praised even in the English Parliament.

Impressed with Freudianism, Aichhorn applied psychoanalytic methods with success to the problem of delinquency. His techniques, unusual even in the experiment-
ing atmosphere of the twenties, won for him the acclaim
of the world of psychology.

After Austria had been liberated from Nazi rule (which
Aichhorn, although Jewish, somehow survived), he was
elected President of the Viennese Psychoanalytic Society.
He wrote a book, *Wayward Youth*, and many books have
been written about him.

Two distinct types of children came under Aichhorn's
care. One group consisted of boys whose dissocial behavior covered an underlying neurosis. With them, Aichhorn
offered approval only in reward for achievement, as "pay-
ment" for increasing socialization. Many of these children had already been overindulged; others had been
neglected. They required not more indulgence, but more
control.

Aichhorn's other group of children concerns us more:
his dissocial boys, without neurosis, who were in constant conflict with their environment. These boys, many
of whom were undoubtedly psychopathic, satisfied their
impulses with indiscriminate, aggressive abandon. They
had not developed sturdy superegos or consciences.

With this second group, all of whom "had been
brought up without affection and had suffered unreason-
able severity and brutality" (4, p. 171), Aichhorn aimed
at satisfying their frustrated desires for love:

First we had to compensate for this great lack of love and then gradually and with great caution begin to make demands upon the children. Severity would have failed completely. Our treatment of this group could be characterized thus: a consistently friendly attitude, wholesome occupation, plenty of play to prevent aggression, and repeated talks with individual members (4, p. 172).

This brief description conveys neither the flavor nor the hazards of such therapy. The first meeting, Aichhorn believed, set the tone of treatment. The interviewer could not be too harsh and thereby antagonize the boy. Nor could he be too loving, for then the child would think him weak. "Our motto was: as far as possible, let the boys alone" (4, p. 172).

The attempt to build an affiliative relation had to be undertaken with great caution. Aichhorn insisted upon a permissive attitude, an avoidance of any belligerence even in response to aggressive attacks. A colleague described an incident of exaggerated aggression, showing the reaction of one boy to this permissiveness:

In the presence of Aichhorn one of the boys attacked another with a large bread-knife, screaming that he meant to kill him. Aichhorn, noticing the exaggeration, did not look around and did not move. The boy, unable to impress his leader, threw the knife on the floor in despair and started to cry bitterly. For days afterwards he was quiet and amenable to discussion (73, p. 242).

Most of the antisocial boys went through the same metamorphosis: ". . . the boys responded to this [permissiveness] with an increased feeling of their own power which found its expression in greater and more frequent acts of aggression; these later gave way to tears of rage, then to a period of sensitivity, and finally to acceptable behavior" (4, p. 178).

The lack of punishment contradicted the boys' past experiences; it was something entirely new in their lives. Unsure of the new environment, perhaps believing they had not been "bad enough," the boys tested the staff with increased aggression. Sudden, sometimes dramatic insight allowed the boys to perceive the almost boundless permissiveness of the staff. The shock of finding that some adults could be kind and understanding opened new emotional possibilities to the boys.

Only emotional crises, Aichhorn believed, broke the boys' defenses against interpersonal relations. Sometimes the staff deliberately promoted such crises:

An aggressive, delinquent boy, whom Aichhorn knew to be "guiltless," operated the school tobacco shop. Noticing a discrepancy in the canteen books, Aichhorn decided to use the situation as a means for instilling a sense of guilt and anxiety in the culprit. He invited the boy to his office and casually asked: "How much do you take in each week?" The boy stated a figure. "Does the money always come out right?"

A hesitating, "Yes," in answer.

"When do you have the most of your trade? In the morning?"

The boy became increasingly restless, but Aichhorn ignored it. Puttering around his office, straightening books, Aichhorn returned again and again to the topic. Suddenly Aichhorn said, "Well, when we get through here I'll go and take a look at your cash."

The boy dropped the book he had been taking down from a shelf.

"What's the matter?"

"Nothing!"

"What's wrong with your cash?"

The boy, overcome with fright, stammered as he stated the missing sum. Aichhorn said nothing, but handed him the cash.

The boy left the room. Ten minutes later he returned and sobbed, "Let them lock me up. I don't deserve your help—I'll only steal again." The boy poured out his story to Aichhorn.

Eventually the money was repaid. The crisis, Aichhorn believed, induced a feeling of guilt which the boy had not known before. After the incident, Aichhorn reported that the boy was "cured."

Aichhorn based his therapy on affection: "We must make good the love of which he has been deprived." Once rapport had been solidly established, the staff increased their demands upon the boys. They criticized and imposed social controls. Using the affectional bonds, they apparently brought the boys to a new sense of social responsibility. Aichhorn reported that his aggressive boys acquired new tolerance for frustration and new consciences. All of the boys, he reported, subsequently became adjusted to society.

Aichhorn's report of success intrigued the scientific world. Yet few dared to copy him. In the 1920's, the method was revolutionary—and even today, few training schools have adopted "milieu therapy." [33]

During the 1930's, Hawthorne Cedar-Knolls based its treatment on Aichhorn's precepts. A research team traced the lives of 81 girls who lived at the school. The report constitutes one of the few evaluations of milieu therapy's impact.

Many types of delinquent girls went through the institution, but one group stood out from the others. Although school therapists did not use the concept of psychopathy, these girls closely resembled the syndrome:

> Early in the work a group of girls was recognized who were asocial but not obviously neurotic. . . . Later it became clear that the feature common to them was an inability to make a real transference to any member of the staff. . . . They acted largely, some of them seemingly exclusively, on impulse and apparently had little or no neurotic or real conflict or sense of guilt. . . . This type of delinquent is readily recognized by the living out of wishes without thought of consequence or regret, and with no real understanding of the "why not" (196).

These girls did not respond to the Aichhorn approach. Therapy did not change their seriously disordered personalities.[34]

Within the last two decades, such schools as Detroit's Pioneer House, Chicago's Orthogenic School, and New York's Wiltwyck have used milieu therapy on young psychopathic children.

Founded in 1946, Fritz Redl's Pioneer House exemplified this approach to the problem. The school treated a small group of severely disturbed children. Although Redl never specifically labeled the boys "psychopathic," that diagnosis seems apt. The children were filled with hate, "whirlpools and rivers and oceans of it." They failed to control their aggression and to postpone their demands for immediate gratification. The "children who hate" could not "establish adequate relations to future experience" nor could they plan their lives with foresight (204).

Redl described the children as "Untaxed by guilt, embarrassment, or shame . . . impulse freedom is guaranteed." The children—have "only a dim, if even existent insight into their own responsibility for what happens to them and the weakest possible resistance in the face of temptation." Typically, the boys had "extremely weak, distorted and confused wishes for object relations with adults. . . ."

Because the Pioneer House children lacked the initial ability of establishing rapport, had insufficient inhibitions, and were retarded in communicative abilities, Redl rejected the psychiatric interview as the sole treatment procedure. He also abandoned the usual methods of education because the children lacked the necessary prerequisites: a high frustration tolerance, sublimative ability, and a capacity for controlling their destructive impulses.

Rather than employ the usual "reformative" methods, Pioneer House attempted to establish an encompassing atmosphere which, in its smallest detail, aimed at the improvement of the youngsters. Every ball game, every meal, every temper tantrum was handled with an eye to the child's treatment. Each individual, from the director to the cook, participated in the program. Even the house itself, its design, furnishings, and upkeep formed an integral part of therapy.

Like Aichhorn, Redl believed that affection is the indispensable center of all treatment: "The children must get plenty of love and affection whether they deserve it or not; they must be assured the basic quota of happy recreational experiences whether they seem to 'have it coming' or not" (204, p. 179).

The Pioneer House program had many goals: "impulse drainage," cultivation of new interests, increasing the child's ability to tolerate frustration. Although the staff allowed wide leeway for regression, they continually tried to develop the child's ability to use inner resources for satisfaction. The recreational activities attempted to inculcate "depersonalized controls," controls which sprang from the "rules of the game." Accepting primitive group codes was an important step toward the acceptance of more important standards.

Controlling the boys' bellicosity was, of course, an ever-present problem. Sometimes the staff ignored belligerence. More often humor, regrouping, or reminding the child of possible results served to inhibit aggression. More rarely, the staff removed a child from the group until he had been calmed, or physically restrained him. At all times, the staff carried out discipline without malice.

The staff utilized Aichhorn's method of precipitating an emotional crisis. Such dramatic displays were followed by therapeutic interviews: the "rub-in" interview brought out certain aspects of reality which the child had ignored (e.g., the reaction of neighbors to back yard cursing); the "guilt-squeeze" interview attempted to "bring to the surface," or instill, feelings of guilt. Other interviews—"expressional," "counter-distortional," or "group"—allowed the children to experience a catharsis and then countered their alibis and hostility with facts.

The "interpretational" interview aimed at making the child aware of his motives. This technique was used when one boy, who was disliked and baited by the others, wished to take a knife along on one of the school outings. David Wineman, one of the school directors, said: "Look, you know darn well you don't want that knife. You're just going to get all the guys against you and that's what you want so you can keep up your complaint to me that they are mean to you. Now look how you're starting the whole thing yourself and then you are going to say the other guys are picking on you . . ." (204, p. 315). The boy left the knife at home.

The withdrawal of community financial support forced the closing of Pioneer House before an adequate assessment of the treatment could be made. All but one of the boys went to foster homes, and posttreatment adjustment has not been reported. Nevertheless, Redl believed the therapy made significant gains in certain important areas. The children seemed better able to communicate verbally, to accept frustration realistically, and to modify their behavior in accord with the *esprit de corps* of Pioneer House. Their aggressive and destructive actions decreased. They became more "sensitive" to social values, and they accepted school rules and routines without rebellion. Furthermore, the children seemed more responsive to the affection of adults.

If the treatment had continued—if the community had responded to the school's need for money—the children might have been transformed. But no money came: "Thus our 'children who hate' went back into the limbo of 'the children that nobody wants'" (21, p. 18).

More fortunate financially has been the Orthogenic School in Chicago. With Bruno Bettelheim as director, the school treats many varieties of emotionally disturbed boys and girls. Bettelheim believes that this melting pot of maladjustment has therapeutic value. The withdrawn child, for example, sees a good deal of aggressive behavior and may seek to try such freedom. The psychopathic child, in turn, may be influenced by his more inhibited comrades.

Bettelheim's therapy calls for an environment in which the child is constantly under treatment. The school draws heavily upon Freud and Dewey, but like all such ventures, develops its own philosophy. The staff is highly permissive of deviant behavior and attempts to satisfy generously the infantile needs of their charges, thereby inducing a "positive relation to the adults who provide for his well being." Each part of the child's life is made as nonthreatening and as pleasurable as possible.

The school maintains its own classrooms, but the stringency and competition of the public school are not to be found. Children are free to leave class at any time, or not to attend at all.

Food, the "great socializer," plays a major role in Orthogenic's therapy. Extra servings are always available at meals, and an unlocked candy and cake chest lures hungry children between times. Bedtime, with its transition into the unreal state of nightmares, is made palatable with snacks, teddy bears, and counselor encouragement. Again in the morning, food greets some children as they reach from the covers, testing the advisability of starting a new day.

The bathroom, too, is a part of the treatment program. Bath-taking, abetted by counselor washdowns and a flo tilla of toy boats, becomes an adventure rather than a threat.

Recognizing that most emotional disturbances originate in the home, the school avoids pseudoparental relationships. Treatment begins with the "simplest and not the most complex relationship." The newcomer is offered casual acquaintanceship, friendship, and care—but not overwhelming love. In time, most children select a mentor. A "love-relationship" occurs, but only after the child's "own experiences have taught him to want such a relationship, after his adjustment has made him ready for it, after he has slowly convinced himself that he can handle it successfully" (21, p. 28).

Once friendly intimacy is established, the child is (figuratively) urged "to change his personality at least in part in the image of the person or persons who are now so important to him. He identifies with them, as we say, and this identification is often the starting point for the organization of his personality" (21, p. 28).

Bettelheim noted three stages in the development of the school's aggressive children, some of whom seemed psychopathic. At first, "their controlling institutions were so underdeveloped that they could neither restrict the socially unacceptable tendencies pressing for release, nor postpone the gratification of those needs which were legitimate" (22). Then, as the bond between the child and the counselor matured, the child felt anxiety if he violated (or wished to violate) the adult's values. In order for the anxiety to operate during this stage, the counselor had to be near the boy. In the third stage, the superego seemed to gain strength and the counselor's physical presence was no longer required.

The child often used illness or injury to bolster his inner controls. One child, with a serious cold, stood in front of an open window. He contracted pneumonia, thus (Bettelheim believes) stopping himself from escaping from the school. Another boy had a cast on his broken arm. He thrust the cast through a window and severely lacerated himself. Bettelheim viewed this as the child's attempt to overcome the desire to hit another boy (22).

The impact of Orthogenic treatment on child personality has never been objectively evaluated. Milieu therapy, however, seems promising for the treatment of psychopathy. Bettelheim, like Aichhorn and Redl, has enthusiastically reported striking behavioral changes in the children. Yet Hawthorne Cedar-Knolls reported almost total failure in its treatment of psychopathic girls.

Each of the four schools embellished the basic philosophy with its own improvisations. These slight variations may explain the differing results. Unfortunately, none of the schools thoroughly traced the effects of its approach on the children's personality.

In summary, the last decades of research into the treatment of child psychopathy have tentatively demonstrated that:

> Except in unusual cases, forced institutional conformity does not improve the child psychopath.
>
> Narcotherapy in some experiments brought temporary relief of symptoms, but in other experiments drugs aggravated the disorder.
>
> Psychotherapy can be useful in the treatment of child psychopathy. Some therapists have been successful, but more therapists report almost total failure.
>
> Milieu therapy has changed the behavior of some psychopaths. Three schools have reported at least temporary success with the method. One school reported complete failure. The treatment's effectiveness in reorganizing the personality has not been ascertained.

The preponderance of evidence, admittedly inadequate and partly contradictory, indicates that milieu therapy offers the most promising answer to the disorder. Milieu therapy, of all the varied approaches, apparently has achieved the most substantial changes in behavior.

III. MILIEU THERAPY: AN EXPERIMENT

Unfortunately, the work of such men as Aichhorn, Bettelheim, and Redl has been hampered by lack of money, personnel, and public cooperation. In consequence, such experiments have often been short-lived or confined primarily to middle-class children whose families could afford the expensive process. Most importantly, milieu therapy has not been subjected to an independent assessment of its effects. The treatment is unique, experimental, eminently promising—but insufficiently tested. Consequently, in 1953, we initiated a series of studies concerned with empirically evaluating the impact of one school, The Wiltwyck School for Boys in New York, representative of the approach of milieu therapy.[35]

Wiltwyck offers an unusual opportunity for evaluating the curative effect of a warm, permissive environment, where individual and group therapy combine their techniques, for Wiltwyck has overcome several of the limitations of the other experiments. Private individuals and public agencies, attracted by Wiltwyck's philosophy, have assured relative financial security for the institution. Top-quality counselors, psychologists, and social workers flock to the school (resulting in an almost one-to-one boy-staff ratio). Thus, though a process of self-criticism and correction continues, Wiltwyck has for several years brought its therapeutic theory into practical application.

Wiltwyck's basic philosophy has been well summarized by its former director, Ernst Papanek: "Punishing teaches the child only how to punish; scolding teaches him how to scold. By showing him that we understand, we teach him to understand; by helping him, we teach him to help; by cooperating, we teach him how to cooperate" (189). This represents the accumulated wisdom of the small group who founded Wiltwyck and particularly of Papanek, its director at the time of the evaluative studies.

As a young man, Papanek studied with Freud and Adler and served in the Austrian parliament. Much of the inspiration for Papanek's work in Europe and later at Wiltwyck can be traced to the influence of Alfred Adler, the founder of "individual psychology." Papanek considers himself an Adlerian and has derived from Adler the conviction that the treatment of disordered children must aim at the re-establishment of "social feeling," by convincing the child, through the structuring of his environment, of the necessity of cooperating with others. While directing education in Vienna, Papanek played an important role, too, in the encouragement of Aichhorn's experiments. After "Anschluss," Papanek migrated to France and established homes for refugee children. With the fall of France, Papanek helped the majority of his children escape to England before he himself was captured by the Germans. The daring (and compassion) of a Nazi guard provided for Papanek's escape to the United States. In America, Papanek headed a Brooklyn school for delinquents before going to Wiltwyck. Under his leadership, Wiltwyck changed from a small orphans' home into a brilliant experiment in the treatment of maladjusted children.[36]

Particularly at the beginning of treatment, the children are allowed to express their pent-up bitterness and antagonism as long as no irreparable damage is done. With no disciplinary cottages, corporal punishments, or harsh scoldings, Wiltwyck attempts only to impress upon the child the consequences of his acts. For example, an aggressive newcomer to Wiltwyck broke 32 windows in the school dining room. After waiting for the boy to quiet down, Papanek explained that some money would be deducted from the boy's weekly allowance to help pay for the damage. Three weeks later, the director called the boy to his office and quietly reinstated the full allowance. Thus, Papanek soothed the boy's bitterness and taught him that authority can help an individual as well as hurt him.

Although Wiltwyck allows its boys to express themselves freely, social responsibility is not ignored. Wiltwyck's 100 students are urged to participate in their community affairs. An elected student council, food committee, job committee, canteen committee, and sports committee cooperate with the staff in the discussion of common problems. Cottage living (with two counselors for every twelve boys), student government, and weekly assemblies give the boys a chance to work out tensions, air hostilities, and train themselves in democratic procedure. These are lessons they sorely need, for most of the boys have been judged incorrigibly delinquent by their parents and by their communities, and many have been previously rejected by other social agencies.

In general, therefore, treatment at Wiltwyck begins by offering the child a loving, permissive environment, so in contrast to the typical background of bitterness and rejection from which so many delinquents have sprung.

After the child has established a relationship with one
of the adults at the school, however, lessons in social responsibility gradually replace permissiveness. The adults
commence to impose controls on the child, but in a nonpunitive manner.

Individual, group, and art therapy supplement the
counselors' efforts. Three psychologists and two psychiatrists work with the most serious cases. Two group therapists meet with other boys. Ten social workers introduce
new children to Wiltwyck, hold weekly interviews with
them, and ease their transition back to city life.

During the winter, Wiltwyck's children (who range
in age from 8 to 14 years) attend classes within the institution. Teachers, skilled in the instruction of emotionally maladjusted children, conduct the ungraded school.
For those who need it, and many do, a special instructor
provides remedial help in reading.

Wiltwyck's counselors, the great majority of whom
are college graduates, participate in a continuing program
of education through group therapy sessions and regular
conferences. Each week the staff meets to discuss one of
Wiltwyck's boys. Usually the case illustrates personality
problems common to several children, thus serving as a
basis for general assessment of treatment.

The pragmatist may well ask: "Does this expensive
and encompassing program cause real changes in the
boys' personalities?" Late in 1953 we attempted a tentative answer to this question by submitting 35 Wiltwyck
children to a battery of personality tests and comparing
the results to those of a control group of 35 boys at a
typical public reformatory, the "New England" school
(169).

The New England school believed that harsh discipline and hard work would reform its inmates. The staff,
most of whom had graduated from high school, lacked
psychological training. Use of a silent disciplinary cottage and corporal punishment maintained order. Though
in contradiction to the Wiltwyck approach, the New
England school was typical of American reformatories.
The contrast offered an excellent opportunity for testing
the relative efficacy of the two philosophies.

In an attempt to measure the children's basic drives,

we used the Adult-Child Interaction Test, other projective personality tests, a values questionnaire, and a sociogram. The boys' responses were analyzed and computed according to months of residence within the schools. We discovered that Wiltwyck made important and desirable changes in its children; New England appeared to have little effect upon its inmates. As a result of the 1953 investigation we found:

The *anxiety* of the Wiltwyck boys significantly decreased the longer the boy was exposed to the school program. At the New England school, insecurity and inner conflict showed a slightly increasing trend.

Authoritarian tendencies among the Wiltwyck boys decreased significantly with length of residence. New England children showed no change.

At Wiltwyck, the school treatment, implemented by an interracial staff, effected a significant decrease in *prejudice*. In New England, prejudice increased with length of stay.

Neither group showed a significant decrease in *aggressiveness*.

More Wiltwyck children viewed the world as good than evil. In New England, the opposite was true.

Wiltwyck children were more satisfied with themselves than were New England children, and they possessed more affirmative ideals.

Wiltwyck children had a more loving ideal of parents and other adults. New England children more often viewed them as punitive.

Wiltwyck children had a greater interest in constructive activities and a better understanding of Christian teachings.

Wiltwyck children chose constructive student leaders. In New England, the leaders showed intense hostility and anxiety.

Wiltwyck children evidenced a much closer attachment to the staff than did New England children.

The 1953 study, therefore, compared the general effects of Wiltwyck to those of the New England school, a reformative environment which differed radically in philosophy and techniques. Since the New England inmates closely resembled the Wiltwyck boys in age, social background, and nature of their disorders, we felt justified in tentatively attributing the changes achieved at the Wiltwyck school to the nature of treatment, rather than to extraneous factors such as incarceration itself.

The 1953 study, while indicating the beneficial results of Wiltwyck's program, led to new and intriguing questions: *Do all types of children respond to Wiltwyck in the same manner? If they differ, in what ways does each respond? How does the treatment affect guilt, aggression, and withdrawal tendencies of the boys? Can Wiltwyck alter the child's view of authority?* And, most important: *Can Wiltwyck do anything for the psychopathic child?*

Between June, 1954, and February, 1955, we investigated the further questions which had been raised by the initial study. During this period of time, 107 children composed the Wiltwyck population. They consisted primarily of Protestant, Negro boys, whose median I.Q. was 90. They averaged 11 years in age, and their average residence at Wiltwyck was 10 months. Before admittance, each child had undergone a thorough psychiatric examination and had been diagnosed as falling into one of four classifications: neurotic, borderline psychotic, behavior disorder, or psychopathic. The nature of these four syndromes of disorder can perhaps best be clarified by a brief description of some illustrative cases:

The 23 withdrawn *neurotic* children felt intense anxiety, inner conflict, and suspicion. Seldom involved in serious delinquencies, these children appeared in court because of neglect, truancy, or bizarre school behavior. Although markedly disturbed, they did not exhibit the usual psychotic symptoms of hallucinations and autistic thinking. "Danny" [37] typified Wiltwyck's neurotic children:

Danny, a 12-year-old Negro boy, seemed continually preoccupied. His "dead pan" face hid intense anxiety and highly volatile emotions. He appeared joyless and enveloped in protective armor. During the intake examination, the psychiatrist noted: "He has no zest or drive and tends to withdraw from all frustration. He is not, however, completely immune to emotional stimulation or incestual fantasies." Danny had not completely lost his powers of concentration, of social comprehension, or his ability to relate to other human beings.

Danny feared his father, although his father had deserted the family several years before. Danny was overly attached to his mother, a prostitute who brought paramours home for rendezvous in the same room with Danny and his brother.

Public agencies supported the family until they discovered the mother's behavior. Late in 1953, a petition of neglect was filed against the mother. Although Danny offered no special school problem and had never been involved in delinquent activities, the court felt that he would benefit from Wiltwyck's treatment.

In January, 1954, Danny entered the school. During his first month, the group counselor described him as "pleasant, quiet, and timid." He exhibited little aggressiveness, but seemed disturbed by sexual problems and compulsively lost his belongings. During his first weeks at Wiltwyck, Danny made no friends. At night, he repeated again and again: "I want to go home. I want to go to my mother."

Five months later, during the research interviews, Danny still showed a high level of anxiety, strong withdrawal tendencies, a confused self-perception, and an unclear concept of family life.

Wiltwyck's six *borderline psychotics*, too, showed signs of intense anxiety, confusion, and suspicion. In addition, they exhibited autistic thinking, hallucinations, and a strong urge to withdraw from reality. Intellectual abilities, social comprehension, and the capacity to respond to others had deteriorated. "Tommy" exemplified the common traits of this small group:

Tommy, an 11-year-old white boy, gave the impression of being an extremely polite, effeminate child. Before admittance, projective test results had shown that Tommy felt "completely rejected, not only by his family but by the whole world." Even though Tommy was intelligent, emotional disturbances blocked his performance. He was preoccupied with monsters and had auditory hallucinations. Voices threatened him as he listened to television or read a book. A hospital psychiatrist found a "paranoid quality to his thinking" and a "fluidity of identification." Sometimes he thought he was Roy Rogers, Superman, or Space Cadet.

Neurological examination showed a normal E.E.G. pattern and no evidence of organic damage. In January, 1954, a New York hospital diagnosed Tommy as schizophrenic but added: "He is in sufficient control of his own impulses to avoid aggressive behavior or running away. His hallucinations are usually benign and are not far removed from the average boy's."

Tommy's mother has been in a mental hospital. Like Tommy, she had auditory hallucinations and "paranoid ideation." She refused to associate with people and talked only in whispers.

Although nondelinquent, Tommy became explosive and aggressive in public school. There Tommy often threw temper tantrums, fell into foaming rages, and tore up his work. Apparent rejection by the teachers seemed to bring forth the outbursts.

Tommy's father, a dull and irresponsible man, minimized the boy's problems. He agreed to send Tommy to Wiltwyck after a court petition of neglect had been filed.

During his first months at Wiltwyck, Tommy posted notes: "I'll come tonight. . . . K."; "You will never be able to catch me. I'll steal everything from this group. . . . K." After a foray of stealing from the other boys, Tommy's aggression subsided. He was then placed under a Wiltwyck psychologist's care.

The majority of Wiltwyck's boys were diagnosed as *behavior disorders*. Sixty-three cases fitted this category of anxious, aggressive, resentful children who "acted out" their conflicts. The primary problem of these children stemmed from their uncontrolled aggressive behavior and their destructive reaction to frustration.

The behavior disorders usually appeared in court because of delinquency or school problem behavior. Two of these children suffered from organic brain damage; five seemed to have become delinquent as a response to their cultural background. The behavior of the vast majority, however, appeared to be the result of brutal, rejectant families and delinquent slum neighborhoods. Although they closely resembled the "average" delinquent, at Wiltwyck the behavior disorders had a great many neurotic traits: nail biting, enuresis, and anxiety.

"Bobby," a 10-year-old Negro child, indicates the typical problems of the behavior disorders. He eagerly sought attention from adults. Handsome and muscular, Bobby had no neurological defects, an average intelligence, and he talked easily. He was, however, very lonely and viewed the world as hostile and threatening.

During an examination at a New York hospital, the psychiatrist noted: "Bobby is anxiety ridden because of an effort to prevent hostile impulses from breaking through. He has found no satisfaction from his environment and has, consequently, withdrawn into himself."

Bobby, the youngest of three children, came from an unstable family. The father, a drunkard, physically abused the mother, rarely contributed to the support of his family, and deserted them at frequent intervals. Since April, 1951, he has not returned. Bobby's mother is a catatonic schizophrenic and is periodically under treatment in state hospitals. When home, she accused the children of poisoning her food and was extremely depressed. In July, 1951, she reentered a mental hospital.

At that time, one of Bobby's sisters went to a foster home and the other sister, a severe behavior problem, was committed to a state institution. The court sent Bobby to live with his grandmother. During his stay there, Bobby began to steal, attacked other children in school, and assaulted his teacher with a knife. The school principal and Bobby's grandmother initiated the court proceedings which led Bobby to Wiltwyck.

During his first weeks at Wiltwyck, Bobby could find no friends. His counselor commented: "He's extremely nervous, wets his bed frequently, and has silly 'jags.'" Bobby seemed to feel that no one liked him and that no one ever could.

Interviewed for the research study after several months at Wiltwyck, Bobby appeared to repress strong aggressive instincts and to feel a pervading anxiety. He had an unclear perception of himself and his parents but seemed to desire friendship with adults. He had not become adjusted to the Wiltwyck environment and could often be found crying piteously or raging bitterly over some imagined rejection.

Only 15 children appeared to be truly *psychopathic* personalities. Aggressive, asocial, highly impulsive children, they exhibited dangerous delinquent tendencies, extreme maladjustment in school, and severe temper tantrums.[38] Unlike the psychotic and neurotic children, they were not highly anxious, withdrawn, or introverted. Furthermore, among the psychopathic children there was a pronounced lack of guilt feelings. In every important respect, they presaged the behavior of that ultimate social enemy, the adult psychopath. "Paul" denoted the psychopathic syndrome:

Paul, a 10-year-old white boy, wore a mask of enmity, creased with scowls and frowns. Extreme aggressiveness and uncontrolled impulsivity at the age of 3½, had brought Paul to the attention of a psychiatrist.

Since first treatment, Paul's aggression, hyperactivity, and destructiveness had increased. In public school, Paul attacked several children, set fire to the teacher, and ravaged the classroom. After one year, the principal suspended him. Then Paul was taught at home, but he drove teacher after teacher from the house. To "have his way," he sometimes resorted to banging his head against the wall. A second psychiatrist concluded: "He has no ability for relating to either adults or children, no comprehension of the consequences of his acts, and no guilt concerning them."

Detailed and frequent neurological examinations have shown no defect or damage in the child's brain.

Paul's family lived in a slum area. His father openly rejected the child and had beaten him severely since infancy. His mother, a weak and ineffectual woman, had no control over the boy.

While stealing from a warehouse, Paul struck a watchman on the head, and the man sustained severe concussions. For this offense, the court remanded Paul to a public home in New York City.

At the home, Paul set fire to the furniture and curtains. He horrified the other children by killing goldfish with pins and pulling out their intestines. From the children's home he was transferred to Wiltwyck in July, 1954.

During the research interview (a month after his arrival), Paul showed no guilt feelings, a hatred of his parents and other authority figures, and such intense hostility that the interview could not be completed. He left the room saying, "Get me out of his hole!"

Our interest focused upon the 15 psychopaths, those "rebels without a cause." While we wished primarily to discover the impact of milieu therapy upon these perhaps "incurable" psychopathic boys, we wanted, too, to analyze the changes induced in other types of boys. In a rough sense, the other children formed a "control group." The boys in each of the four diagnostic categories were further divided in terms of length of residence at the school. Those in residence 0-8 months were considered "new arrivals." Although submitted to the same type of general treatment at approximately the same age, the boys differed strikingly in basic character. Thus, one could estimate the *relative* effects of milieu therapy upon the psychopathic boys in contrast to the less difficult cases.

As a first step, in 1954, all 107 children submitted to an array of interviews, tests, and observational ratings. These measures aimed at tapping three interconnected areas of the children's character: their unconscious processes, their conscious values, and their actual behavior. By studying unconscious drives, we hoped to ascertain the changes in the underlying motivations of the child. By measuring conscious values, we wished to discern whatever changes there might be in social attitudes. By various observational ratings, we sought to relate these inner dynamisms to the outer behavior of the child. In the previous Wiltwyck study, certain standard tests (such as the Adult-Child Interaction Test) were used. In 1954 we supplemented these measures with several new tests specifically designed for psychopathic children. (The reader interested in the details of these tests, should consult the first edition of this book (168).) In general, however, they were designed to reveal the following aspects of the children's character and behavior:

(1) *Aggression:* It can safely be said that the greatest social menace of the psychopath, and indeed of many delinquents, lies in his frightening aggressiveness. One of our goals, therefore, lay in examining Wiltwyck's effect on aggressive tendencies. Several measures were used to gauge the aggression of the children. The "Rover Test," one of the approaches, pictured a dog in a variety of situations, all of them frustrating. As we presented the pictures to the children, we asked, "What does Rover want to do?" The child could pick one of three possible alternatives. One of them pictured Rover reacting with aggression, another showed him withdrawing from the threat, and the third offered a neutral, sometimes assertive response. A typical situation illustrated Rover being scolded by his master. With each picture, a question was asked. For example:

> Does Rover want to bite his master?
>   (the aggressive choice)
>
> Does Rover want to show how sad he feels?
>   (the withdrawn choice: the picture shows
>   Rover sulking in a corner)
>
> Does Rover want to shake hands and make friends?
>   (the neutral choice)

As one might expect, the psychopathic children, toward the beginning of treatment, more often chose an aggressive reponse, while the neurotics and psychotics more often picked a withdrawan alternative.

(2) *Withdrawal tendencies:* The "Rover test" furnished scores on each child concerning his tendency, in the face of frustration, to withdraw from the threat. Because withdrawal from reality constitutes one of the major symptoms of neurotic and psychotic children, this measure seemed particularly appropriate in estimating Wiltwyck's effects on such boys.

(3) *Guilt:* As the treatment of the average delinquent, particularly the psychopath, depends on the reorientation of his conscience—or indeed, on building a conscience out of nothing—we deemed it a particularly important area of study. As a measure of conscience (those internalized feelings of guilt which prevent the violation of generally applicable rules of conduct), we constructed ten stories, each ending with a question. Every story described a situation in which "Bob" had violated some standard of behavior in American society. After each story, we asked, "How does Bob feel?" A typical story read: "Bob and Jack fought one day. Bob pulled a knife and stabbed Jack. How does Bob feel?" The responses included such answers as:

> "Bob felt grand. He hated Jack."
>   (satisfaction)
>
> "Bob was scared. Jack might get him."
>   (fear of external punishment)
>
> "Bob felt sorry. He had hurt Jack."
>   (internalized guilt)

Thus the answers could be categorized as exhibiting satisfaction, fear, or guilt. The psychopathic children, at the start of treatment, chose the lowest proportion of "guilty" responses.

(4) *Attitude towards authority:* One of the disordered child's most disturbing, although often justified, characteristics is his bitter attitude toward society and its representatives. The psychopathic child, of course, refuses even to recognize authority, much less admire or obey it. Thus, evaluating changes in the children's views of authority became one of our objectives. Again, we called upon "open-ended" stories as a way of analyzing the child's character. In these stories, "Bob" transgressed accepted behavior. At the end of the story, an authority figure (mother, teacher, policeman) appeared on the scene. The children were asked, "What does the (authority figure) do?" A typical story said: "Bob came home very late one night. He had fallen down and hurt himself. What did his father do?" Typical answers included:

"He whipped Bob for being late."
(punitive response)

"He took Bob to the hospital because he was sick."
(supportive)

"His father was mad."
(punitive)

"If he was hurt bad, his father bandaged him."
(supportive)

The psychopathic children revealed the most fearful view of authority: 56 per cent of their answers described the authority figure as punitive.

(5) *Self-perception:* During the interviews, we asked a variety of direct questions aimed at uncovering the child's view of himself, his ideal self, and his "ego-ideals." For example, 20 personality traits were read to each child. The interviewer asked: "Does this describe you? Are you (strong, bad, smart, kind, cruel, etc.)?" We did not expect the children to give an accurate description of themselves. Rather, we anticipated that we could estimate the extent to which the child admitted negative qualities and

the degree to which he exhibited a differentiated, realistic self-concept. Some boys responded with a flat answer, others with a differentiated response: "Sometimes I'm bad and get in trouble; other times I'm good or try to be good." We asked the children, too, such direct questions as: "What do people like best about you?" "If you could be anyone in the whole world, whom would you be?" "What is a good boy like?" At the beginning of treatment, none of the psychopathic boys believed that others liked him for his inner qualities and none of them gave a positive response to the question about their ideal of the "good boy." Typically, too, the psychopathic boys wished to become a power figure—"Samson," "Superman," "the President."

We supplemented these various measures of the child's fantasies and inner processes with several ratings of his overt behavior.[39] Each counselor at Wiltwyck rated the behavior of his charges in such areas as the boy's hostility, overt destructiveness, impulsivity, and degree of suggestibility. Since the counselors wake the child in the morning, eat, play, talk, and stay with him until he is in bed, we believed their judgments would be most valuable in analyzing the behavior of the children. The counselors did not know our specific purpose or method of treating the data; thus, we expected that they would judge the boys in as objective a fashion as possible.

Another behavioral test touched on the children's response to frustration. The ability to meet frustration with calm realism marks the socially mature child. The psychopathic boy, faced with frustration, often gives reign to bitter fury. Neurotic and psychotic children, on the other hand, more often turn their aggression inward, burning out their rage in deeply repressed channels. Wiltwyck's environment might be expected to increase the child's ability to accept frustration realistically. To find out if it does, we asked the counselors to arrange a controlled test. On a day when the children normally expected to be allowed to play, their counselors informed them that their cottages were dirty and that they had to be thoroughly cleaned by the children. Although this substitution of work for play constituted a mild frustration, we did not believe it would markedly interfere with the process of treatment. The counselors observed and rated the children's response immediately after the announcement. In their initial response to the frustration, Wiltwyck's psychopaths reacted with either aggression or hyperactivity while the neurotics and psychotics either accepted the situation realistically or withdrew sullenly, refusing to help.

This array of personality tests, questionnaires, and behavioral ratings served as our tools in assessing Wiltwyck's effect on its severely maladjusted children. By bringing to bear different approaches on different levels —projective tests, open-ended stories, direct questions, an experimental situation, and observational ratings— we hoped to measure objectively important aspects of the child's personality. After the initial testing in 1954, a sample of boys (who had been new arrivals in September, 1954) were retested in 1955 and again went through a series of interviews and observations. Thus, we were provided with "before-and-after" measures of changes in the children; moreover, because the data lent itself to quantification, we could treat the evidence in a statistical fashion. We could estimate, in other words, the changes, over time, which had occurred in different types of children in different "layers" of their behavior and character—and, through the use of statistical tests, suggest which of these changes should be attributed merely to "chance" and which might have resulted from the nature of milieu therapy.[40]

What changes occurred?

The evidence suggested that milieu therapy had a decisively positive effect not only on the "behavior disorders," but, most importantly, upon the psychopathic children. Statistical analyses of the evidence indicated that the level of internalized guilt of the psychopaths and behavior disorders markedly increased, their view of authority became less fearful and punitive, and their aggression subsided. In several significant sectors of character, Wiltwyck created desirable changes.

In the case of neurotic or prepsychotic children, however, the treatment induced less marked improvement. The general pattern of the results can be seen in Table 5-1.

TABLE 5-1

Summary of Major Results from the Wiltwyck Studies

Measures	Psychopaths and Behavior Disorders	Neurotics and Borderline Psychotics
Aggression ("Rover Test and "Guilt Stories")	Decreased*#	No change
Withdrawal tendencies (Rover Test)	No change	Decreased*#
Internalized guilt	Increased*#	No change
Hostile view of authority	Decreased*#	Decreased#
Negative perception of self	Increased#	Increased#
Differentiated perception of self	No change	No change
Reaction to frustration (as indicated in the experimental situation)	Increased realism	Increased aggression
Counselors' ratings of:		
Aggressive behavior	Decreased	No change
Withdrawn behavior	No change	Decreased
Control over impulsivity and destructiveness	Increased	No change
Realistic self-perception	Increased#	Increased*#
Positive ego-ideals	Increased#	Decreased#

* $p < 05$ in comparisons between boys in residence 0-8 months and boys in residence 9-23 months.

\# $p < 05$ in test-retest results using each boy as his own control. Withdrawal tendencies for neurotics and psychotics showed a significant change only when mean group scores were used.

As the chart indicates, Wiltwyck seemed to have less influence on the *neurotic* and borderline-*psychotic* children than on the behavior disorders and psychopaths. Such boys exhibited a decreased tendency to choose withdrawn fantasies on the "Rover test," and they appeared less fearful in their answers to the "authority stories." Their counselors noted, in the 1955 rerating of the boys, some decrease in anxiety. Yet, they moved only slowly and erratically towards a "cure."

At the beginning of this section we described a neurotic, "Danny," and a psychotic, "Tommy." By once again looking at these two boys, we can trace the effects of therapy in more individual terms:

When Danny began treatment, he was tense, anxious, and unhappy. He retired from contact with the world and hid his feelings behind a timid, passive front. His father had deserted the family, and his mother, a prostitute, had neglected the child.

During the early months, he kept to himself in the cottage group and seemed disturbed by his sexual development.

In June, 1954, five months after he entered the school, Danny had not markedly changed. He still had a high level of anxiety, strong withdrawal tendencies, and confused self-perception.

During counseling by his social worker, Danny gave way to "paranoid" fantasies. He accused the school and his parents of attacking him. The social worker gradually counteracted the fantasies by consistent friendliness and warmth.

A Wiltwyck psychologist guided Danny in individual psychotherapy. At first, with the psychologist, Danny expressed "negative" feelings about Wiltwyck, the other boys, and his father. His ambivalent sexual feelings came to the surface. The psychologist found that Danny was bothered by his relation to his mother. The mother, herself a paranoid personality, berated Danny's father, society, and the school.

In the fall of 1954, a rash spread over Danny's face and body. Medical examination did not uncover an organic malfunction. The other boys in the school, who had never been very friendly with Danny, now avoided him completely. Fearful of "catching" the rash, they isolated him.

At Christmas time, Danny expected a visit from his father. Even though his mother hated the father, Danny felt some love for him. Christmas passed, however, without the father's coming to the school. Danny's disappointment was evident.

By February, 1955, Danny seemed to have improved. No longer shunned by the other boys, he often "joined in the fun." He had formed warm relations with his counselor, social worker, and psychologist. His relations

with his parents bothered him considerably, but psychotherapy had given him slightly more insight. His counselor reported that Danny's anxiety had decreased slightly,
his rash had disappeared, and his paranoid fantasies had
ended.

Whenever frustrated, however, Danny withdraws and
still spends much of his time brooding. He feels inferior
to the other boys and, as his counselor expressed it, "feels
very sorry for himself."

When tested in 1955, Danny's aggressive fantasies had
decreased, and his view of authority had become less
punitive. His self-concept was more differentiated. His
withdrawal fantasies, however, had not decreased, and his
internalized guilt had not changed.

It appears that Wiltwyck helped Danny in several important ways. It brought him out of his emotional isolation, changed his view of authority, and gave him greater
self-insight. The therapy had not, it seems, radically
changed his tendency to withdraw from reality.

"Tommy," a borderline psychotic, had many of the
same problems as Danny:

When he entered Wiltwyck early in 1954, Tommy
was a severely disturbed child. Voices threatened him,
hallucinations pervaded his thinking, and he felt rejected
by the world. In public school, Tommy had often thrown
aggressive rages in response to teacher discipline. His
mother, a paranoid, lived in a mental hospital. His irresponsible father was unable to cope with the boy.

During his first months at Wiltwyck, Tommy posted
threatening notes throughout the school and stole from
the other boys. A Wiltwyck psychologist took him in
treatment. Deep guilt over his mother's commitment to a
mental hospital appeared in psychotherapy. Whenever
he felt that he was losing the therapist's support, Tommy
became aggressive. At the same time, however, he showed
a fear of expressing hostility. Testing by the school psychologist showed that Tommy was an "oral character,"
that he had intense castration fears, and that he felt keen
rivalry with his father.

At first, Tommy's social worker had difficulty establishing rapport. Tommy blamed the worker for his coming

to Wiltwyck. As his acceptance of the school increased, his hostility to the worker diminished.

In his cottage group, Tommy kept apart from the other boys. The children jibed him as a "fat boy."

In time, Tommy lost weight, and his relations with the other boys improved. He was often bullied, but after several months he began to fight back when attacked. His withdrawal from the group gradually decreased.

His "benign" hallucinations continued. Every night as he went to bed, Tommy told himself the story of "Terror Tim," a masked robber. Often the boy identified with the adventurous, imaginary figure. After about eight months of treatment, Tommy fantasied less about "Terror Tim."

By February, 1955, Tommy's condition had not markedly improved. He had begun to regain weight, and he was still called "fat boy." He seldom participated in group activities but spent his time absorbed in fairy tales and comic books. At times, he took the role of comic characters. Near his bed, he kept a club which he called "Herman" and endowed it with almost human characteristics. His counselors noted feelings of inferiority, particularly concerning his genital development. He was still subject to vast mood swings, although his aggressive explosions had decreased. When frustrated, he withdrew into an emotional shell.

On the 1955 tests, Tommy's aggressive fantasies seemed to have decreased slightly. His withdrawal fantasies had not changed, nor had his view of authority figures. In certain areas, Tommy seemed to have retrogressed: His self-perception was less differentiated than before; he admitted fewer negative qualities concerning himself, and his ego ideals had become more fantastic.

Tommy seemed to have gained less from the Wiltwyck therapy than Danny. Neither boy decreased his withdrawal fantasies. Together, they represent a fairly typical response of neurotic and psychotic boys to Wiltwyck.

The *"behavior disorders"* at Wiltwyck—more or less typical of American delinquents—changed more strikingly than did the neurotics and psychotics. In four important traits, the study indicated radical change in this type of boy. The children's aggressive fantasies, as well as their aggressive behavior in the school, significantly decreased. Milieu therapy, at least as judged by the boys' responses to open-ended stories, strengthened the conscience and the internalized guilt of the behavior disorders; counselor ratings noted that the boys' control over impulsivity and destructiveness had also increased. The children exhibited a significant improvement in their tendency to view authority figures as "supportive" rather than fearful or threatening. And, too, in their response to direct questioning, the boys shifted from an admiration for "power figures" to a greater expressed liking for "positive" models, such as George Washington Carver, Albert Schweitzer, and their counselors. Certain other important aspects of their behavior did not, however, undergo change: the boys still responded with aggression, for example, to the experiment eliciting reactions to frustration.

The degree of change in the behavior disorders can best be illustrated by a comparison of their test results to the answers of "normal children." We first validated the tests used at Wiltwyck by administering them to a sample of middle-class children drawn from a Boston suburb. At the beginning of their stay at Wiltwyck, the behavior disorders offered many more "pathological" responses to the tests than did the normal school children. Yet, by the completion of their stay, the same children had proportionately *fewer* aggressive fantasies, a *less* fearful view of authority, and approximately the same level of guilt as did the suburban boys. Thus, Wiltwyck seems to socialize these antisocial children—at least in the sense of bringing them much closer to middle-class norms in contemporary American society.

The progress of one boy, "Bobby," typifies the reaction of behavior disorders to milieu therapy as offered at Wiltwyck:

When he came to Wiltwyck, Bobby was a lonely, aggressive child who hated the world. He had a history of stealing, unprovoked attacks on other children, and problem behavior in school. Often anxiety overcame him, and he withdrew from the outside world.

His family had been disrupted by mental disease. His

mother and one sister lived in mental hospitals. Another sister was in a foster home. The father had deserted his family.

Interviewed a few months after his arrival, Bobby seemed to repress strong aggressive desires and to feel intense anxiety. He had not adjusted to the Wiltwyck environment. Frustration caused either rage or withdrawal.

In time, counseling by his social worker increased Bobby's feelings of security and acceptance. He formed warm relations with his cottage counselor and gradually became friendly with the other boys. He joined the school choir, and his singing won him applause. His aggression decreased markedly. His acceptance of restrictions improved and, although he still "talked back," he carried out instructions.

In February his counselor reported that Bobby's anxiety had decreased greatly. When frustrated, he no longer exploded in hostility, although he sometimes broke into tears.

In February, 1955, the tests showed several important changes in Bobby. His aggressive fantasies had decreased. His internalized guilt had increased. His self-perception was much more differentiated, and he was able to admit many more negative qualities about himself. His view of authority had become more friendly, and his withdrawal fantasies had decreased. When asked what he disliked about Wiltwyck, he replied: "I like everything about it. There's nothing wrong."

Milieu therapy helped Bobby (as it did most other behavior disorders) in modifying his aggression, in changing his view of authority, and in controlling his desires in accord with society's restrictions.

The *psychopathic* child, like the *psychopathic* adult, has a distinct personality syndrome. Certain of his traits could be distinguished by the tests we used. The psychopathic children had much less guilt and a much more punitive view of authority than did the behavior disorders, the neurotics, or the normal children. The psychopaths had greater aggressive fantasies and less withdrawal fantasies than did the neurotics or the public school boys.

The Wiltwyck study helped to clarify two theoretical problems. First, it indicated that the child psychopath's need for love is not extinguished. The Wiltwyck counselors rated all the psychopathic children as having a strong craving for attention. In addition, four of the psychopaths in the longitudinal study improved their relations with counselors. Thus, an affectional bond could be established with these child psychopaths.

Second, the study indicated that psychopaths, as children, have no more intense aggressive fantasies than do other delinquents. The fantasy aggression of the psychopaths was no greater than that of the behavior disorders —although it was greater than that of the neurotics and the normal children. Apparently the psychopaths, who are certainly aggressive in overt behavior, "act out" more than the other children primarily because they lack internalized controls.

As previous chapters have shown, the psychopath is supposed to be unresponsive to therapy. Yet both the 1954 and the 1955 studies showed that milieu therapy improved the child psychopath in many important ways. The evidence indicated that the psychopaths had greatly decreased their aggressive fantasies and that this important transition was also mirrored in behavior. Notoriously lacking in conscience, the psychopathic children also exhibited a significant increment in internalized guilt, as well as greater control over impulsivity. Their attitude toward authority became more friendly and their ego ideals more positive. In most important aspects —aggression, guilt, view of authority—the psychopathic boys closely approached the scores of the "normal," suburban children.

The case of "Paul," whom we mentioned earlier, is a typical example pointing up the effects of milieu therapy on the psychopathic child:

Upon entering Wiltwyck, Paul was an extremely aggressive, uncontrolled child. He had been expelled from public school for attacking other children and his teacher. During a robbery, he struck a watchman over the head. Sentenced for the crime, Paul went on a rampage in the children's home.

His parents had severely disciplined Paul but had been

unable to control him. The father openly rejected the boy.

Interviewed in early July, 1954, Paul showed hatred of his parents, strong hostility, and little guilt. He had no friends in the school.

Paul's explosiveness shocked even the Wiltwyck staff, long accustomed to such hostility. During the first months of treatment, he fought constantly, refused to obey authority, and was friendly with nobody.

His counselor tried to guide Paul into activities which would allow harmless release for his aggression. Paul fished in the brook which runs through the Wiltwyck grounds. He caught fish by clubbing them with a stick. His prowess as a fisherman won the respect of the other boys, and his aggression toward human beings decreased.

Paul reluctantly joined a dancing group. At first the instructor allowed Paul to interpret rhythms by himself to release his pent-up energy. Later, Paul participated in group dancing. After many months, he appeared in a dancing show given at the school.

Paul's relations with his counselor and the boys in his cottage improved. By February the counselor had established rapport with Paul. Although still impulsive, Paul's control of his behavior had greatly increased. He no longer attacked the other children, and his hostility toward the school had disappeared.

Re-interviewed in February, 1955, Paul's aggressive fantasies had decreased, his view of authority had become more friendly, and his recognition of his own negative traits had increased. His internalized guilt had increased greatly but was still below the "normal" level. His feelings of rejection were strong. When asked what people liked about him, he replied: "Nothing!"

Although greatly improved, Paul required further treatment. At the end of the interview, Paul talked about a bow and arrow he was making. "I want to put sharp points on it," he said. Then he asked, "What do you think will kill a man faster, a bullet or an arrow?" Obviously, Paul's aggressiveness had not completely disappeared. By February, 1954, Paul had been in the school only nine months.

More striking improvement can be seen in "Miguel,"

a child psychopath who had been treated for 13 months. Miguel spent the first nine years of his life in a Puerto Rican orphanage. His parents were divorced immediately after Miguel's birth. Unable to support her children, the mother placed them in an institution.

In 1951, the mother accompanied a male friend to New York. Later she sent for the children. In New York, Miguel displayed destructive, hostile explosiveness. He refused to attend school, stayed away from home at night, stole, and destroyed property throughout the neighborhood.

In late 1953, Miguel's stepfather brought the boy before a New York court and complained of his "incorrigibility." The court remanded Miguel to New York's Youth House.

At Youth House, Miguel pretended that he could not speak English. He formed no affectional relations. He did not control his emotions: during temper tantrums he ran, fought, crawled, yelled, and screamed. Psychiatric examination uncovered "marked feelings of rejection," aggression, "longstanding defiant behavior," and "apprehension about establishing relations."

Sent to Wiltwyck in January, 1954, Miguel had difficulty in adjusting to the school. During the first months, he was hostile, sucked his thumb, and had enuresis. In June, his counselor reported that Miguel "wanted friends among the boys, but had no close relationships."

In the 1954 interview, Miguel had strongly aggressive fantasies, very low guilt, and a highly punitive perception of authority. He had no clear conception of himself. He admitted few negative qualities, and said he "hated" Wiltwyck.

During the intervening months, Miguel participated both in group therapy and in individual therapy. His aggressive conduct diminished, and his random impulsivity came under more rational control. He became very dependent on the group therapist and followed him everywhere in the school. His relations with the other boys improved, but he still had no close friends among the boys.

In the 1955 interviews, Miguel's personality seemed to have undergone important alterations. His internalized guilt greatly increased, and his extremely hostile view of authority was almost eradicated. His aggressive fantasies had decreased slightly.

Thus, in milieu therapy, society may well have an effective instrument for the treatment of psychopathy. Our study indicates that the psychopathic child, if treated in a permissive environment, can be changed. Boys like Paul and Miguel need not become adults like William Cook or Josef Borlov. In light of the causative background of psychopathy, the therapy offered at Wiltwyck would seem particularly appropriate for children such as Paul and Miguel. The warm, supportive environment could serve to satisfy the children's dependency needs which had so long been frustrated by their families. The consistency, nonpunitiveness, and social controls imposed by the Wiltwyck staff could provide the prerequisites for the establishment of a conscience. By removing the child from his typically rejecting environment and placing him, sometimes for years, in a totally new social situation, the treatment achieves a radical alteration in the usual experience of psychopathic personalities.

What influences at Wiltwyck created the changes? Milieu therapy mobilizes the entire environment against the child's disorder. Psychotherapy, group therapy, and art therapy, social workers, counselors, and psychologists converge in treating the child. Moreover, the treatment necessarily removes the child from his family and his social environment. Consequently, one finds it difficult to isolate the particular causes of change, Yet, one can suggest that four factors may play primary roles in altering the boys: the rapport between children and counselors; the absence of punitive frustration; the subtle but powerful social control exerted not only by the adults but also by the boys' leaders, and individual and group psychotherapy.

A boys' rapport with Wiltwyck adults seems closely related to his improvement. A quarter of a century ago, August Aichhorn observed, "The most important thing [in curing delinquents] is the child's feeling for the counselor." Fortunately, our study offered an opportunity, although not a perfect one, for checking the relationship between rapport and certain changes in the boys. At the beginning of the research, we asked each counselor to describe his relation to each boy.

Thirty-seven per cent of the boys were judged by the counselors to have "warm" relations with at least one staff member;[41] 29 per cent were designated as having erratic relations ("sometimes cool"); 32 per cent were denoted as having "friendly but distant" relations; and 2 per cent were marked as having "cool" relations. In general, the counselors seemed wary of overrating the degree of rapport.[42]

Comparing these ratings of rapport with the children's performance on the (independent) personality tests uncovers some significant relationships:

Those children with whom any counselor claimed a warm relation had fewer aggressive fantasies than those with whom counselors had distant or cool relations.

Those children with whom any counselor claimed close relations evidenced greater internalization of guilt than those with whom the counselors had erratic, distant, or cool relations.

Those children with whom any counselor claimed close relations more often viewed authority figures as supportive and friendly than did those with whom the counselors had erratic, distant, or cool relations.

Those children with whom any counselor claimed close relations more often had a "loving" ideal of good parents than did those with whom the counselors had distant, cool, or erratic relations.

In general, boys who were designated as having close relations with a counselor possessed greater social maturity. They had fewer aggressive desires, "sturdier consciences," and more friendly attitudes toward authority. In these traits, they differed from children who had changeable or cool relations with the staff. These facts gave rise to an interpretive problem: Does the warm relationship cause these personality traits, or is it the traits themselves which make possible the warm relations? The evidence indicated that rapport may simply be correlated with nonaggressiveness in the child and with a relatively more friendly view of authority. At the beginning of treatment, for example, counselors more often described themselves as having a warm relation with the nonaggressive children. Thus, since significant differences existed before treatment really began, we assumed that rapport does not *cause* a decrease in aggression or an increase in friendly views of authority. On the other hand, changes in the children's level of internalized guilt came about only after a long spell of treatment. It would appear, therefore, that a close adult-child relationship leads the child to identify with the counselor, to absorb some of the counselor's standards, and thus, to fortify the child's level of internalized guilt.

A second element in the Wiltwyck environment, the absence of brutality and punitiveness, would also seem to play an important role, particularly in changing the psychopathic boys.

In part, the establishment of rapport depends on the adult's nonpunitive attitude. These children need to see that adults can be kind. Permissiveness may also account for the children's decrease in aggressive desires. Punishment is, of course, frustrating—and frustration tends to increase aggression. Permissiveness removes at least one cause of the children's hostility. By allowing the boys to "act out" their aggression in socially harmless ways, the school provides an outlet for hostility. Permissiveness probably influences the child's view of authority figures. Most of the boys had never before associated with a nonpunitive, supportive adult. At Wiltwyck the staff is friendly, and the child's view of authority figures is modified.

In addition to rapport and permissiveness, the influence of group living may account for some of the improvements. Before coming to Wiltwyck, many of the boys belonged to street gangs. Group pressures then encouraged antisocial behavior. At Wiltwyck, on the other hand, each group is guided by counselors. Group influence turns the boy in a positive, socializing direction. The school submits the child to a new kind of social control, a type which the psychopathic boys may never have experienced.

The boy leaders themselves seem to be an aid to the "therapeutic" pressure of the group. In the 1953 study, an analysis of Wiltwyck's boy leaders (detected by a sociogram) showed them to be low in authoritarianism, anxiety, and aggression. They were secure and well adjusted in comparison to the other boys.

In the present research, counselor ratings offered a further opportunity for assessing the personalities of the child leaders. The staff named 12 boys as consistently leading at the school. These leaders were bigger and older than the average boy. More importantly, as indicated by our tests, the leaders had significantly lower aggressive scores and significantly greater internalized guilt than the average Wiltwyck child.

The combined influence of the child leaders and the counselors creates a group atmosphere which probably plays an important part in increasing inner controls of the antisocial boys.

Another factor should be mentioned—individual counseling. Throughout a boy's stay, he has opportunities for many talks with his counselor, the social workers, the psychologist, and other staff members. The rapport established is important, but also the talks themselves probably give the boy greater insight into his problems and personality. The children's increased willingness to admit negative traits about themselves—a tendency which we noted in direct interviews with the boys—may well be due to the individual counseling.

These four factors—adult-child rapport, permissiveness, group influence, and individual counseling—may account for the changes which we have traced in the children at Wiltwyck. With each child, one factor may be more important than another. On the whole, however, the relation seems to be this:

> *Rapport:* increases a desire to be socialized.
> *Permissiveness:* decreases aggression and punitive views of authority.
> *Group influence:* increases behavioral control
> *Counseling:* increases children's self-understanding.

Does milieu therapy permanently change these boys? Only the future will tell. It is axiomatic in modern social science that the situation helps determine behavior and personality. The Wiltwyck environment, a new "situation," causes radical alterations in personality. When the children return to their homes (generally in slum neighborhoods), the "situation" again changes, and their actions and attitudes may change with it.

"Claude Brown," a former Wiltwyck boy, has poignantly analyzed this problem in his brilliant discussion of "Harlem, My Harlem" (31). After achieving a reputation as "the worst boy in the neighborhood," Brown was sent to Wiltwyck.

> Following a two and a half years stay at Wiltwyck, I returned to my dear old Harlem. I was then thirteen. In a few weeks I became uncomfortably aware of not being able to fit in anymore. There were many new vices to learn, but somehow I just could not pick up where I had left off. Having no alternative, however, I set out to reestablish myself in the old community . . . (31, p. 379).

He became, once again, a gang leader and a "pusher of horse." After he was shot in a gang fight, the courts sent Brown to the Warwick Training School where, he remarked, "I had learned many new ways of crimes. I had also become well acquainted with many of New York City's teenage criminals" (31, p. 381). Yet, after release —and two more commitments to Warwick—Brown underwent a radical change: "I moved out of Harlem, and got a job. Most of my spare time was spent in Harlem, taking the ribbing and laughing that my attending evening high school evoked from my old street corner cronies. They laughed for three years. When I entered college there were no more laughs" (31, p. 381). Today, Brown continues as a student at a major American University.

Whether one can regard Brown as typical of Wiltwyck boys—or whether one can legitimately credit Wiltwyck for his transformation—demands answers which can be furnished only by a systematic follow-up study of the boys as they enter adulthood. Yet the extent of change in the boys' characters during their residence in the school offers substantial hope that the treatment may exert lasting, beneficial effects.

NOTES

1. Sheldon and Eleanor Glueck found that 80 per cent of parolee convicts commit at least one other offense within five years of their release.

2. The state later revoked the agreement.

3. Mohr and Heaver found a higher proportion of cures in "psychopaths" than did the Gluecks with nonpsychopaths. The Gluecks, however, used more rigorous methods and traced even unreported crimes. In all probability, use of the Gluecks' methods would have further decreased the small proportion of success found by Mohr and Heaver.

4. Heaver (109) based diagnosis on five major traits: lack of concern for others, impulsivity, inability to learn from experience, instability, and emotional immaturity.

5. Selection based on severe anti-social behavior.

6. "Levels of loyalty" meant, in essence, explaining to the soldier why he should obey his officers.

7. After a three month study, the Army concluded that 78 per cent had adjusted to military life. No evaluation was made of the specific adjustment of psychopaths.

8. The major criterion for diagnoses of psychopathy was nonresponsiveness to treatment.

9. Paper and pencil tests like the Bell Adjustment Inventory were used.

10. Because of this "guilt," it may be incorrect to call Harold a psychopath. Nevertheless, this anxiety was constricted to one area, incestuous desires, and it failed to exert any type of socialized control over Harold's behavior. It seems more akin to a fearfulness of fatherly retaliation than an internalized conscience. Possibly hypnoanalysis might reveal this same type of incestuous anxiety in other psychopaths.

11. Quoted in O'Donnel (183).

12. Quoted in Curran and Mallinson (50).

13. Benjamin Karpman, although a believer in the "noncurability" of psychopaths, has reported several cases of successful therapy. Karpman believes, however, that these patients were not "true" psychopaths. From his point of view, psychopathy is caused only by "idiopathic" (unknown, presumably constitutional) causes; if psychogenic causes can be found in the patient's past, Karpman maintains that he is not a psychopath (130, pp. 305-325).

One of Karpman's patients, Jerry Briggs, had most of the symptoms which other social scientists would diagnose as psychopathic. Karpman himself called Briggs a neurotic because of his intense mother hatred, a "psychogenic cause." Briggs, a famous bandit, came from a vain, social-climbing family and was severely rejected by his eccentric, cigar-smoking mother. After an early crime, the boy was committed by his mother to reform school. He had a long history of antisocial behavior: stealing, shoplifting, gun-running, gambling, and armed robbery.

Briggs was caught and sentenced to prison for stealing

$130,000 from a mail truck. In prison, psychotherapy helped, and he made a good adjustment. Some years after release, however, Briggs committed suicide. Therapy, while not lifting him to a "normal" level, at least reduced his criminality.

14. Neither Adatto, nor Train, nor Freyhan specified the basis for diagnosis of psychopathy.

15. Diagnosis based on severe antisocial behavior.

16. One other experiment confirmed Silverman's findings that Dilantin Sodium benefits psychopaths. Only one patient, however, was given the drug, and he was later shown to be an epileptic. See Brill and Walker (29).

17. Diagnostic criteria were not stated by either Hill or Shouron.

18. Severe antisocial behavior was the major criterion of diagnosis.

19. Darling's cases included: a neurotic with an intense fear of smothering, a manic-depressive who had stolen a car and who drank heavily, and a paranoid who had attacked an attendant and planned an escape.

20. Cited in Almansi and Impastate (10). Golden's patients had great anxiety and marked depressive characteristics—traits which a true psychopath almost never has.

21. Banay's patients, although antisocial, apparently included both neurotics and psychotics. The twelve cases who did not respond to treatment were paranoids.

22. Cited in Lindner (154, p. 491).

23. Evidence presented in this article (66) suggests that the operation should be used with great caution and only on cases with temporal lobe foci.

24. A number of experiments generally utilizing the therapeutic community approach are described in Gibbens (78), Mackwood (160), Fenton (67), and Lieberman and Siegel (149).

25. Castration has often been advocated for so-called sexual offenders. While some follow-up studies on castrated sexual offenders, such as that conducted on discharges from Herstedvester, suggest that they are less likely to commit further sexual crimes than noncastrated offenders, the evidence is by no means conclusive.

26. See Bender (18). The article contains a succinct description of the child psychopath.

27. Case descriptions of the psychopathic boys pictured them as extremely aggressive, "lacking in good judgment," affectively superficial, and indifferent.

28. Robert was diagnosed as a "primary" behavior disorder. His basic problem was uninhibited, aggressive behavior. The line between this diagnosis and psychopathy seems particularly vague

in Robert's case, so the results of his treatment have relevance
to the issue of psychopathic therapy.

29. Szurek found that the factor which best predicts therapeutic success is the presence or absence of parental affection
in the patients' lives. Without previous warmth, therapy is
difficult.

30. Szurek believes that the psychopathic child can be cured
only by furnishing him with warmth, security, firmness, and
fairness. Friedlander's methods, although labeled "psychoanalysis," seem to meet these requirements—at least in Billy's
case.

31. One major therapeutic approach, nondirective counseling,
has not been tried on psychopathic children. George D. Watt
used the method on 11 delinquent boys at Utah State In-
dustrial School. Evaluation indicated that seven of the boys
had achieved at least two of the aims of the therapy: free
expression and greater insight. Comparison with a control
group showed that the 11 cases made statistically significant
improvements on the MMPI (particularly on hypochondriasis,
psychasthenia, and schizophrenia) and on the California Test
of personality. Nondirective counseling, though useful for
normal delinquents, does not seem applicable to psychopathy.
Psychopaths lack the desire for change which seems prerequisite
for successful nondirective therapy. See Watt (264).

32. "Milieu" therapy is not ordinary group therapy. Group
treatment attempts to establish a new experience for the child;
but the experience is not one which encompasses his entire life.
Few attempts have been made to use group therapy with child
psychopaths. Some of the more promising experiments with
serious juvenile delinquents have involved "controlled activity
groups" and discussion groups. See Shulman (226), also
Gertsen (76). The effect of these experiments on the few
child psychopaths included in their samples has not been
evaluated.

33. The Children's Village of Ska near Stockholm, in some
ways similar to Aichhorn's school, consciously attempts to instill infantile attitudes in the children. Regression is encouraged.
Children drink from bottles and become dependent upon the
staff. The value of this method, which presumably allows more
complete identification, has not been ascertained.

34. Diagnoses are often retrospective judgments. Perhaps because rapport was *not* established, certain girls were later tabbed
as "unable" to form a relation. There may well have been
girls who, at the beginning of treatment, were truly psychopathic; but who, because they *did* form an attachment and *did*
respond to treatment, were excluded from this group of
"failures."

35. Statements made about Wiltwyck's policy refer only to the period 1953-1955. Chapter 6 of the previous edition of this book presents a complete description of the studies which are briefly summarized in this section. Those readers who are interested in the methods of the study, the reliability and validity of the measures which were utilized, and the exact statistical results should consult this chapter as well as the appendix of *Psychopathy and Delinquency* (168).

36. Papanek now serves as an Associate Professor of Education at Queens College, New York.

37. Case names have been changed.

38. Kings County and Bellevue hospitals, where the children were diagnosed before placement in Wiltwyck, did not use the psychopathic label. They called such children "active aggressive personalities" or, occasionally, "passive aggressive personalities." They did recognize the character syndrome which we have termed the "psychopathic personality" but preferred the other labels with their less opprobrious connotations.

39. Other questionnaires concerning the child's values and perception of the environment were used but failed to provide any significant or interesting results. They are described in *Psychopathy and Delinquency* (168).

40. The conclusions which follow are based on two approaches. One "longitudinal," the other "cross-sectional." Twenty-five boys who had been new arrivals in 1954 were reexamined in 1955. The longitudinal data provided by this approach was supplemented by a cross-sectional analysis of the test results of all 107 cases. The 107 boys were divided into three categories: those who had resided at the school for one week to eight months (relatively new arrivals), those who had lived at Wiltwyck for nine to twenty-three months (an average length of stay), and those who had been at the school for 23 months or more (the "old-timers"). By comparing the test responses of these three groups, one could achieve some estimate of changes in the boys. In the statistical analyses, to provide sufficient numbers, the "behavior disorders" were joined with the "psychopaths" while the "neurotics" and "psychotics" were joined together. Festinger's or Wilcoxen's nonparametric formulas and the corrected X^2 test were used to estimate significance. The results of the "cross-sectional" study and of the "longitudinal" study were almost entirely complementary.

41. With many children, different counselors had different types of relations. For the above summary, the "warmest" rating given each child by any counselor was used in assigning him to a category.

42. Recent studies have shown that therapists often overestimate their rapport with a patient. Teuber and Powers (255)

analyzed the counselor-child relations in the Cambridge-Somerville Study and found that the counselor's reported better relations between the boys and themselves than did the boys.

6

The Psychopath, the Law, and Society

Psychopathy represents the most expensive and most destructive of all known forms of aberrant behavior . . .

ROBERT LINDNER

On April 20, 1931, two men accosted the driver of a Baltimore milk wagon. The middle-aged driver, John W. Anderson, stopped his truck. The two men climbed aboard and asked Anderson for his money. The driver resisted, and there was a brief struggle. Although both bandits carried guns, only one used his—to shoot and kill the driver. John Anderson left a wife and three children. His murderer, Herman Webb Duker, was a psychopath. As a child, Duker had been rebellious and vicious. He had served nine months in the New York City Reformatory. After release, he went to Baltimore and broke into apartments and stole $2,000.

At 18, Duker was committed to the Maryland School for Boys. Psychiatrists diagnosed him as a "psychopath of the chronic delinquent type, with some sexual psychopathy and with a marked tendency toward the runaway reaction" (261, p. 211). But the laws of Maryland did not recognize psychopathy as "insanity." Thus Duker could neither receive mental hospital treatment, nor could he be permanently segregated from society. Duker escaped from the Maryland school.

While committing another crime in New York City, he was apprehended and sentenced to 18 months in the Elmira Reformatory. Because of his aggressive, belligerent behavior, Duker's term was stretched to 31 months. Once again, a psychiatrist diagnosed him as a "psychopathic personality."

Like Maryland, New York laws did not recognize psychopathy as "insanity." Duker missed another opportunity for treatment. In January, 1931, he was released.

171

On April 20, he shot and killed John Anderson in Baltimore.

Duker's case illustrates the inadequacy of present social and legal policy with its blindness to the facts of psychopathy. If Duker could have been cured while at the reform schools, or if he had never been released, Anderson might still be alive.

At his trial, Duker stood before the court in brazen, guiltless defiance. On advice of counsel, he pleaded guilty to first degree murder. His lawyer did not use insanity as a defense, for Duker "knew the difference between right and wrong."

The testimony of five psychiatrists and a voluminous report on his past life, however, marked the defendant as a pathologically deformed person. Judge Joseph Ulman recounted:

> Duker's twenty-two years of life unfold types and degrees of activity that indicate a grossly distorted personality. He is not merely a youthful delinquent who has achieved a precocious maturity in crime. As a small child he exhibited an appalling and inhuman cruelty to animals which persisted for many years. The full record of his robberies and like crimes will never be known. He confesses many for which he was never apprehended; and says that after committing them he experienced an unusual sense of peace and satisfaction— almost of exaltation—a release from his nervous restlessness. This is certainly not the common experience of normal criminals. He has for years suffered from serious abnormalities in the sex sphere. None of these peculiarities is at all obvious to superficial examination. On the witness stand he presents the picture of an alert, courageous and peculiarly plausible individual. His apparent normality, coupled with his abnormal career, is itself an evidence of his pathological condition.
>
> What is that condition? With a degree of unanimity that reflects credit upon every medical witness in this case, the Court is assured that Duker is a "psychopathic personality." This is the conclusion reached by the present and former medical officers of the Supreme Bench, whose freedom from bias was to be presumed. It is the conclusion reached in 1928 by Doctor Partridge, then psychiatrist of the Maryland School for Boys, and in 1930 by Doctor Christian and the late Doctor Harding, Superintendent and Psychiatrist, respectively, of Elmira Reformatory—long before the murder had been committed. It is the same conclusion reached by

Doctor Truitt, employed by the defense, and by Doctor Tanyhill and Doctor Gillis, employed by the State, for the purposes of this hearing. The "battle of experts," so often and so properly denounced as characteristic of American criminal trials, did not occur in this case (261, p. 215).

Under contemporary law, Duker was fully responsible for his actions. Yet the trial evidenced the incongruity of a test based on "the knowledge of right and wrong":

> To paraphrase the views expressed by every expert witness in this case, the psychopathic personality is emotionally unbalanced so that he does not respond normally to what his conscious mind tells him. He knows the consequences of wrong-doing, but impulses beyond his control sway his actions regardless of the result to himself or to others . . . Every witness in this case agreed that Duker has not the normal emotional and moral impulses and controls—and every witness concluded that he is "not fully responsible" for his actions (261, p. 217).

The jury convicted Duker of first-degree murder. Judge Ulman, in sentencing the defendant, had only two choices: life imprisonment or execution. Every psychiatric witness testified to the peril of imprisoning Duker:

> Doctor Guttmacher says of Duker that he is potentially one of the most dangerous types of individuals that society knows; that in a penal institution he would not be amenable to authority, and would be among the leaders in rebellion against it. Doctor Truitt, interrogated by the Court specifically as to how he thinks Duker would respond to the discipline of imprisonment for life in the Maryland Penitentiary replied that "the outlook would be unfavorable." The court had, then, to decide between life imprisonment and hanging for a man who is legally sane, medically of abnormal psychology, and socially extremely dangerous. Moreover, he is socially dangerous and a menace to the life of others whether he be at large or confined in prison. And it must not be forgotten that prison guards are human beings—and that administration of law "for the protection of society" applies to them as well as to other citizens (261, p. 218).

Convinced of Duker's extreme dangerousness, Judge Ulman sentenced him to be "hung by the neck until dead." As he passed sentence, Ulman stated: "This action is a confession of social and legal failure" (261, p. 219).

Society had had the opportunity of giving Duker the intensive treatment which he so obviously required. In New York, in Elmira, and in the Maryland schools, Duker's life might have been changed; but it was not. Even admitting a failure in treatment, different laws might have segregated Duker early in life.

Knowing that Duker was legally, but probably not morally responsible for his crimes, Judge Ulman was well aware of the implications of his decision:

> Duker is a mentally abnormal person, and I knew him to be so when I sentenced him to hang. There is something very ugly about that bald statement. Even a judge who believes in capital punishment would hesitate a long time before he imposed the death sentence upon a person known to be mentally irresponsible. I do not believe in capital punishment . . . society confesses its own failure every time it exacts a life for a life (261, p. 229).

Neither the public nor Maryland's governor understood the reasoning of Ulman's decision. People showered the judge with letters and praised him for a courageously vindictive punishment. The governor, Albert C. Ritchie, perhaps with justification, questioned the fairness of hanging a man who was "not responsible" for his crime. The Governor commuted Duker's sentence to life imprisonment, stating: "What I cannot understand is how the Court could first decide—as it did—that Duker's mental disorder should be considered in mitigation of punishment, and that he should not be hanged; and then sentence him to be hanged anyhow, not for his crime, but because the penitentiary is the only place to which he could be committed." [1]

I. THE PSYCHOPATH AND LEGAL POLICY

The Duker case highlighted two questions which have long puzzled legal philosophers. Is the psychopath responsible for his acts? And, how can we best protect society from his depredations?

Nonresponsibility for an act due to mental disorder was first introduced into the common law in 1724. An English court held that a man was irresponsible if "he doth not know what he is doing, no more than . . . a wild beast" (87).

A century later, the quaint "wild beast test" was superseded by the famed M'Naghten decision, a case which set the bounds for contemporary standards of legal responsibility. In 1843, M'Naghten, a parnoiac, murdered Sir Robert Peel's secretary. The killer had mistakenly believed that the secretary was the statesman himself. The courts judged M'Naghten mentally irresponsible. The House of Lords attacked the court's decision.

The judges' reply constitutes the precedent upon which American and English law now bases its standard of criminal responsibility: a plea of insanity depends on establishing that "at the time of committing the act, the party accused was labouring under such a defect of reason, from disease of the mind, as not to know the nature and quality of the act he was doing, or, if he did know it, that he did not know he was doing what was wrong" (85, p. 99).

Thus, in modern America a man, although insane, is considered legally responsible unless he is found by the jury not to know the difference between right and wrong. In a minority of states, the criminal is assumed to be legally irresponsible—even if he does know that his act was "wrong"—if the crime was committed under the influence of an "insane, irresistible impulse." In most cases, a psychopath is tabbed as legally sane and responsible.

These criteria seemed more plausible before modern science discarded the theory of faculty psychology. At that time, man's brain was sometimes depicted as a conglomeration of independent compartments, each recording or controlling a different species of idea or action. Some facultative theories held for a special "moral sense" which enabled the individual to distinguish right from wrong. If functioning correctly, "moral reason" controlled or repressed "irrational impulse."

Contemporary research, on the other hand, has inseparably linked the conscious and the unconscious, the rational and the irrational. Man's nature is an interdependent, interrelated structure. One federal judge graphically stated the current position: "The modern science of psychology . . . does not conceive that there is a separate little man in the top of one's head called reason whose function it is to guide another unruly little man called instinct, emotion, or impulse in the way he should go." [2]

Moreover, the criminal law ignores the complexity of causes which prompt man's behavior. Probably no criminal, whether mentally disordered or not, deliberately decides to commit an "evil" act. His behavior cannot reasonably be depicted as the conscious choice of an independent free will. Rather, the actions of all criminals come from a complicated interplay of biological, social, and psychological causes. Thus, it is unrealistic to try arbitrarily to distinguish the "sane" from the "insane" criminal on the basis of these criteria. The impracticality of this task has been pointed out by Hervey Cleckly: "The law, at least theoretically, operates on the assumption of an absolute contrast, an either-or standard by which one must pronounce patients totally insane (irresponsible) or totally sane (responsible). This, as nearly all psychiatrists will admit is neither in accordance with reality nor conducive to fair and useful action" (40).

Based as they are on such faulty premises, the tests of responsibility become, in practice, highly confused. Neither the lay jurist nor the trained psychologist can abstract "moral faculty" and trace its functioning. The result is that confused testimony makes the issue of responsibility a legal quagmire. Even were it possible to distinguish irresponsible from responsible criminals on the basis of some test which would identify the former as those whose actions were based on false beliefs, society would then be counting its most dangerous criminals as the ones whose actions were least deserving of punishment.

In theory, the tests of insanity are unrealistic; in practice, they are unwieldy. The psychopath, together with other criminals, is punished by imprisonment although imprisonment rarely changes him. Later he is released, and he repeats his patterns of behavior.

If the psychopath were declared irresponsible, two new possibilities would be open. He would, in all probability, be sent to a mental hospital where the best instruments of modern treatment could be applied. Even in a therapeutically advanced hospital, as our review of treatment showed, the psychopath might still be unreformed. In the event that treatment failed, the psychopath could be permanently segregated by commitment. His release would be dependent, not upon the crime he had committed, but upon the cure of his disorder.

If treated early in life, Herman Duker might have been cured. Milieu therapy, as the Wiltwyck study indicates, could probably have lessened his aggression, increased his inner controls, and helped him to internalize the standards of society. He might, if treated correctly, have formed relationships which would have broken through his callousness.

If treatment failed, Duker should not have been returned to society. Yet he "served his sentence" and, under present law, he had to be released. Legal recognition of Duker's mental abnormality and "irresponsibility" would not have been "softness"; it would have been a realistic, necessary step in the protection of society.

Unfortunately, many judges hesitate to abandon the prevailing standards of responsibility for fear of destroying punishment's effectiveness as a deterrent of criminal behavior. This position arises from the theoretical premises of the criminal law. As Roscoe Pound has commented: ". . . historically, our substantive criminal law is based upon a theory of punishing the vicious will. It postulates a free agent confronted with a choice between doing right and doing wrong and choosing freely to do wrong. It assumes that the social interests . . . are to be maintained by imposing upon him a penalty corresponding exactly to the gravity of his offense" (194).

Punishment does not, as we have seen, deter the psychopath. He is incapable of moral control, and rational weighing of consequences is alien to his nature. In any case, the risk of permanent commitment in a mental hospital seems a reasonably stronger deterrent than the threat of a few years in prison.

The psychopath's neurological and environmental background creates a mental disorder which makes him dangerous. Both for the safety of society and in fairness to the psychopath, he should be "treated" instead of "punished."

Acknowledging irresponsibility of action assumes that

human beings have a varying capacity for free choice. Some men, unhampered by biological, social, or psychological defects, can utilize this potentiality to its highest degree. In the psychopath, the sphere of conscious choice has been diminished by restrictions of environment and neurological structure.[3] The psychopath does not choose to be a wicked man. His margin of freedom is slight.

For years, social and medical scientists have recognized the dangerous inadequacies in the existing tests of criminal responsibility. Even in 1838, five years before the M'Naghten decision became the accepted standard, psychiatrist Isaac Ray called moral knowledge a "fallacious" test of criminal responsibility (203). Modern psychiatric groups have repeatedly recommended the abandonment of the standard.[4]

Increasingly, many progressive members of the legal profession agree. In 1928 Sheldon Glueck stated: "It is evident that the knowledge tests unscientifically abstract out of the mental make-up but one phase or element of mental life, the cognitive, which, in this era of dynamic psychology, is beginning to be regarded as not the most important factor in conduct and its disorders" (87). In the same year, Justice Cardoza concurred: "Everyone recognizes that the present [legal] definition of insanity has little relation to the truths of mental life" (35, p. 32).

Glueck and Cardoza advanced beyond the legal thought of the 1920's. Only recently has the profession as a whole begun to adopt their viewpoint. A recent federal court decision marks the first official recognition of this trend.

Monte Durham, the defendant in this historic trial, had for many years been in and out of hospitals and prisons. At 17 the Navy discharged him with the comment that he suffered "from a profound personality disorder which renders him unfit for Naval Service" (2, p. 864). Two years later, car-stealing netted him a probationary sentence. He attempted to commit suicide. After a short sojourn in Washington mental hospitals, Durham returned to society and began passing bad checks.

Arrested for forgery and sentenced to jail, Durham exhibited signs of mental disorder. Examination at St.

Elizabeth's hospital resulted in diagnosis of "psychosis with psychopathic personality." After 15 months of hospital treatment, he was released as "recovered" and returned to jail to serve the remainder of his sentence.

Paroled from jail, Durham broke the conditions of his release, headed for the South and again forged checks. He was returned to St. Elizabeth's hospital, and this time diagnosed as a psychopathic personality, "without mental disorder." Eventually discharged, he broke into a home and was returned to the hospital. After insulin shock treatments and 16 months of hospitalization, he went on trial.

During the trial, Durham's mother testified that he "seemed afraid of people" and had asked her to enclose his windows with steel bars. Durham's own testimony was confused and hallucinated:

Q: Do you remember writing it?
A: No. Don't you forget? People get all mixed up in machines.
Q: What kind of a machine?
A: I don't know. They just get mixed up.
Q: Are you cured now?
A: No, sir.
Q: In your opinion?
A: No, sir.
Q: What is the matter with you?
A: You hear people bother you.
Q: What? You say you hear people bothering you?
A: Yes.
Q: What kind of people? What do they bother you about?
A: (No response.) (2, p. 865).

A psychiatrist, called as an expert witness, repeatedly testified that Durham was "of unsound mind." Yet he could not absolutely certify that the defendant was legally insane. "If the question of the right and wrong were propounded to him," the psychiatrist said, "he could give you the right answer" (2, p. 868). By any other standard, however, Monte Durham suffered from a mental aberration.[5] Nevertheless, the trial judge held Durham legally responsible, and imprisoned him.

In 1954, Durham's case was carried to the United States Court of Appeals. Circuit Judge Bazelon, recognizing the issues involved, asked the prosecutor, the defending counsel, and a "friend of the court" to file complete briefs on the problem of criminal responsibility. Because of several legal errors, Judge Bazelon reversed the lower court's decision.[6] Most importantly, the court formulated a new test of criminal responsibility: ". . . an accused is not criminally responsible if his unlawful act was the product of mental disease or mental defect" (2, pp. 874-875).

The judge hoped that the new standard would avoid a "misleading emphasis on cognitive" abilities. He reflected: "In attempting to define insanity in terms of a symptom (i.e., irresistible impulse or moral knowledge), the courts have assumed an impossible role, not merely one for which they have no special competence" (2, p. 872). Although the Durham decision clearly reflects an advance in American law, only one jurisdiction, Maine, had adopted it by 1961, and many eminent lawyers attacked it. Both Jerome Hall and the American Law Institute have criticized the vagueness of its terms and argued for the usefulness of a revised, modernized "M'Naghten rule" (106).

The Durham test of criminal responsibility would help clarify the legal issues. Courts would no longer ascertain the defendant's "moral knowledge." Nor would they determine his exact state of mind while he committed the crime. Yet the court would be faced with deciding whether the defendant's crime was *caused* by "mental disease" or "mental defect." This, too, is a complex problem. During the Durham case, for example, the psychiatric witness responded to the judge's persistent questions: ". . . I can't tell how much the abnormal thinking and the abnormal experiences in the form of hallucinations and delusions—delusions of persecution—had to do with his anti-social behavior" (106, p. 873). Yet the witness was convinced that Durham was of unsound mind."

In an attempt to simplify further the legal problem of responsibility, the American Law Institute has proposed another test. Formulated by Sheldon Glueck, the new standard recognizes the pervading influences of mental disorder on crime. "A person is not responsible for criminal conduct," this criterion states, "if it was committed substantially under the influence of a mental disease or defect." The advantage of the test is that it does not require exact specification of the role played by mental disorder in a particular crime. Yet, the Law Institute specifically excluded the psychopathic personality from consideration as a mentally diseased person. Although no state is bound to accept proposals of the American Law Institute, its recommendations exert a wide influence over the profession.

These proposed tests of criminal responsibility, though striding across a mire of confusion, leave the status of the psychopath ambiguous. Is he, or is he not, mentally diseased? Asociality, aggression, guiltlessness, and lovelessness set the psychopath apart from the normal human being—just as hallucinations or delusions characterize the psychotic. Yet many lawyers and psychiatrists argue that the psychopath—like the neurotic, the confirmed alcoholic, and the drug addict—is not "diseased." [7]

Judge Ulman, in rendering his decision to hang Herman Duker, expressed the practical problem:

> "Responsibility," whether mental responsibility or moral responsibility or social responsibility, is a concept about which it is useless to argue. Opinion concerning it is not the result of reason, but rests in emotion or belief. To me it was clear that a judge pronouncing sentence had to disregard altogether this kind of philosophical consideration. When an individual is attacked, his right of self-defense is absolute, and he need not stop to inquire whether his attacker is acting voluntarily or by reason of compulsions beyond his control. When society is subjected to attack, either actual or potential, and whether by one who is responsible or by one who is irresponsible, those charged with its protection *must* repel the attack, using such means as are available for the purpose (261).

The problem of responsibility, a vital philosophical issue, still hinders the criminal law in its task of protecting society from the psychopath. A provocative suggestion by psychiatrist Thomas Szasz might go far in resolving the perplexities of criminal responsibility. Szasz has criticized the standard tests as well as the new Durham rule. He has pleaded for "publicly verifiable criteria of rendering judgement" rather than the highly debat-

able opinions now proffered by expert witnesses, and he
has noted, with much justification, that contemporary
psychiatry cannot provide a "scientific distinction between mentally sick and mentally healthy persons . . ."
(242). Szasz has concerned himself, too, with the way in
which the "psychiatrization of the law" may subvert the
ethics of an "open society" by, implicitly, putting the
goal of "good individual and public health" above that
of "individual choice and responsibility." Thus, Szasz has
concluded:

> In this dilemma, it seems to me that the most dignified,
> and psychologically and socially most promising, alternative
> is not to consider mental illness an excusing condition.
> Treating offenders as responsible human beings, even though
> sometimes they may not be individually 'blameworthy,' offers
> them the only chance, as I now see it, of remaining 'human'
> and possibly becoming more so (242).

He wishes, therefore, that the courts act *as though
all* people were responsible for their decisions. Informed
by a concern for the open society, Szasz's suggestion does
not mean that the law would blindly ignore the causes
of crime or that the courts would simply punish the
criminal for his self-chosen wickedness. Szasz argues
that juries should consider all of the "human circum-
stances" which lead a person to crime and that sentences
should be based on scientific evidence as well as ethical
considerations.

A revolutionary proposal by Sheldon Glueck would,
like Szasz's suggestion, bypass the problem of determining responsibility. Glueck has proposed the establishment
of a "treatment tribunal" as society's most effective defense. His revision would separate the two functions of
criminal law: determination of guilt, and imposition of
sentence. During the trial, the judge and jury would ascertain only the guilt or innocence of the defendant. If
found guilty, the criminal would be remanded to a treatment tribunal. This board, composed of behavioral scientists, would then handle the disposition of the case.
The individual's sentence would depend, not upon an
arbitrary definition of "responsibility," but rather upon

a scientific evaluation of the nature and causes of his behavior.

This legal dichotomy would leave the complicated issue of treatment to experts who have training and experience. Most judges, while highly capable of deciding the issues arising during a trial, are unqualified for the difficult task of prescribing differential treatment (75).

Under our present system, as Sheldon Glueck discerned, judges must "prescribe in advance the length of time the patient should be kept in the hospital and then hold him there the full period or discharge him ahead of time, whether cured or not" (85, p. 100). The treatment tribunal would eliminate prescription of the exact period of time required for reformation. Sentences would be, within broad statutory limits, indeterminate. The nature of the criminal's disorder, his response to treatment, and his danger to society would be reviewed periodically by the board. A prisoner would be released when he seemed likely to make a satisfactory adjustment to society.

The treatment tribunal would fit the sentence to the criminal and not to the crime. Contemporary law imposes a specific punishment for a specific crime: the more serious the crime, the greater the punishment. Often, dangerous individuals receive light sentences because they are caught while committing minor crimes. This prevailing "pay as you go" plan neither protects society nor prevents crime. The long-range interests of society require that sentencing be based, not on the nature of the crime, but on the nature of the criminal.

Western criminal law seems now to be based largely on a pattern outlined, in 1764, by Cesare Beccaria, a Milanese nobleman. Revolted by the favoritism and brutality of European justice, Beccaria attempted to establish a universal standard. "Pleasure and pain are the only springs of actions in beings endowed with sensibility" (16), he wrote. Therefore, by instant infliction of pain on the wrongdoer, crime could be stopped. The punishment, he believed, should not be erratic: "If an equal punishment be ordained for two crimes that injure society in different degrees, there is nothing to deter men from committing the greater as often as it is attended with greater advantage" (16).

Beccaria's theory, enlightened and laudable for his times, conflicts with modern knowledge of human nature. Crime, particularly the crimes of a psychopath, does not come from the decision of a "vicious will." Criminal acts are not reasoned calculations of the degrees of pleasure and pain involved. The criminal, when he commits a crime, rarely thinks of being caught.[8]

Severe punishment neither reforms the criminal, nor does it prevent crime. Wisconsin has a mild criminal code; yet it ranks among the lowest in number of violent crimes committed. Southern states, possessing highly punitive laws, have the highest rates of violent criminalism. George Bernard Shaw detected the inadequacy in the Beccarian theory: ". . . the flaw in the case of Terrorism is that it is impossible to obtain enough certainty to deter. The police are compelled to confess every year, when they publish their statistics, that against the list of crimes reported to them, they can set only a percentage of detections and convictions" (219, p. 36).

The establishment of a treatment tribunal, although contravening the Beccarian standard of "justice," would protect society more thoroughly, particularly from the psychopaths.[9] Its aim would not be to punish a man for his crimes; it would be to protect society.[10]

Glueck explained: "The legal and institutional provisions for the protection of society must be based not so much upon the gravity of the particular act for which an offender happens to be tried, as upon his personality, that is, upon his dangerousness, his personal assets, and his responsiveness to peno-correctional treatment" (88).

Bringing about such a revolution in legal thought is not impossible. Indeed, California has already established a system which, in some ways, resembles the treatment tribunal. After the courts sentence a felon to prison, California's Adult Authority assumes responsibility for his treatment and release. Every sentenced criminal passes through a reception center, where he undergoes thorough social-psychological examination. Officials recommend a general treatment plan for the individual. On the basis of this plan, the prisoner is assigned to an institution which best meets the needs of his maladjustment. His release date, roughly set by statute,[11] is dependent on the Authority's judgment of his progress. Recently, Maryland has copied many aspects of California's system; its courts now sentence the criminal, not the crime.

In recent years, several states have revised their methods of treating juvenile delinquency. California, Massachusetts, Minnesota, Texas, and Wisconsin have established "youth correction boards" (57). After appearance in court, delinquents are remanded to the administrative board. Each youth's sentence and treatment is then determined and his release date set at the board's discretion. Many of the states are, however, hampered by insufficient treatment facilities.

Although most Western countries still attempt formal estimates of the offender's degree of responsibility—France refers to "*le caractère délictueux*"; Belgian courts gauge the offender's ability to control his actions; Czechoslovakia assesses responsibility in terms of the danger of a person's action to society; England, formally, utilizes the right and wrong rule—while most nations, in other words, have not radically revised the formula, a movement towards reform can be seen in several countries. The French penal code, the Cuban Code of Social Defence of 1936, and the Swedish Act of 1945 specify "mental disorder" as a reason for suspending the usual punishments. Further, they recognize the irrational elements which motivate psychopathic—indeed, all criminal —actions and they place the burden of proof upon the prosecution. England, in its Mental Health Act of 1959, has taken perhaps the greatest step forward, since the Act legally recognizes the existence of the psychopathic personality and provides that such persons may receive treatment in a mental hospital rather than being submitted to punishment.

Americans are beginning to recognize that their legal system does not furnish adequate protection. Treatment tribunals, in one of several forms, may offer a more effective instrument of social control. Nevertheless, the combination of public apathy and prejudice hinders their further development.

By themselves, of course, treatment tribunals will not eliminate crime, nor do they offer a final answer to psychopathy. It would be useless for a treatment tribunal to commit a psychopath to an institution which could do nothing to cure him. The psychopath needs special attention. Intensive and patient therapy is essential for his rehabilitation.

Well-trained personnel, public cooperation, and the effective utilization of scientific knowledge, together with a reoriented criminal code, could do much to alleviate criminality.

II. THE PSYCHOPATH AND SOCIAL POLICY

Our laws can be changed to protect society from psychopathy. Declaring the psychopath irresponsible, preferably with the additional establishment of treatment tribunals, would be beneficial and realistic protective measures. Yet legal changes are not enough. We must apply more effective methods of treatment—and treatment is contingent upon accurate diagnosis. In the control of psychopathy, progress in social science must accompany or precede progress in the law.

Social science has moved slowly forward. Measures have been developed for distinguishing the psychopath —the conscienceless, aggressive, asocial individual—from other deviants. For the adult psychopath, unfortunately, cures are difficult. Psychotherapy and hypnoanalysis have, apparently, rehabilitated some psychopathic personalities. The needs of the time require a great increase not only in the application of these methods, but in thorough evaluation of their results.

If every means of treatment has been tried and has failed with a particular individual, there seems to be only one sound alternative for the protection of society: unlimited custody. This is an expensive alternative, and one which civilized man hesitates to adopt. But Billy Cook, Josef Borlov, and Herman Duker have shown the dangers of this hesitation. Exile need not be irrevocable. Examinations might indicate important changes which would justify release.

Many states have already enacted "habitual criminal" laws which allow permanent incarceration after a certain number of felonies have been committed. The "habitual criminal" is frequently a psychopath; but, too frequently, such criminals have already cost society dearly.

Unlimited custody should be used *only* in those cases where extensive treatment has failed, and where every predictive instrument indicates the dangerousness of the individual. Society should not condemn a man to life custody unless it has exhausted all other resources.

Some social commentators, like Judge Ulman, advocate execution of the hardened psychopath. Lifetime imprisonment, they believe, would be taking a risk: the psychopath endangers his warders and fellow convicts.

George Bernard Shaw saw no greater cruelty in executing the "incurable criminal" than in incarcerating him for life. Execution, Shaw declared, would end the suffering of the convict, protect the lives of the guards, and offer true safety to society. After describing some psychopathic personalities, Shaw added:

> Now you cannot get rid of these nuisances and monsters by simply cataloguing them as subthyroidics and superadrenals or the like. At present you torment them for a fixed period, at the end of which they are set free to resume their operations with a savage grudge against the community which has tormented them. That is stupid. Nothing is gained by punishing people who cannot help themselves, and on whom deterrence is thrown away. Releasing them is like releasing the tigers from the Zoo to find their next meal in the nearest children's playing ground. . . .
>
> . . . It was a horrible thing to build a vestal virgin into a wall with food and water enough for a day; but to build her into a prison for years as we do, with just enough loathsome food to prevent her from dying, is more horrible: it is diabolical. If no better alternatives to death can be found than these, then who will not vote for death? If people are fit to live, let them live under decent human conditions. If they are not fit to live, kill them in a decent humane way. Is it any wonder that some of us are driven to prescribe the lethal chamber as the solution for the hard cases which are at present made the excuse for dragging all the other cases down to their level, and the only solution that will create a

sense of full social responsibility in modern populations (219, pp. 50-51, 54-55)?

Despite Shaw's arguments, his suggestion that the psychopath's life be extinguished seems unjustified. Execution is irrevocable; custody can be ended. New treatments may be developed, or misdiagnoses occur.

Perhaps the case described by Raymond Corsini, San Quentin psychologist, was misdiagnosed. Or perhaps, as many "prison hands" believe, a spontaneous and inexplicable transformation took place:

> The prison psychologist often sees the processes of change where the uncontrollable psychopath finally becomes mature. There is a sudden influx of insight, remorse, and conscientiousness. . . .
>
> One particular inmate, diagnosed as a psychopathic personality, explained that while engaged in a conversation with some prison associates he became suddenly aware that their conversation was distasteful. He realized in a flash of insight the consequences of his past actions and the nature of his present attitude. He backed away from the group, feeling a revulsion for them. He walked around the prison overwhelmed by the intensity of the insights he was experiencing. He literally changed overnight in his psychological make-up, becoming an earnest, seeking, conscientious, ambitious person (41, p. 112).

This spontaneous recovery seems in conflict with contemporary knowledge of psychopathy. Yet it serves to illustrate the dangers of execution. Diagnoses, like all human judgments, can be mistaken. Execution of psychopaths, because they are psychopaths, would end all possibility of correcting fallacious diagnoses or mistaken predictions.

In future years, effective treatment for psychopathic personalities may be discovered. Psychotherapy, aided perhaps by hypnoanalysis and drugs, shows promise. Further development may prove that these or other methods can cure even the most hardened cases.

Since execution precludes the possibility of better treatment, spontaneous "conversion," or correcting mistaken diagnoses, it hardly seems a just solution to society's problem. Thus, permanent custody represents the most effective and the fairest protection for society. Tragically, one hundred years of scientific research have not produced a more satisfactory answer.

Fortunately, social science has developed a more successful treatment for child psychopathy. If present knowledge were applied extensively, the delinquent child need not become the dangerous adult.

The Wiltwyck project indicates that "milieu therapy" can do much to countermand psychopathy. The aggressive drives of the psychopathic children markedly declined, their friendly acceptance of authority gained, and (most importantly) their internalized guilt significantly increased. Combined psychological therapy, sustained acceptance, and realistic punishment in the form of "consequences" changes the psychopathic child into a more socialized individual. Some of the children's personalities underwent basic transformation.

Apparently, the reorientation of child psychopaths requires a complete change in environment. Possibly, in a few cases, schools, guidance clinics, or social work could provide the prolonged therapy necessary for socializing the child. For most child psychopaths, nevertheless, curing the pervasive disorder depends on total reorientation of the environment.[12]

Unfortunately, there are few schools which approximate the Wiltwyck climate. To make deep inroads on the problem of psychopathy, the milieu therapy "idea" must be extended. Public reformatories have the physical facilities, but neither the philosophy nor the staff for accomplishing this task. Wider application of effective treatment requires an alteration in the reformatory and in the public attitude toward child psychopaths. The emphasis must be placed on "curing"—not punishing, "training," or "educating"—such children.

Effective treatment also requires money. And the public is loath to open its pocketbook. When financial troubles forced the closing of Detroit's Pioneer House, Fritz Redl justifiably exclaimed: ". . . we are still having trouble in recovering from our amazement that, in one of the richest cities in the United States with its pride and world-wide fame in the non-human aspects of en-

gineering, it would remain impossible to create adequate
treatment channels to rescue these five lives" (204, p.
315).

Milieu therapy is expensive—very expensive. The cost
of treating one boy for one year at Wiltwyck is over
$4,500. Thus, for the average length of residence, treat-
ment costs $7,000. Nevertheless, this is a small price to
pay when compared to the financial toll which the un-
cured psychopath exacts. Table 6-1, for example, is the
record—and the cost to society—of one San Quentin
psychopath.[13]

TABLE 6-1

Age	Item	Cost
6	Arrest, trial, and probation for stealing from mailboxes	$ 300
7-12	Arrests, trials, probation, and losses from many petty thefts	$1,000
14	One year's maintenance in California reform school and cost of repairs to school property	$2,400
17	Trial, psychiatric examinations, arrest for assault with intent to kill	$ 400
	One year's maintenance in mental hospital and treatment	$2,000
19	Losses, trial, and arrests for several burglaries	$2,000
	Maintenance for four months in county jail	$ 400
	One year of probation	$ 400
20	Losses from burglaries; one year's maintenance in Iowa's mental hospital	$2,000
22	Faked enrollment in Maritime Service, then Air Corps; discharged from both as unfit for service	$ 400
23	Losses from robberies and maintenance in Colorado prison for one year	$3,000
25-29	Losses from burglaries and maintenance for four years in San Quentin	$9,000
	Total:	$23,100

In less than three decades of life, this psychopath directly cost society $23,100. As the years pass, this sum
will multiply. Add estimates of the cost of police services

and of losing the man's constructive labor, and the estimate soars.

For less than one-third the financial burden, society might have changed the life of this man.

Effective treatment, assuming its availability, probably depends upon discovering the disorder early in the person's life. Identifying the child psychopath is a problem too long ignored by students of the disorder. In the last 20 years, however. Sheldon and Eleanor Glueck, Herman Mannheim, and many others have been developing predictive instruments for use with adult criminals and juvenile delinquents. Although not specifically aimed at the prediction of psychopathy, these tests should work as well, perhaps better, for psychopathic criminals. Certainly the use of such tests with psychopaths should be intensively investigated.

The Gluecks have constructed actuarial tables for adult prisoners, relating backgrounds and prison records to postincarceration behavior. They discovered that a variety of factors distinguished the convicts who later committed crimes from those who did not (89) (91) (90).

In 1944 the army used these tables with 200 prisoners in military rehabilitation centers (215). Applying the Glueck scales retrospectively, army researchers discovered that 170 of the inmates had a 60 per cent chance of failure at the time of their induction. Twenty more had a 50 per cent chance of failure.[14] If the tests had been used before induction, a majority of the delinquents would probably have been rejected.

The Glueck instruments could be of great value in the handling of adult psychopathy. If the test had, for example, been applied to Herman Duker before parole from the reformatory, he might not have been released. The test, when used retrospectively, predicted that Herman Duker had had a 95 per cent chance of total failure (261). The murder of John Anderson proved the "prediction" correct.

The correct prediction of psychopathy in children has even greater importance. The effectiveness of treatment, many studies have shown, apparently diminishes with increasing age. The Gluecks' work *Unraveling Juvenile*

Delinquency offers strong hope that the disorder can be detected early in life.

From their comparison of delinquents with nondelinquents, the Gluecks selected the social and psychological factors that most clearly demarcated the two groups. Choosing independent factors which were present early in the child's life, the Gluecks constructed three statistical tables. The tests consisted of weighted scores based on the incidence of delinquency in relation to each trait. One table drew its materials from the boys' social backgrounds; another, from psychological traits on the Rorschach test; and a third, from traits diagnosed through psychiatric interviews.

In the last few years, several studies have demonstrated the high predictive value of the social scale. Bertram J. Black and Selma J. Glick applied the test to 100 boys at the Hawthorne Cedar-Knolls School. Tracing the backgrounds of the children, the researchers assigned each boy a weighted score. They studied five factors in making the judgment: paternal discipline, maternal supervision, paternal affection, maternal affection, and family cohesiveness. The authors concluded: "It could have been determined very early in the lives of the 100 boys that they were headed for delinquent careers, in other words, that in over 90 per cent of the instances they were likely to develop into serious delinquents" (24, p. 22).

In 1952 Harvard researcher Richard E. Thompson furnished further evidence of the test's predictive value. Thompson chose 100 case studies from the Cambridge-Somerville experiment. Using the five social factors, Dr. Eleanor T. Glueck made judgments on the behavior of each boy. Since the Cambridge-Somerville experiment included a follow-up study, it provided an independent check of the Glueck scale. In 91 per cent of these cases, Dr. Glueck correctly predicted whether the boy became delinquent in later years. Moreover, as Thompson noted: "[The scale] maintained its high reliability when specifically applied to boys as young as six years. Its predictive power was maintained on boys of ethnic origin that was different from that of the series on which it had originally been constructed; on a group whose intelligence quotients were higher than those in the original group; on boys of somewhat better economic status than in the original sample . . . ; and it was just as effective when checked on boys residing in more privileged city areas" (257).

These studies have done much to confirm the value of the Glueck scales.[15] Now, for the first time, prediction is being attempted on the basis of the Gluecks' work. In New York, the Glueck tables are being applied in slum areas as children enter school. Half of the children whom the test predicts will become delinquent are receiving extensive counseling; the other half, used as a critical test of the scales' validity, are left to the usual school and community devices. The Gluecks' recent *Predicting Delinquency*, indicates that the experiment seems to be successful. Another decade, however, will be required before the validity of these particular instruments is established.

In other areas, researchers are measuring the predictive value of such instruments as the Minnesota Multiphasic Personality Inventory.[16] Interim reports indicate that these tests, too, can weed out future criminals—particularly when the tests are applied to adolescents. There appears to be reasonable hope that criminality and psychopathy can be predicted relatively early in a person's life. *If* this hope is fulfilled by future experiments, our society will be faced by a major question of policy. Should society, either through legal or private agencies, intervene in the operation of the family? How can such an intrusion take place without violating basic civil liberties? No one can answer these questions with facility and, surely, all of us would prefer to utilize voluntary methods of preventing psychopathy. Occasions may well arise, nevertheless, when families producing incipient psychopathic personalities will refuse treatment. Intervention might be advised in such cases as in a case where parents refused to quarantine their child if he suffered from measles. If the more hopeful results of the Cambridge-Somerville and Wiltwyck experiments can be trusted, such intervention would better protect society and the incipient criminal.

The implications of intervention for individual liberty

are so serious, however, that we believe such an action cannot be justified. Rather, we would advocate offering services to families in a way which would be likely to lead to their being accepted.

Closely allied with the study of prediction is the study of causation. At present, it seems logical to presume that a combination of lovelessness in childhood and a defective brain produces psychopathy. The growth of guidance clinics, social work, and early medical care may possibly aid in preventing the disorder. An effective preventive policy depends, however, on extending our knowledge of causation.

Every improvement in social policy, whether it be altering the legal structure, expanding "milieu therapy," or increasing research into various phases of the disorder, depends on changing the public attitude. The present atmosphere is supercharged with aggression. Revenge, in its most primitive form, pervades both the theory and the application of our modern instruments of social control. The criminal law and the prison often serve as legitimized outlets for society's repressed aggression.

The heinous crimes perpetrated by psychopaths call forth bitter savagery from the public.[17] After a recent murder by two psychopathic boys, a prominent newspaper columnist thundered: "From the record so far you would just have to say that these punks are plain bad, poison mean, inhuman little animals who deserve no consideration, no clemency. Society didn't make them that way, either. The rottenness must dwell within a man who kills strangers for fun when the killer himself is not insane." The columnist advocated immediate execution of the boys.

The columnist's outburst is not uncommon. In fact, most of our social and legal structure is based on vengeance. Unfortunately, vindictiveness does nothing to solve the problem. It only impedes realistic solutions. Revising the legal system and providing effective treatment of the disorder depends on altering the public's attitude. Society's protection from psychopathy requires realism, not vituperation.

The control of psychopathy obviously demands several

important changes in contemporary social policy. Some of these improvements only the trained lawyer or the social scientist can initiate. Others can be aided by every individual in his role as a citizen. All of the changes depend on the cooperation and support of the public. These seem to be the minimum requisites of an effective policy:

The criminal law must be revised in consonance with our knowledge of the causes and nature of psychopathy. Tests of criminal responsibility should be discarded in recognition of the fact that some of the most dangerous criminals would not be considered legally responsible by any plausible test.

Criminal law should abandon its emphasis on the nature of the offense and concentrate instead on the nature of the offender.

The sentencing of psychopaths should, ideally, be placed in the hands of a "treatment tribunal" which would emphasize rehabilitation rather than punishment.

Experimentation in the treatment of adult psychopathy should continue. Until an effective therapy is developed, the hardened adult psychopath should be placed under custodial care.

The use of milieu therapy for the treatment of child psychopathy should be expanded.

Research into causation, as well as treatment and prediction, must be stepped up.

The public must be weaned from its vindictive attitude and brought to one of realistic appraisal of its own best interests.

Many of these improvements are interdependent. Legal changes without effective treatment are inadequate; research discoveries, if unimplemented, do little good. Gordon Allport's observations on conquering the problem of racial and religious prejudice apply equally to psychopathy: "Since the problem is many-sided, there can be no sovereign formula. The wisest thing to do is to attack on all fronts simultaneously. If no single attack has large effect yet many small attacks from many directions can have large cumulative results" (9, p. 507).

Perhaps the most practical place to start the task would be in changing reform school practices. The decreased fantasy aggression, increased acceptance of society's standards, and newly formed consciences developed through milieu therapy indicate that we do have methods for successful treatment of child psychopathy (as well as for milder forms of delinquency). With changes in philosophy, with increased financial support, and with an improvement in personnel, many reform schools could reproduce the effectiveness of milieu therapy.

Some final words about the seriousness of the psychopathic problem: It cannot be stated too often that the disorder takes a costly toll in money, in corrective efforts, and in lives. We have already discussed, very cursorily, the financial burden of psychopathy. One psychopath in his twenties has already bled society of $23,100; his older comrade, in a full lifetime, costs probably three times that much.

How prevalent is this critical disorder? Because of the confusion over diagnosis, no one can give an accurate answer. Many estimates have, however, been made. Some scientists believe that psychopaths constitute a large proportion of all criminals. San Quentin psychologist Raymond Corsini reckoned: "Psychopaths make up the bulk of prisoners" (41, p. 112). Sheldon Glueck places the proportion lower, at around 20 per cent of all criminals (86). Ecuadorian psychiatrists found 13 per cent of Quito prison convicts were psychopathic (49). Eighteen per cent of British inmates were so diagnosed (121). United States naval officials calculated that their training centers contained 26 per cent psychopaths (50). Each year, approximately 180,000 criminals are incarcerated in American prisons. Using a conservative estimate of 10 per cent, it would seem that 18,000 of these were psychopathic.

Fewer estimates have been made of the proportion of psychopaths among juvenile delinquents. In their most recent study, Glueck and Glueck found that 7 per cent of incarcerated juvenile delinquents were psychopathic (89). In the Wiltwyck study, 14 per cent of the boys suffered from the disorder. Using the midpoint, 10 per cent, 3,000 juvenile psychopaths should be added to the 18,000 adults.

Finally, psychopaths can be found in mental hospitals

as well as in prisons. Kirson Weinberg believes that 2.6 per cent of all hospital admissions are psychopaths (266). Other scientists have found a higher incidence: Royal Naval Hospitals admissions include 5 per cent psychopathic patients (60); American army hospitals, in 1938, contained 36 per cent psychopaths (50); and Hervey Cleckly figured that psychopaths accounted for 31 per cent of the psychiatric beds in a Georgia hospital (38). Again using a conservative figure, 5 per cent, 24,000 psychopaths reside in American mental hospitals.

By adding these figures, we arrive at the estimate that over 45,000 psychopaths are in the custody of American institutions. Admittedly, this is only a reasonable guess. Since this includes no judgment on the number of psychopaths outside institutions, the true incidence is undoubtedly higher.

Such gaugings of the cost and extent of psychopathy only begin to measure the danger of the disorder. The psychopath commits twice as many crimes as the average convict, and his crimes are of the most critical nature (262). His guiltlessness creates an unusual propensity for bizarre sexual activities.[18] He often uses drugs, and more often peddles them (12). Thus his pernicious activities affect many lives, and unhappiness follows in his wake. Norman Mailer even suggests ". . . that the psychopath may indeed be the perverted and dangerous frontrunner of a new kind of personality which could become the central expression of human nature before the twentieth century is over." In his provocative essay, "The White Negro," Mailer romanticizes the psychopathic personality and identifies "hipsters" as a philosophic elite drawn from the ranks of psychopaths (161). And, too, he tends to overstress the danger of psychopathy in contemporary America; he "modestly," estimates that "there are ten million Americans who are more or less psychopathic." Nevertheless, his major point deserves consideration: he argues that the violence, the fast rate of social change, and the contradictory nature of twentieth century civilization provide fertile ground for psychopathy.

. . . the psychopath is better adapted to dominate those mutually contradictory inhibitions upon violence and love which civilization has exacted of us," he points out, "and if it be remembered that not every psychopath is an extreme case, and that the condition of psychopathy is present in a host of people including many politicians, professional soldiers, newspaper columnists, entertainers, artists, jazz musicians, call-girls, promiscuous homosexuals and half the executives of Hollywood, television, and advertising, it can be seen that there are aspects of psychopathy which already exert considerable cultural influence (161, p. 203).

There is obvious danger in the psychopath's relation to the political order. We have discussed briefly the criminal's preference for an authoritarian regime (3). In Hermann Goering's life, we have shown what can happen when a fertile political situation and a psychopathic personality concur. The malignancy of a psychopath who gains political power can hardly be overemphasized.

The American political structure is not immune. The life of political boss David Stephenson warns Americans of the danger of psychopathic demagogues.

Born in 1892, in a small Texas town, Stephenson participated in petty crimes and carried a gun as a young child. He gained a reputation for flamboyance, lying, and pleasure-seeking exhibitionism. During drinking sprees, he liked to orate in the town square.

Stephenson hated his parents. His father died when the boy was young, his life ruined by oppressive manual labor. Stephenson's mother detested her son. The antipathy between them never ceased. In later life, when Stephenson was making over $900,000 a year, he refused to send a penny to his mother—who worked as a waitress.

Stephenson married twice. At 22 he wedded the winner of an Oklahoma beauty contest. Three months later he deserted her and their unborn child. She divorced him on grounds of sadistic cruelty. Stephenson's other marriage ended also in divorce. The second wife complained of his sadistic sexual activities and his thievery from her mother.

During World War I, Stephenson served in the National Guard, but never went overseas. After the war, he bragged about fictitious war experiences. He lived from day to day, skipping from job to job.

In the early 1920's, Stephenson had a stroke of luck. A friend of his, a petty Indiana politician, hired him as an assistant in establishing a state Ku Klux Klan. Stephenson relished the work. When his friend died, Stephenson inherited the Klan leadership with its enormous power.

Within the next few years, he built an extensive machine. He extended honorary memberships to 700 Indiana clergymen. He formed the "Horse Thief Detectives" to carry out the bullying work of the organization. Hundreds of thousands of Indianians flocked to join the Klan. If they did not, the "detectives" exerted pressure.

Throughout the state, Stephenson held rallies and gave vent to his uninhibited drives. At a meeting in an open field, he flew over the people in a red airplane, painted with gold crosses. The airplane swept to a landing in the middle of the crowd. Stephenson gave a brief rabble-rousing speech and then flew back into the clouds.

Stephenson acquired a palatial house. He gave raucous parties that were attended by "the best people" in Indiana. During the parties, Stephenson had photographers weaving among the crowds. To the pictures taken by the photographers, Stephenson added faked pornographic details and used the negatives to blackmail his guests.

Stephenson's power extended over the political structure of the state. Even though reports of his graft, robberies, and strange sexual behavior persisted, Stephenson suppressed them before they reached the courts. At the height of his influence, Stephenson jokingly declared: "I'm the embodiment of Napoleon." In Indiana, at least, no one laughed at the joke.

In 1925 Stephenson kidnapped Madge Oberholtzer, a worker in the Department of Public Institutions. In his private railroad car, he raped her. Afterwards, Miss Oberholtzer tried to poison herself with bichloride of mercury. Stephenson and his chauffeur took her from the train and placed her in an automobile. For hours, the two drove the girl around. She pleaded to be taken to a doctor. Stephenson refused, and watched with curiosity as she died.

The story of her death leaked out, but Stephenson was unafraid. "My word is law," he declared. His power, however, could not stop the public uproar, and Stephenson was indicted.

No Indiana lawyers wanted to handle the case, and the courts were frightened. An honest prosecutor was finally discovered, but the state refused to pay his traveling expenses to the trial.

After his arrest, Stephenson gave way to an almost paranoid episode. The Imperial Wizard of the Klan, he believed, was persecuting him. Evidence began to pile up against Stephenson as witness after witness overcame timidity. A final piece of testimony convicted Stephenson of murder. The medical report showed that Madge Oberholtzer had died, not from the bichloride of mercury, but from an infection caused by teeth wounds on her body. Stephenson was sent to prison (274).

In 1955, at age 63, David Curtis Stephenson was paroled from prison, his power gone, his fortunes at their nadir. Stephenson ruined himself, yet he remained in power long enough to trail agony through the state.

The crimes of a Stephenson, of a Duker, of a Cook revolt society. Psychopathy, and all of its execrable consequences, has plagued every human society. Dostoyevsky's inspired portrait of Fyodor Karamazov testifies that psychopathy is not confined to modern America.

It is the part of wisdom to understand the problem of psychopathy and not to give way to emotion. We have the tools to solve the problem: we know the nature and character of the psychopath's affliction; we know how to distinguish him from other "mentally diseased" people; we know, at least rudimentarily, what causes psychopathy. And, if the Wiltwyck study is a true indication we know how to change the psychopathic child and avoid the vicious fruits of his maturity.

If society has the will, it can protect itself against this most dangerous and, at the same time, most lonely of human beings.

NOTES

1. The governor also questioned the validity of sentencing a man because of a prediction concerning his peril to society.

2. Durham vs. United States, 1954. U.S. Court of Appeals,

Wash., D.C., 214 F. 2d, 862, Federal Reporter, West Publishing Co., St. Paul, p. 864.

3. For a discussion of the complicated issue of criminal responsibility and free will, see Glueck (85).

4. Both a report made by the Royal Commission on Capital Punishment and an American report by the Committee on Forensic Psychiatry of the Group for the Advancement of Psychiatry agreed that the M'Naghten rule should be abandoned.

5. At times Durham was labeled "psychopathic," at other times, "psychotic." Almost all psychiatrists who examined him agreed, however, that he was mentally abnormal.

6. Among other errors, the lower court did not recognize that the burden of proof of Durham's sanity lay with the prosecution; incorrectly dismissed as "no evidence" all psychiatric testimony because the witness could not certify that the defendant failed the right-wrong test; and did not weigh the "whole evidence."

7. In the discussions at the American Law Institute, Manfred Guttmacher wished to add "major (mental disease)" to the criterion for irresponsibility. This addition, depending upon its interpretation, could rule out psychopathic personality.

8. A treatment tribunal would not eliminate whatever element of deterrence punishment exerts. Men would still be incarcerated and often for longer periods.

9. Beccaria's work deserves credit, for it modified the brutality of his times and controlled the favoritism of the courts. Voltaire described a typical criminal case of the century. A young man, the Chevalier de la Barre, sang some sacrilegious songs in a tavern one night. Vindictive neighbors complained. As punishment, the "criminal" had his tongue pulled out at the roots, his right hand cut off, and was burned at the stake by a slow fire.

10. Under a treatment tribunal, the rights of the criminal would be protected: statutes might roughly determine sentences, counsel and witnesses might appear at the tribunal, annual reviews of each case would be required, and an appellate tribunal would have to be established. See Glueck 227-229.

11. The Glueck proposal allows broad indeterminate sentences, set by law. Such limitations seem necessary for the protection of individuals who might otherwise be condemned for life merely because they are diagnosed as having a particular type of character.

12. The fact that the Cambridge-Somerville counseling largely failed in treating psychopaths, while Wiltwyck succeeds, supports this assertion. Such a position runs counter to the social-work theory that children should never be removed

from their parents. Apparently, with psychopathic children, a separation is advisable.

13. Estimates of the cost of arrests, trials, and incarceration are taken from the *World Almanac*'s average figures for 1954. Estimates of cost of losses are taken from the convict's records.

14. The army designated 130 of the inmates as "psychopathic personalities." Of these, 88 per cent received highly delinquent predictive scores on the Glueck scales.

15. D. Tiedman has noted that the Glueck scales were constructed on the basis of a population in which there were 50 per cent delinquents. In normal areas, with other proportions of delinquents, Dr. Tiedman believes that the scales will not accurately differentiate the nondelinquents.

16. For a discussion of current predictive devices, see Ohlin (184). Also see Elio Monachesi: Prediction of Criminal Behavior, in Vernon Branham and Samuel Kutash: *Encyclopedia of Criminology*, New York, Philosophical Library, 1949.

17. *The Authoritarian Personality* research has demonstrated that, ironically, criminals themselves are the most intemperate in their condemnation of crime, advocacy of stern punishment, and acceptance of conventional moral values.

18. The term "sexual psychopath" has gained wide currency in recent years. Many social scientists have pointed out that the label is a misnomer. Most sexual deviants are not psychopaths. The true psychopath, while sexually uninhibited, is not the sex "maniac."

"Sexual psychopath" laws have been enacted which permit the permanent imprisonment of offenders. Edwin Sutherland suggested that these laws are unnecessary: the sexual offender usually does not repeat his crime; imprisonment does not cure him; and the states which have instituted the laws have not witnessed a drop in sexual crimes. See Edwin Sutherland: "Sexual Psychopath Laws." *Journal of Criminal, Criminology, and Police Science*, 40:545-554, 1950.

Bibliography

1. ABRAHAMS, JOSEPH, AND McCORKLE, LLOYD. "Group Psychotherapy at an Army Rehabilitation Center." *Diseases Of The Nervous System*, 8:50-62, 1947

2. ADATTO, CARL. "Observations on Criminal Patients During Narco-analysis." *Archives of Neurology and Psychiatry*, 62:82-92, 1949

3. ADORNO, T. W., AND OTHERS. *The Authoritarian Personality*. New York, Harper, 1950

4. AICHHORN, AUGUST. *Wayward Youth*, New York, Viking, 1935

5. ALDINGTON, RICHARD. *Lawrence of Arabia, A Biographical Enquiry*. London, Collins, 1955

6. ALEXANDER, FRANZ. "The Neurotic Character." *International Journal of Psychoanalysis*, 11:292-313, 1930

7. ALLPORT, G. W. *Basic Considerations for a Psychology of Personality*. New Haven, Yale University Press, 1955

8. ALLPORT, GORDON. *Becoming*. New Haven, Yale University Press, 1955

9. ALLPORT, GORDON. *The Nature Of Prejudice*. Cambridge, Addison-Wesley, 1954

10. ALMANSI, J. AND IMPASTATE, DAVID. "The Use of Electroshock Therapy in Correctional Institutions." *Handbook of Correctional Psychology* (ed.: Lindner, R. and Seliger, R.). New York, Philosophical Library, 1947

11. ALPERS, B. Hypothalamic Destruction. *Psychosomatic Medicine* 2:286, 1944

12. AUSUBEL, DAVID P. "The Psychopathology and Treatment of Drug Addiction in Relation to the Mental Hygiene Movement," *Psychiatric Quarterly Supplement*, 22:219-250, 1948

13. BALDWIN, A. L., KALHORN, J., AND BREESE, F. H. Patterns of Parental Behavior. *Psychological Monographs*, No. 3, 1945

14. BANAY, R. S. AND DAVIDOFF, L. "Apparent Recovery of a Sex Psychopath After Lobotomy." *Journal of Criminal Psychopathology* 4:59-66, 1942

15. BANDURA, ALBERT AND WALTERS, RICHARD. *Adolescent Aggression*. Row Peterson, Chicago, 1959

16. BECCARIA, C. *An Essay on Crimes and Punishments*. London, F. Newburry, 1770

17. BENDER, LAURETTA. "Post-encephalitic Behavior Disorders in Childhood." In NEAL, JOSEPHINE B.: *Encephalitis.* New York, Grune & Stratton, 1942

18. BENDER, LAURETTA. Psychopathic Behavior Disorders in Children. *Handbook of Correctional Psychology* (ed.: Lindner, R. and Seliger, R.). New York, Philosophical Library, 1947, pp. 360-377

19. BENDER, LAURETTA, AND COTTINGTON, FRANCES. "The Use of Amphetamine Sulphate (Benzedrine) in Child Psychiatry." *American Journal of Psychiatry*, 99:116-121, 1942

20. BERLIT, B. "Statistical Study of Hereditary Taint in a Selected Group: Siblings and Parents of 362 Officers and Inmates of a Hospital in Saxony." *A. Ges. Neurol. Psychiat.*, 52, 1935

21. BETTELHEIM, BRUNO. *Love is Not Enough.* Glencoe, Free Press, 1950

22. BETTELHEIM, BRUNO. Somatic Symptoms in Superego Formation. *American Journal of Orthopsychiatry*, 18:649-658, 1948

23. BIRNBAUM, KARL. The Psychopathic Criminal. *Journal of Nervous and Mental Disease*, 2:543-553, 1917

24. BLACK, BERTHAM J. AND GLICK, SELMA J. *Recidivism at the Hawthorne-Cedar-Knolls School.* Research Monograph No. 2, Jewish Board of Guardians, New York, 1952

25. BOWLBY, JOHN. *Maternal Care and Mental Health*, Geneva, World Health Organization, 1952

26. BOWLBY, JOHN, AINSWORTH, M., BOSTON, M., AND ROSENBLUTH, D. "The effects of Mother Child Separation, A follow-up Study," *British Journal of Medical Psychology*, 1956, vol. 29

27. BOWLUS, D. E., AND SHOTWELL, ANNA. "A Rorschach Study of Psychopathic Delinquents." *American Journal of Mental Deficiency* 52:23-30, 1947

28. BRADLEY, G. "E.E.G. Patterns of Children With Behavior Disorders." *Connecticut State Medical Journal*, 6:773-777, 1942

29. BRILL, N. K. AND WALKER, E. F.: "Psychopathic Behavior With Latent Epilepsy." *Journal of Nervous and Mental Disease*, 101:537-549, 1945

30. BROMBERG, WALTER. "Dynamic Aspects of Psychopathic Personality." *Psychoanalytic Quarterly*, 17:58-70, 1948

31. BROWN, CLAUDE. "Harlem, My Harlem," *Dissent*, Vol. VIII, Summer, 1961, No. 3

32. BURGUM, MILDRED. "Constructive Values Associated With Rejection." *American Journal of Orthopsychiatry*, 10:319, 1940

33. CALDWELL, J. M. "The Constitutional Psychopathic State: I. Studies of Soldiers in the U. S. Army." *Journal of Criminal Psychopathology*, 3:171-179, 1941

34. CAMERON, NORMAN. "Paranoid Conditions and Paranoid States," *American Handbook of Psychiatry*, edited by Silvano Arieti, 1959, Basic Books, New York

35. CARDOZA, B. *What Medicine Can Do For The Law.* New York, Harper, 1930

36. CASON, H. AND PESCOR, M. J. "A Statistical Study of 500 Psychopathic Prisoners." *Public Health Reports*, 61:557-574, 1946

37. CHORNYAK, J. "Some Remarks on the Diagnosis of the Psychopathic Delinquent." *American Journal of Psychiatry*, 97:1327-1331, 1941

38. CLECKLY, HERVEY. *The Mask of Sanity.* St. Louis, C. V. Mosley, 1941

39. CLECKLEY, HERVEY. "Psychopathic States," *American Handbook of Psychiatry* (ed.: Arieti, Silvano). New York, Basic Books, 1959

40. CLECKLY, HERVEY. "The Psychopath Viewed Practically." In LINDNER, ROBERT AND SELIGER, R. V.: *Handbook of Correctional Psychology.* New York, Philosophical Library, 1947

41. CORSINI, RAYMOND. "Criminal Psychology": In BRANHAM, VERNON AND KUTASH, SAMUEL: *Encyclopedia of Criminology.* New York, Philosophical Library, 1949

42. CORSINI, RAYMOND J. "Psychodrama with a Psychopath." *Group Psychotherapy*, 1958, 11, 33-39

43. CORSINI, RAYMOND. "The Method of Psycho-drama in Prison." *Group Psycho-therapy*, 3:321-326, 1951

44. CRAFT, M. J. *Mental Disorder in the Defective, Mental Health*, 17:95-99, 1958

45. CRAFT, M. J. "Personality Disorder and Dullness." *Lancet*, 1959, Vol. 1

46. CRAFT, M. J. "Psychopathic Personalities: A Review of Diagnosis, Aetiology, Prognosis, and Treatment." *The British Journal of Criminology*, January, 1961, Vol. 1, No. 3

47. CRAWFORD, PAUL L. "The Relative Sensitivity of the LAIS, WAIS, and Porteus Maze in Differentiating Between Psychopathic and Psychotic Patients in a Mental Hospital." *Psychological Service Center Journal*, 11:93-97, 1959

48. CRUVANT, A., AND YOCHELSON, LEON. "The Psychiatrist and the Psychotic Psychopath; A Study in Interpersonal Relations." *American Journal of Psychiatry*, 106:498-594, 1950

49. CRUZ, J. "Estudio de Las Personalidades Psyicopaticas en

Nuestra Criminalidad." *Arch. Crim. Neuropsiquiatry*, 3:38-50, 1939

50. CURRAN, D. AND MALLINSON, P. "Psychopathic Personality." *Journal of Mental Science*, 90:266-286, 1944

51. CUTTS, K. K. AND JASPER, H. H.: "Effects of Benzedrine Sulphate and Phenobarbital on Behavior Problem Children with Abnormal E.E.G.'s." *Archives of Neurology and Psychiatry*, 41:1138-1145, 1939

52. DARLING, H. F. "Definition of Psychopathic Personality." *Journal of Nervous and Mental Disease*, 101:121-126, 1945

53. DARLING, H. F. "Shock Treatment in Psychopathic Personality." *Journal of Nervous and Mental Disease*, 101:247-250, 1945

54. DARLING, H. F. AND SANDALL, J. W. "Treatment of the Psychopath." *Journal of Clinical and Experimental Psychopathology*, 13(3), 1953 (Sept.)

55. DAVIDOFF, E. AND GOODSTONE, G. L. "Amphetamine-Barbituate Therapy in Psychiatric Conditions." *Psychiatric Quarterly*, 16:541-548, 1942

56. DAVIS, K. "Extreme Social Isolation of a Child." *American Journal of Sociology*, 45:554-565, 1940

57. DESMOND, THOMAS C. "Youth Correction Authority Plan." *Encyclopedia of Criminology* (ed.: Branham, Vernon and Kutash, Samuel). New York, Philosophical Library, 1949

58. DOLLARD, J., DOOB, L., MILLER, N. E., MOWRER, O. H., AND SEARS, R. R. *Frustration and Aggression*. New Haven, Yale University Press, 1939

59. DUBOIS, C. *The People of Alor*. University of Minnesota Press, 1944.

60. EAST, W. N. "Psychopathic Personality and Crime." *Journal of Mental Science*, 91:426-466, 1945

61. EATON, JOSEPH AND WEIL, R. J. *Culture and Mental Disorders*, Free Press, Glencoe, Ill. 1955

62. EHRLICH, S. K. AND KEOGH, R. P. "The Psychopath in a Mental Institution," *A.M.A. Archives of Neurology and Psychiatry*, 76:286-295, 1956

63. EISNER, E. A. "Relationships Formed by a Sexually Delinquent Adolescent Girl." *American Journal of Orthopsychiatry*, 15:301-308, 1945

64. ELLINGSON, R. J. "Incidence of E.E.G. Abnormality Among Patients with Mental Disorders of Apparently Non-Organic Origin," *American Journal of Psychiatry*, 1954, Vol. III, pages 263-275

65. ESSEN-MOLLER, E. "Individual Traits and Morbidity in a Swedish Rural Population," *Acta Psychiat. et. Neurol.*, 1956, Scand. Supp. 100

66. FALCONER, M. A. AND SCHURR, P. "Surgical Treatment of Mental Illness," *Recent Progress in Psychiatry*, Vol. 3, New York, Grove Press, 1959

67. FENTON, N., *An Introduction to Group Counseling*, 1957, Department of Corrections, State of California, Sacramento

68. FIELD, MINNA. "Maternal Attitudes Found in 25 Cases of Children with Primary Behavior Disorder." *American Journal of Orthopsychiatry*, 10:293-311, 1940

69. FRANKENSTEIN, CARL. *Psychopathy: a Comparative Analysis of Clinical Pictures*. Grune and Stratton, New York, 1959

70. FREEMAN, WALTER, AND WATTS, JAMES W. "Prefrontal Lobotomy: the Problem of Schizophrenia." *The American Journal of Psychiatry*, 101:739-748, 1945

71. FREUD, A. AND BURLINGHAM, D. *Infants Without Families*. New York, International Universities Press, 1944

72. FREYHAN, F. A. Psychopathology of Personality Functions in Psychopathic Personalities. *Psychiatric Quarterly*, 25:458-471, 1951

73. FRIEDLANDER, K. *The Psychoanalytic Approach to Juvenile Delinquency*. London; Kegan, Paul, Trench, Tribner, 1947

74. FULTON, J. F. AND INGRAHAM, F. D. "Emotional Disturbances Following Experimental Lesions of the Base of the Brain." *Journal of Physiology*, 90:353, 1929

75. GAUDET, FREDERICK J. "Sentencing Behavior of Judges." In VERNON BRANHAM AND SAMUEL KUTASH: *Encyclopedia of Criminology* New York, Philosophical Library, 1949

76. GERSTEN, CHARLES. "Group Therapy with Institutionalized Delinquents." *Journal of Genetic Psychology*, 80:35-64, 1952

77. GIBBS, E. L. AND LENNOX, W. G. "Classification of Epileptic Patients and Control Subjects." *Archives of Neurology and Psychiatry*, 50:111, 1943

78. GIBBENS, T. C. N. "Recent Trends in the Management of Psychopathic Offenders." *British Journal of Delinquency*, 2:103-116, 1951

79. GIBBENS, T. C. N., POND, D. A., STAFFORD-CLARK, D. "A Follow-up Study of Criminal Psychopaths." *British Journal of Delinquency* V. 6, 1955

80. GILBERT, G. M. "Hermann Goering: Amiable Psychopath." *Journal of Abnormal and Social Psychology*, 43:211, 1948

81. GLASER, EDWARD AND CHILES, DANIEL. "An Experiment in the Treatment of Youthful Habitual Offenders at the

Federal Reformatory, Chillicothe." *Journal of Clinical Psychopathology*, July, 1948, 376-425

82. GLUECK, BERNARD. A Study of 608 Admissions to Sing Sing Prison. *Mental Hygiene*, Vol. II, 1918, 85-151.

83. GLUECK, BERNARD JR. "Changing Concepts in Forensic Psychiatry." *Journal of Criminal Law, Criminology, and Police Science*, 45:125 (No. 7), 1954

84. GLUECK, BERNARD JR. "Psychodynamic Factors in the Sex Offender." *Psychiatric Quarterly*, 28:1-21, 1954

85. GLUECK, SHELDON. *Crime and Justice*. Cambridge, Harvard University Press, 1945, p. 99.

86. GLUECK, SHELDON. Introduction to ROBERT LINDNER: *Rebel Without A Cause*. New York, Grune and Stratton, 1944.

87. GLUECK, SHELDON. *Mental Disorder and the Criminal Law*. Boston, Little, Brown, 1927, 13

88. GLUECK, SHELDON. "Principles of a Rational Penal Code." *Harvard Law Review*, 41:453-482, 1928

89. GLUECK, SHELDON AND ELEANOR. *500 Criminal Careers*. New York, Knopf, 1930

90. GLUECK, SHELDON AND ELEANOR. *After-Conduct of Discharged Offenders*. London, Macmillan, 1945

91. GLUECK, SHELDON AND ELEANOR. *Criminal Careers in Retrospect*. New York, The Commonwealth Fund, 1943

92. GLUECK, SHELDON AND ELEANOR. *Unraveling Juvenile Delinquency*, Cambridge, Commonwealth Fund, 1950

93. GLUECK, SHELDON AND ELEANOR. *Physique and Delinquency*, Harpers, New York, 1956

94. GOLDFARB, W. "Psychological Privation in Infancy and Subsequent Adjustment." *American Journal of Orthopsychiatry*, 15:247-255, 1945

95. GOTTLIEB, J. S., ASHLEY, M. C., AND KNOTT, J. R. Primary Behavior Disorders and the Psychopathic Personality. *Archives of Neurology and Psychiatry*, 56:381-400, 1946

96. GOULDS, G. A. "Attitudes Toward Self and Others of Psychopaths," *Journal of Individual Psychology*, 16, 1960

97. GOUGH, H. G. "A Sociological Theory of Psychopathy." *American Journal of Sociology*. 53:359-366, 1948

98. GOUSTER, MONTZ. Moral Insanity. *Revue Des Sciences Medical*, 5:181-182, 1878. Abstracted in *Journal of Nervous and Mental Disease*

99. GRANT, J. D. AND GRANT, M. Q. "A Group Dynamics Approach To The Treatment of Non-conformists in the Navy," *American Academy of Political and Social Science*, 322:126-135, 1959

100. GREEN, EUGENE, SILVERMAN, DANIEL, AND GEIL,

GEORGE. "Petit Mal Electro-Shock Therapy of Criminal Psychopaths." *Journal of Criminal Psychopathology*, 5(4):667-695, 1944

101. GREENACRE, PHYLLIS. "Problems of Patient-Therapist Relationship in the Treatment of Psychopaths." ROBERT LINDNER AND R. V. SELIGER, Eds.: *Handbook of Correctional Psychology*. New York, Philosophical Library, 1947

102. GREENACRE, PHYLLIS. "Conscience in the Psychopath." *American Journal of Orthopsychiatry*, 15:495-509, 1945

103. GREENBLATT, MILTON. "Electro-encephalographic Studies of Homicidal Psychopaths." In P. SOROKIN: *Eplorations in Love And Altruistic Behavior*. Boston, Beacon Press, 1950

104. GURVITZ, MILTON. "Developments in the Concepts of Psychopathic Personality." *British Journal of Delinquency*, 2:88-102, 1951

105. GURVITZ, MILTON. "Intelligence Factor in Psychopathic Personality." *Journal of Clinical Psychology*, 3:194-196, 1947

106. HALL, JEROME. *Studies in Jurisprudence and Criminal Theory*. New York, 1958; American Law" Institute's Tentative Draft, No. 4

107. HALLER, B. L. "Some Factors Related To The Adjustment of Psychopaths on Parole from a State Hospital." *Smith College Studies of Social Work*, Vol. 13, 1942

108. *Handbook of Mental Disorders*, Boston, 1952

109. HEAVER, W. L. "A Study of 40 Male Psychopathic Personalities: Before, During, and After Hospitalization." *American Journal of Psychiatry*, 100:342-346, 1943

110. HEINICKE, C. *Some Antecedents and Correlations of Guilt and Fear in Young Boys*. Harvard University Ph.D. Dissertation, June, 1953

111. HENDERSON, DAVID. *Psychopathic States*. New York, W. W. Norton, 1939

112. HEUSER, K. D. "The Psychopathic Personality: Rorschach Patterns of 28 Cases." *American Journal of Psychiatry*, 103: 105-112, 1946

113. HILL, DENNIS. "Amphetamine in Psychopathic States." *British Journal of Addiction*, 44:50-54, 1947

114. HILL, DENNIS. "E.E.G. in Episodic Psychotic and Psychopathic Behavior," *E.E.G. Clinical Neurophysiology*, 4:419-442, 1952

115. HILL, D., POND, D. A., MITCHELL, W., AND FALCONER, M. A., "Personality Changes Following Temporal Lobectomy for Epilepsy." *Journal of Mental Science*, 183:18-27, 1957

116. HILL, D. AND WATTERSON, D. "Electro-encephalographic

Studies of the Psychopathic Personality." *Journal of Neurology and Psychiatry*, 5:47-64, 1942

117. HOLLINGSHEAD, AUGUST AND REDLICH, FRITZ, *Social Class and Mental Illness*, John Wiley, New York, 1958

118. HOLZBERG, JULES D., AND HAHN, FRED. "The Picture-Frustration Technique as a Measure of Hostility and Guilt Reactions in Adolescent Psychopaths." *American Journal of Orthopsychiatry*, 22:776-797, 1952

119. HOOTEN, ERNST. *Crime and the Man*. Cambridge, Harvard University Press, 1939

120. HUNT, J. M. *Personality and the Behavior Disorders*, Vol. II, Ronald Press, 1944.

121. HYLAND, H. H. AND RICHARDSON, J. C. "Psychoneuroses in the Canadian Army Overseas." *Canadian Medical Association Journal*, 47:432-442, 1942

122. JENKINS, RICHARD. "Review of Psychopathy and Delinquency," *American Journal of Orthopsychiatry*, 1957

123. JENKINS, RICHARD L. "The Psychopathic or Antisocial Personality," *The Journal of Nervous and Mental Disease*, 131:318-334, 1960. JENKINS, R. L. AND HEWITT, L. "Types of Personality Structure in Child Guidance Clinics," *American Journal of Orthopsychiatry*, 14:84-94, 1944

124. JENKINS, R. L., AND GLICKMAN, S. "Common Syndromes in Child Psychiatry." *American Journal of Orthopsychiatry*, 16:244-261, 1946

125. JOHNSON, A. M. AND SZUREK, S. A. "The Genesis of Anti-Social Acting-out in Children and Adults." *Psychoanalytic Quarterly*, 21:323-343, 1952

126. JONES, MAXWELL. *Social Psychiatry*. London, Tavistock, 1952

127. JONES, MAXWELL. "The Concept of the Therapeutic Community." *American Journal of Psychiatry*, 112:647-650, 1956

128. KAHN, EUGENE. *Psychopathic Personalities*. New Haven, Yale University Press, 1931

129. KALLMAN, FRANZ J. *The Genetics of Schizophrenia*. New York, J. J. Augustin, 1939

130. KARPMAN, BENJAMIN. "Autobiography of a Bandit." *Journal of Criminal Law, Criminology and Police Science*, 3:305-332, 1946

131. KARPMAN, B. "On the Need of Separating Psychopathy into Two Distinct Clinical Types: the Symptomatic and the Idiopathic." *Journal of Criminal Psychopathology*, 3:137, 1941

132. KARPMAN, B. "Psychopathy in the Scheme of Human Typology." *Journal of Nervous and Mental Disease*, 103:276-288, 1946

133. KARPMAN, B. "Seven Psychopaths: A Correlative, Non-Statistical Study of Predatory Crime." *Journal of Clinical Psychopathology and Psychotherapy*, 6:299, 1944

134. KARPMAN, B. "The Sexual Psychopath." *Journal of Criminal Law, Criminology, and Police Science*, 42:184-198, 1951

135. KAVKA, JEROME. "Pinel's Conception of the Psychopathic State: an Historical Critique," *Bulletin of the History of Medicine*, 23:461-468, 1949

136. KENNEDY, A. "Psychopathic Personality and Social Responsibility," *Journal of Mental Science*, 1954, Vol. 100: p. 873

137. KINBERG, OLOF. On the Concept of "Psychopathy" and the Treatment of So-called "Psychopaths." *Theoria*, 12:169-180, 1946

138. KNIGHT, ELIZABETH M. "A Descriptive Comparison of Markedly Aggressive and Submissive Children." *Smith College Studies in Social Work*, Vol. 4, 1933

139. KOREY, S. R. "The Effects of Benzedrine Sulfate on the Behavior of Psychopathic and Neurotic Juvenile Delinquents." *Psychiatric Quarterly*, 18:127-137, 1944

140. KUTASH, S. B. "Performance of Psychopathic Defective Criminals on the T.A.T." *Journal of Criminal Psychopathology*, 5:319-340, 1943

141. LANGE-EICHBAUM, W. *Genie, Irrsinn, und Ruhm*, Muenchen, E. Reinhardt, 1956

142. LANGE, JOHANNES. *Crime and Destiny*, New York, C. Boni, 1930

143. LASSNER, RUDOLPH. "Psycho-Drama in Prison." *Group Psychotherapy*, 3:77-91, 1950

144. LEONARDO, R. A. "Criminal Psychopaths and the Electroencephalogram." *Medical World*, 56:101-104, 1947

145. LEWIS, HILDA. *Deprived Children*, Oxford, London, 1954

146. LEVY, DAVID. *Maternal Overprotection*. New York, Columbia Press, 1943

147. LEVY, DAVID. "Primary Affect Hunger." *American Journal of Psychiatry*, 94:643-652, 1937

148. LEVY, SOL. "Personality Factors in a State Prison." *Journal of Clinical and Experimental Psychopathology*, Jan.-Feb., 1952

149. LIEBERMAN, D. AND SIEGEL, B. A. "A Program for Sexual Psychopaths in a State Mental Hospital," *American Journal of Psychiatry*, 113:801-807, 1957

150. LINDNER, ROBERT. "Experimental Studies in Constitutional Psychopathic Inferiority." Part I, *Journal of Criminal Psychopathology*, 3:252-276, 1943. Part II, *Journal of Criminal Psychopathology*, 4:484-500, 1943

151. LINDNER, ROBERT. "Psychopathy as a Psychological Problem." *Encyclopedia of Psychology*. New York, Philosophical Library, 1948

152. LINDNER, ROBERT. "Psychopathic Personality and the Concept of Homeostasis." *Journal of Clinical Psychopathology and Psychotherapy*, 6:511, 1945

153. LINDNER, ROBERT. *Rebel Without a Cause—The Hypnoanalysis of a Criminal Psychopath*. New York, Grune & Stratton, 1944

154. LINDNER, ROBERT. "Therapy." In BRANHAM, V. C. AND KUTASH, S. B. *Encyclopedia of Criminology*, New York, Philosophical Library 1949

155. LINDNER, ROBERT. "The Rorschach Test and the Diagnosis of Psychopathic Personality." *Journal of Criminal Psychopathology*, 5:69-93, 1943

156. LINDSLEY, D. B., AND HENRY, C. E. "The Effect of Drugs on Behavior and the E.E.G. of Children with Behavior Disorders." *Psychosomatic Medicine*. 4:140-149, 1943

157. LIPPMAN, HYMAN. "Difficulties Encountered in the Psychiatric Treatment of Chronic Juvenile Delinquents." In Eissler, K. R. *Searchlights on Delinquency*. New York, International Universities Press, 1949

158. LIPTON, HARRY. "The Psychopath." *Journal of Criminal Law, Criminology, and Police Science*. 40:584-596, 1952

159. LOWRY, L. G. "Personality Distortion and Early Institutional Care." *American Journal of Orthopsychiatry*, 10:576-586, 1940

160. MACKWOOD, J. C. "Remedial Education Psychotherapy During Penal Detention," *The Roots of Crime* by EAST, NORWOOD, Butterworths, London, 1954

161. MAILER, NORMAN. "The White Negro," *Voices of Dissent*, Grove Press, Inc., New York, 1958

162. MARTIN, JOHN BARTLOW. *Break Down the Walls*, New York, Ballantine Books, 1951

163. MASLOW, A. H. *Motivation and Personality*, New York, Harper, 1954

164. MASON, I. "An Index of the Severity of Criminalism or Psychopathy," U. S. Army Medical Dept. *Bulletin*, 75:110-114, 1944

165. MAUGHS, S. B. "A Concept of Psychopathy." *Journal of Criminal Psychopathology*, 2:329-356, 465-499, 1941

166. McCANN, WILLIS H. "The Psychopath and the Psychoneurotic in Relation to Crime and Delinquency." *Journal of Clinical and Experimental Psychopathology*, 9:551, 1948

167. McCORD, WILLIAM AND JOAN; AND THURBER, EMILY.

"Some Effects of Paternal Absence on Male Children." *Journal of Abnormal and Social Psychology*, 64:361-369, 1962

168. McCORD, WILLIAM AND JOAN. *Psychopathy and Delinquency*, 1956, Grune and Stratton, New York

169. McCORD, WILLIAM AND JOAN. "Two Approaches to the Cure of Delinquents." *Journal of Criminal Law, Criminology, and Police Science*, 44:442-467, 1953

170. McCORD, WILLIAM AND JOAN AND GUDEMAN, JON. *Origins of Alcoholism*, Stanford University Press, Stanford, 1960

171. McCORD, WILLIAM: PORTA, JUDITH, AND McCORD, JOAN. "The Familial Genesis of Psychoses." *Psychiatry*, 25:60-71, 1962

172. McCORD, WILLIAM AND JOAN, AND VERDEN, PAUL. "Sexual Deviance Among Lower-Class Adolescents," *International Journal of Social Psychiatry*, 8:165-179, 1962

173. McCORD, WILLIAM AND JOAN; AND ZOLA, IRVING. *Origins of Crime*, New York, Columbia University Press, 1959. McCORD, WILLIAM AND JOAN "A Follow-up Report on the Cambridge-Somerville Youth Study," *The Annals of the American Academy of Political and Social Science*, 322:89-96, 1959

174. "Mental Deficiency Committee of Royal Medico-Psychological Association Report." *Journal of Mental Science*, 82,247-257, (May, 1937)

175. MICHAELS, J. J. *Disorders of Character*, Springfield, C. C. Thomas, 1955

176. MOHR, PETER. "Die Forensische Bedeutung der Psychopathen." *Schweiz Arch. Neurol Psychiat.* 60:244-268, 1947

177. NAEGELSBACH, H. "Zur Graphollgischen Beurteilung Psychopathischer Talle." *Z. Angew. Psychol.*, 49:258-269, 1935

178. NELSON, J. L. AND ZIMMERMAN, J. "Psychopathic States with Psychotic Reactions." *Psychiatric Quarterly*, 14:49-60, 1940

179. NEWELL, H. W., "The Psycho-dynamics of Maternal Rejection," *American Journal of Orthopsychiatry*, 4:387-401, 1934. NEWELL, H. W., "A Further Study of Maternal Rejection," *American Journal of Orthopsychiatry*, 6:576-589, 1936

180. NEWKIRK, P. R. "Psychopathic Traits are Inheritable." *Diseases of the Nervous System*, 18, 52-54, 1957

181. NEWMAN, H. H., FREEMAN, F. N., AND HOLZINGER, K. J. *Twins: A Study of Heredity and Environment*, Chicago University Press, Chicago, 1937

182. NILSON, LENNART. "Frontal Lobotomy in Sweden." *Nurs. Times*, London, 45:447-451, 1949

183. O'DONNEL, L. P. "The Problems of Treating Psychopaths." *Psychiatric Quarterly*, 14:248-254,1940

184. OHLIN, L. E. *Selection for Parole*. New York, Russell Sage Foundation, 1951

185. ORDRONAUX, JOHN. "Moral Insanity." *American Journal of Insanity*, 29:313, 1873. Abstracted in *Journal of Mental Science*, 20:145, 1874

186. OSTROW, M., AND OSTROW, M. "Bilaterally Synchronous Paroxysmal Slow Activity in the Encephalograms of Non-Epileptics." *Journal of Nervous and Mental Disease*, 103:346-358, 1946

187. PALMER, H. *Psychopathic Personalities*. London, Peter Owen, 1958

188. PALMER, HAROLD. *Psychopathic Personalities*. Philosophical Library, New York, 1957

189. PAPANEK, ERNST. "Training School-Program and Leadership." *Federal Probation*, June, 1953

190. PARTRIDGE, G. E. "A Study of 50 Cases of Psychopathic Personality." *American Journal of Psychiatry*, 7:953-973, 1928

191. PARTRIDGE, G. E. "Current Conceptions of Psychopathic Personality." *American Journal of Psychiatry*, 10:54, 1930

192. PICHOT, P. "Le Questionnaire PNP." *Revue Psychologique Applique*, 8:199-219, 1958

193. PLOWITZ, PAUL. "Psychiatric Service and Group Therapy in the Rehabilitation of Offenders." *Journal of Correctional Education*, 2:78-80, 1950

194. POUND, ROSCOE. Introduction to F. B. Sayre: *Cases on Criminal Law*, Rochester, N. Y., The Lawyers Cooperative Publishing Co., 1927

195. POWERS, EDWIN, AND WITMER, HELEN. *An Experiment in the Prevention of Delinquency*, New York, Columbia Press, 1951

196. POWDERMAKER, FLORENCE: LEVIS, H. T., AND TOURAINE, G. "Psychopathology and Treatment of Delinquent Girls." *American Journal of Orthopsychiatry*, 7:61, 1937

197. PRITCHARD, JAMES C. *A Treatise on Insanity*. Philadelphia, Haswell, Barrington and Haswell, 1835

198. PRITCHARD, R., AND ROSENZWEIG, S. "The Effect of War Stress Upon Childhood and Youth." *Journal of Abnormal and Social Psychology*, 37:329-344, 1942

199. PUNTIGAM, F. "Verursacht die Encephalitis post Vaccinationen bei Jugendlichen kriminogene Personlichkeitsveranderungen?" *Ost. Ztchr. Kinderheilk. Kinderfursorge*, 1950, 4, p142-159

200. RABINOVITCH, RALPH. "A Differential Study of Psychopathic Behavior in Infants and Children. Round Table," *American Journal of Orthopsychiatry*, 21:231-237, 1951,

201. RABINOVITCH, RALPH. "Psychopathic Delinquent Children-1949 Round Table." *American Journal of Orthopsychiatry*, 20:233-265, 1950

202. RABINOVITCH, R. D. "Round Table on Psychopathic Behavior in Children." *American Journal of Orthopsychiatry*, 22:223-267, 1952

203. RAY, ISAAC. *Medical Jurisprudence of Insanity*. Boston, Little, Brown, 1838

204. REDL, FRITZ AND WINEMAN, DAVID. *Controls From Within*. Glencoe, Free Press, 1954

205. REINHARDT, JAMES MELVIN. *The Murderous Trail of Charles Starkweather*, Thomas, Springfield, Ill., 1960

206. ROBIN, A. A. "A Controlled Study of the Effects of Leucotomy." *Journal of Neurology, Neurosurgery, and Psychiatry*, 21:51-57, 1958

207. RODGERS, TERRY. "Hypnotherapy and Character Neuroses." *Journal of Clinical Psychopathology*, 8:519-524, 1947

208. RODGERS, T. "A Dynamic Study of the So-called Psychopathic Personality." *Journal of Nervous and Mental Disease*, 107:43-54, 1948

209. ROSANOFF, A. J. "The Etiology of Child Behavior Difficulties." *Psychiatric Monographs*, 1, 1943

210. ROSEN, ALBERT. "Differentiation of Diagnosis Groups by Individual MMPI Scales." *Journal of Consulting Psychology*, 1958, 22, 453-457.

211. ROSOW, H. M. "Some Observations on Groups Therapy with Prison Inmates," *Archives of Criminal Psychodynamics*, 1955, Vol. 1

212. SCHACTEL, A. H. AND LEVI, M. B. "Character Structure of Day Nursery Children as Seen Through the Rorschach." *American Journal of Orthopsychiatry*, 15:213-222, 1945

213. SCHMIDEBERG, MELITTA. "The Analytic Treatment of Major Criminals: Therapeutic Results and Technical Problems. Psychology and Treatment of Criminal Psychopaths." *International Journal of Psychoanalysis*, 30:197 abstract, 1949

214. SCHMIDEBERG, MELITTA IN EISSLER, K. R. *Searchlights on Delinquency*. New York, International Universities Press, 1949

215. SCHNEIDER, ALEXANDER J. N., LA GRONE, CYRUS W., GLUECK, S., GLUECK, E. "Prediction of Behavior of Civilian Delinquents in the Armed Forces." *Mental Hygiene*, 28:456-475, 1944

216. SCHNEIDER, K. *Psychopathic Personalities*. London, Cassell, 1958

217. SEARS, R., MACCOBY, E., AND LEVIN, H. *Patterns in Child Rearing*. Evanston, Row, Peterson, 1956

218. SESSIONS-HODGES, R. "The Impulsive Psychopath: A Clinical and Electro-physiological Study." *Journal of Mental Science*, 91:476-482, 1945

219. SHAW, GEORGE BERNARD. *The Crime of Imprisonment*. New York, Philosophical Library, 1946

220. SHELDON, WILLIAM H. *Varieties of Delinquent Youth*. New York, Harper, 1949

221. SHERMAN, LEWIS J. "Retention in Psychopathic, Neurotic, and Normal Subjects." *Journal of Personality*, 25:721-729, 1957

222. SHERMAN, M., AND HENRY, T. R. *The Hollow Folk*. New York, Thomas Y. Crowell, 1933

223. SHOTWELL, A. M. "A Study of Psychopathic Delinquency." *American Journal of Mental Deficiency*, 51:57-62, 1946

224. SHOVRON, J. J. "Benzedrine in Psychopathy and Behavior Disorders." *British Journal of Addiction*, 44:58-63, 1947

225. SHOWSTACK, N. "Treatment of Prisoners at the California Medical Facility." *American Journal of Psychiatry*, 112:821-824, 1956

226. SHULMAN, H. H. "Delinquency Treatment in the Controlled Activity Group." *American Sociological Review*, 10:405-414, 1945

227. SILVERMAN, D. "Clinical Studies of Criminal Psychopaths." *Archives of Neurology and Psychiatry*, 50:18, 1943

228. SILVERMAN, D. "E.E.G. and the Treatment of Criminal Psychopaths." *Journal of Criminal Psychopathology*, 5:439-466, 1944

229. SILVERMAN, D. "The Electroencephalogram of Criminals." *Archives of Neurology and Psychiatry*, 52:38-42, 1944

230. SIMMONS, D. J. AND DIETHELM, O. "Electroencephalographic Studies of Psychopathic Personalities." *Archives of Neurology and Psychiatry*, 55:410-413, 1946

231. SIMMONS, D. J. AND ROCKWELL, F. "The Electroencephalogram and Personality Organization in the Obsessive-Compulsive Reactions." *Archives of Neurology and Psychiatry*, 57:71-77, 1947

232. SIMON, B., O'LEARY, J. L., AND RYAN, J. J. "Cerebral Dysrhythmia and Psychopathic Personalities: A Study of Ninety-Six Consecutive Cases in a Military Hospital."

Archives of Neurology and Psychiatry, 56:677-685, 1946

233. SIMON, BENJAMIN, HOLTZBERG, JULES, D., AND UNGER, JOAN. "A Study of Judgment in the Psychopathic Personality." *Psychiatric Quarterly,* 25:132-150, 1951

234. SLATER, E. T. O., "Psychiatric Genetics," Part II, in *Recent Progress in Psychiatry,* edited by G. Fleming and A. Walk, Vol. 3, New York, Grove Press, 1959

235. SLATER, E. T. O. "Psychotic and Neurotic Illnesses in Twins," M.R.C. Special Report Series, 1935, no. 278, H.M.S.O.

236. SLATER, E. T. O. "Psychopathic Personality as a Genetical Concept." *Journal of Mental Science,* 94:277, 1948

237. STAFFORD-CLARK, D.; POND, DESMOND; AND DOUST, J. W. L. "The Psychopath in Prison: A Preliminary Report of a Cooperative Research." *British Journal of Delinquency,* 2:117-129, 1951

238. SLAWSON, JOHN. "Treatment of Aggression in a Specialized Environment." *American Journal of Orthopsychiatry,* 13:384-441, 1943

239. SUTHERLAND, EDWIN. "Sexual Psychopath Laws." *Journal of Criminology, Criminal Law, and Police Science,* 40:543-554, 1950

240. SYMKAL, ANTHONY, AND THORNE, FREDERICK C. "Etiological Studies of Psychopathic Personality." *Journal of Clinical Psychoolgy,* 7:299-316, 1951

241. SYMONDS, P. M. *The Psychology of Parent-Child Relations.* New York, D. Appleton-Century Co., 1939

242. SZASZ, THOMAS. "Criminal Responsibility and Psychiatry." *Legal and Criminal Psychology,* ed. Hans Toch, Holt, Rinehart and Winston, New York, 1961

243. SZUREK, S. A. "Notes on the Genesis of Psychopathic Personality." *Psychiatry,* 5:1-6, 1942

244. SZUREK, S. A. "Some Impressions from Clinical Experience with Delinquents." *Searchlights on Delinquency,* (ed.: Eissler, K. R.) New York, International Universities Press, 1949

255. TEUBER, HANS LUCAS AND POWERS, EDWIN. "Evaluating Therapy in A Delinquency Prevention Program." *Psychiatric Treatment,* Vol. 21, Baltimore, William and Wilkins Co., 1955

256. THOMPSON, G. N. *The Psychopathic Delinquent,* Thomas, Springfield, Illinois, 1953

257. THOMPSON, RICHARD E. "A Validation of the Glueck Social Prediction Scale for Proneness to Delinquency." *Journal of Criminal Law, Criminology, and Police Science,* 43:451-470, 1952

258. THORNTON, NATHANIEL. "The Relation Between Crime

and Psychopathic Personality." *Journal of Criminal Law, Criminology, and Police Science,* 42:199-204, 1951

259. TONG, J. "Stress Reactivity in Relation to Delinquent and Psychopathic Behavior.", 1959 cited by Michael Craft in "Psychopathic Personalities: A Review of Diagnosis, Aetiology, Prognosis, and Treatment." *British Journal of Criminology* Vol. 1, No. 3, Jan., 1961

260. TRAIN, GEORGE. "Pentothal Sodium: An Aid to Penologic Psychotherapy." *Handbook of Correctional Psychiatry* (ed.: Lindner, Robert, and Seliger, Robert), 641-666. New York, Philosophical Library, 1947

261. ULMAN, JOSEPH. *A Judge Takes the Stand.* New York, Knopf, 1933

262. VAN VORST, R. B. "An Evaluation of the Institutional Adjustment of the Psychopathic Offender." *American Journal of Orthopsychiatry,* 14:491-493, 1944

263. WALKER, C., AND KIRKPATRICK, B. "Dilantin Treatment for Behavior Problem Children with Abnormal E.E.G." *American Journal of Psychiatry,* 103:484-492, 1947

264. WATT, GEORGE. "An Evaluation of Non-Directive Counseling in the Treatment of Delinquents." *Journal of Educational Research,* 42:343-352, 1949

265. WEBER, LOUIS. "Working With a Psychopath." *Journal of Abnormal and Social Psychology,* 47:713-721, 1952

266. WEINBERG, KIRSON S. *Society and Personality Disorders.* New York, Prentice-Hall, 1952

267. WHEELAN, L. "Aggressive Psychopathy in One of a Pair of Uniovular Twins: A Clinical and Experimental Study." *British Journal of Delinquency,* 2:130-143, 1951

268. WHITAKER, C. A. "Ormsby Village: An Experiment with Forced Psychotherapy in the Rehabilitation of the Delinquent Adolescent" *Psychiatry,* 9:239-250, 1946

269. WHITE, ROBERT. *The Abnormal Personality.* New York, Ronald Press, 1948

270. WHITING, J. AND CHILD, I. L. *Child Training and Personality: A Cross-Cultural Study.* New Haven, Yale University Press, 1953

271. WITTELS, F. "The Criminal Psychopath in the Psychoanalytic System." *Psychoanalytic Review,* 24:276-291, 1937

272. WOLBERG, L. "The Character Structure of the Rejected Child." *The Nervous Child,* 3:74-88, 1944

273. WOLFE, B. M. "The Later Adjustment of Sixteen Children Diagnosed as Psychopathic Personality." *Smith College Studies in Social Work,* 13:156-157, 1942 (abstract)

274. ZINK, H. "A Case Study of a Political Boss." *Psychiatry,* 1:527-533, 1938

Index